T,

I hope this book becomes us[illegible] journey to finding the truth [illegible] and your development of y[illegible] self-discovery. I am always there to support you in whichever direction you choose.

love Just. xxxx. feb. 17th 1997.

CW00421019

Ways of Enlightenment

Ways of Enlightenment

Buddhist Studies at Nyingma Institute

DHARMA PUBLISHING

Dharma Publishing

NYINGMA EDUCATION SERIES

Ways of Enlightenment

Library of Congress Cataloging-in-Publication Data

Ways of enlightenment : Buddhist studies at Nyingma Institute.
p. cm. – (Nyingma education series)
Based on Mi-pham-rgya-mtsho's Mkhas 'jug.
ISBN 0-89800-255-9
ISBN 0-89800-254-0 (pbk)
1. Buddhism—Doctrines. I. Mi-pham-rgya-mtsho, 'Jam-mgon 'Ju, 1846–1912. Mkhas 'jug. II. Series.
BQ4132.W39 1993 294.3'42–dc20 93-1546

Copyright © 1993 by Dharma Publishing. All rights reserved. No part of this book, including text, maps, tables, charts, and illustrations may be reproduced without written authorization. Unauthorized reproduction is a violation of the laws of the United States of America and/or international copyright conventions. For information, write: Dharma Publishing, 2425 Hillside Avenue, Berkeley, CA 94704.

This publication is sponsored by Dharma Enterprises, U.S.A.

Research for *Ways of Enlightenment* was compiled and edited by Dharma Publishing staff.

Typeset in Adobe Trump Mediaeval with Trump Mediaeval Outline initials. Printed and bound by Dharma Press, U.S.A.

10 9 8 7 6 5 4 3 2 1

Contents

SECTION FOUR
Fundamental Awakening   63

SECTION FIVE
Training for Freedom   83

SECTION SIX
Ways to Enlightenment 101

SECTION TEN
Instant Sense Fields

SECTION ELEVEN
Interdependent Co-operation

SECTION TWELVE
Powerful Properties

SECTION THIRTEEN
Expressions of Time   199

SECTION FOURTEEN
World of Suffering   205

SECTION FIFTEEN
Causes and Conditions 225

SECTION SIXTEEN

Reality of Freedom   259

SECTION SEVENTEEN

Path of Liberation   267

Charts, Maps, and Illustrations

Publisher's Introduction

The Nyingma school of Tibetan Buddhism, the tradition of the Ancient Ones, traces its lineage of realization back through seventh century Tibet to the Buddha, the Guide of the World. The blessings of this lineage, embodied in the practice, writings, and compassionate activity of countless masters, have led thousands of individuals to freedom and lasting happiness.

In 1972, Tarthang Tulku, an accomplished Nyingma lineage holder, founded the Nyingma Institute in Berkeley, California for the purpose of introducing Westerners to the theory and practice of the Buddhist teachings. During the past twenty years, over 100,000 Westerners from all walks of life have attended classes and seminars at the Institute and at Nyingma Centers in Germany, Holland, and Brazil. Through programs in relaxation, basic meditation, and Buddhist psychology and philosophy, developed under the guidance of Tarthang Tulku, Institute students have been encouraged to explore the Buddha's teachings.

Over the years, Dharma Publishing has supported this educational process by producing books that expand the base of knowledge for Western Dharma students. The Translation Series includes Sūtras, biographies of Dharma masters, texts on analytic meditation and Abhidharma, and more advanced works such as Longchenpa's Trilogy of Finding Comfort and Ease. The Crystal Mirror Series presents historical perspectives on the Dharma, while the Nyingma Psychology Series offers teachings helpful to practice in daily life.

For at least ten years, Dharma Publishing has wanted to bring out an introductory but comprehensive guide for Buddhist studies that could benefit Nyingma Institute students as well as individuals interested in studying independently. In the early 1970's, Tarthang Tulku had introduced some of his students to a text that could provide the foundation for such a project: Lama Mipham's encyclopedic Gateway to Knowledge, the mKhas-pa'i-tshul-la-'jug-pa'i-sgo-zhes-bya-ba'i-bstan-bcos, or Khenjug. Organized around the Ten Topics of Expert Knowledge, the Khenjug includes all the fundamental subjects of Dharma study.

The text of the Khenjug proved difficult for beginners. Lama Mipham's intended audience was already knowledgeable and his treatment of the most basic subjects is often brief. An excellent commentary to the Khenjug exists, composed by Khenpo Nuden, but the commentary too requires substantial background to be used successfully.

In the late 1980's, with the encouragement of Tarthang Tulku, members of the Dharma Publishing staff once again took up the Khenjug, compiling a list of several hundred basic subjects for background research. This list was presented to Tarthang Tulku, who clarified various subjects and recommended particular Sūtras, Śāstras, and Abhidharma texts for study. Staff members compiled passages from these texts, organizing the wide variety of material in accord with the structure of the Khenjug.

To study the hundreds of subjects contained within the Ten Topics requires a basic understanding of the Buddha, Dharma, and Sangha, the three trainings, and the three vehicles, and the historical development of the Dharma lineage. The present book begins with an introduction based on these themes, followed by a discussion of the most basic Dharma subjects drawn from seven of the Ten Topics of the Khenjug. A second volume will survey the remaining three topics, whose content reveals the profound and vast vision of the Mahāyāna.

Ways of Enlightenment can only hint at the vast ocean of wisdom that the teachings contain—each of Lama Mipham's Ten Topics would require a whole book to discuss in detail. This volume is best seen as an introductory study guide for Western students: a resource for developing familiarity with key concepts and terminology, the structure of the path and maps of consciousness, and sources essential for further study. In the future it will surely be possible to develop better vocabulary, arrive at a deeper understanding, explore more subtle distinctions, and create a clearer presentation.

If the seed of the Dharma is to take root and flourish in Western culture, the ground must be well prepared. Preparation includes the study of philosophy and history, combined with regular meditation practice and the application of the teachings directly in everyday life. In the Nyingma tradition, such a many-sided approach is considered vital.

When joined together from the outset, study and practice foster a deep experiential appreciation for the potential of our human existence. Intellectual understanding based on study and experiential understanding based on practice support one another; together they begin to illuminate the structure of the path. Knowledge of Dharma history demonstrates the level of commitment required to follow the path and reveals the beauty of the results in the lives of great masters. The student learns patience and determination, and is protected from disappointment and discouragement.

When students of the Dharma can verify the teachings through direct experience, confidence in their own understanding and in the Dharma both develop naturally. Confidence in turn generates the sustained engagement necessary for effort to bear fruit, and the taste of this fruit helps knowledge to deepen into complete certainty. This certainty forms the link to the lineage of light—-at once the inner wisdom of the Dharma and our own deepest truth. The Western heart cherishes individual freedom, but it is only through such direct knowledge that the freedom to choose becomes meaningful.

In Tibet, transmission of the lineage of enlightened knowledge depended on making a particular kind of connection to a teacher who possessed realization of the inner meaning of the texts. Under the insightful guidance of such a teacher, the student proceeded along the path of direct, unequivocal experience.

To follow such a path was never easy, and today it is more difficult than ever. There is little in Western culture or ways of thinking that supports the all-important relationship between Dharma student and Dharma teacher. Moreover, it is rare to meet a teacher who is fully trained in the lineage and also experienced in working with the underlying patterns of the Western mind. Western Dharma students often lack the traditional prerequisites for successful study and practice: a basic knowledge of Buddhist thought, well-developed confidence in the teachings, a stable commitment, and wholehearted devotion.

Still, if our resolve to study the Dharma is strong, such difficulties can become an inspiring challenge. As we develop knowledge, we discover that confidence, commitment, and devotion come forth naturally. When we ourselves know what the tradition of the Awakened Ones stands for, the blessings of the lineage can guide us on the path. With such a foundation, the longevity of the Dharma in the West can become a reality.

Exactly one hundred years ago, in 1893, the first Buddhist teachers set foot in America to attend the World Parliament of Religion. During the last half of this century, the Dharma has truly begun to enter Western culture, not just as an exotic curiosity but as a spiritual path. If this generation of Dharma practitioners can make a genuine connection to the teachings of the Enlightened One, a Western Buddhist way of life may unfold as a new chapter in the history of the Dharma. With the profound wish that *Ways of Enlightenment* will support the making of this connection, this volume is dedicated to Western students of the Dharma.

SECTION ONE

Buddha: The Awakened One

CHAPTER ONE

Light of the World

Over two thousand years ago, there lived an Indian prince Siddhārtha, "He Whose Aim Will Be Accomplished." Vividly aware of human suffering, Prince Siddhārtha determined to penetrate the root cause of frustration and pain and discover a more deeply satisfying way of life. After the accomplishment of his purpose, he became known as the Buddha, the Awakened One.

The Life of the Buddha

Born into the ancient world in a time before Greece was beginning its Golden Age, Siddhārtha Gautama belonged to the royal family of the Śākyas, rulers of a kingdom in the plains of northern India. When the child was conceived, his mother, Queen Māyā, dreamed that a beautiful white elephant, the symbol of wisdom and royal power, was descending into her womb. During the time she carried the child, Māyā's contentment was so profound that it inspired the king to set aside matters of state and turn to spiritual practice. She uplifted all those around her, encouraging friendliness and compassionate action. Throughout the kingdom of the Śākyas, all intrigue and struggle ceased for ten months.

Birth and Childhood

In the springtime, Queen Māyā gave birth in the garden of Lumbinī beneath a flowering tree. At the birth of the child, a deep peace descended upon the kingdom. Jealousy, greed, depression, and fear vanished; even fierce animals grew gentle toward each other. For seven days the child was honored in the Lumbinī garden by gods and men, by villagers and courtiers, as the king distributed gifts and food to all. On the seventh day, Queen Māyā died and was reborn in the heavenly realms.

King Śuddhodana soon welcomed Asita the rishi, a holy man from the Himalayas. Asita predicted that Prince Siddhārtha would become either a great king ruling the four quarters of the earth or an Awakened One, a Buddha. Gazing at the child, the rishi wept as he foretold the child's special destiny, and the king anxiously implored him to speak the truth.

"I see no misfortune or hindrance for Siddhārtha.
I lament for myself, O Master of Men.
For I am old and worn. He will be a Buddha;
honored by the world, he will preach the Dharma.

"But I will not be present
to gaze upon him with joyful eyes." (LAL VII)

As he grew to young manhood, the child appeared to conform to the ways of the world but continually astounded those around him. When Siddhārtha was carried into the temple to receive the gods' blessings, the statues rose from their places and bowed to him. When the king bestowed ornaments and jewelry upon him, the child gave them all away. While attending school, he amazed his teachers and inspired the other children with his knowledge of language, philosophy, and mathematics.

A few years later, when wandering through the fields around a farming village, Siddhārtha seated himself beneath a tree and spontaneously entered a deep meditative state. All day long the shadow of the tree did not move, but remained steady, shading the prince. His father discovered him there and for a moment glimpsed his son's true nature:

"There he sits, like a fire blazing on a mountaintop,
like the moon surrounded by clusters of stars.
My whole body trembles to see him deep in meditation,
glowing like a brilliant lamp." (LAL XI)

King Śuddhodana quietly removed his crown and royal insignia, raised both hands above his head, and bowed twice to the seated prince. Coming out of meditation, young Siddhārtha spoke to his father with great authority: "In working the field of the mind, O father, seek nothing from another."

Fearful that his only son would leave home to become a seeker of truth, the king began to surround the young prince with beauty and pleasure and protected him from all sight of suffering.

Mastery: Skills and Pleasures

When Siddhārtha grew to manhood, he followed his father's wish that he should marry. He chose the wise and virtuous princess Gopā, whose hand he won by proving himself master of the worldly arts and sciences.

Siddhārtha had no equal in wrestling, archery, running, swimming, handling elephants, horsemanship, chariot driving, and feats of strength. His knowledge of poetry, grammar, and composition knew no bounds; his excellence was unsurpassed in painting, sculpture, instrumental music, dance, and song as well as crafts and commerce. He demonstrated complete mastery of magic and the mysteries of nature, astrology, traditional Indian scriptures, debate, religious ceremonies, and yoga.

Gopā, whose qualities mirrored those of Siddhārtha, was clearly a perfect partner for the prince. Her purity of heart and independent judgment shone forth in her demeanor and actions. Unmoved by luxury and finery, utterly forthright in speech, she was unswayed by customs and opinions. When she chose to go unveiled in the presence of everyone, and the courtiers objected, she gently replied:

"Whether seated, standing, or walking,
the noble-minded shine, unveiled . . .
The assemblies of gods know my conduct,
my virtues, my restraint, and my modesty.
Why should I veil my face?" (LAL XII)

Gopā and Siddhārtha lived in unsurpassed delight, in the most elegant dwellings, surrounded by attendants and entertainments of all kinds. The king built three palaces for the prince and his wife and saw to their every need, still hoping that his son would not abandon his royal position to go the way of the seeker.

Decision: Departure and Practice

During four visits to the gardens outside the royal city, the prince saw four sights: an old man, life nearly spent, abandoned by his family; a man disfigured and diseased, gripped by pain; a lifeless corpse on its way to burial, followed by grieving relatives; and a tranquil renunciate intent on liberation. Deeply impressed with the inevitability of suffering and inspired by the renunciate's serenity, the prince resolved to renounce his kingdom to search for the end of suffering. Siddhārtha's heart and mind fully opened, and he embraced the inevitable suffering that human beings have endured since time immemorial. In dream after dream, Siddhārtha saw beings languishing in endless frustration and suffering.

He approached his father, the king, and requested permission to depart on the quest he had chosen.

"Lord, I seek four things. If you can but give them to me, I shall remain here, and you will always see me in this house; I will never leave.

"I desire, my lord, that old age should never take hold of me; that I should always possess the radiance of youth; that I should always be in perfect health, and that sickness should never strike me; that my life should be endless, and that there should be no death."

The king was overcome with sorrow at these words. "What you ask, my son, cannot be done; in these matters I am powerless. Even the sages who live for aeons are not free from the fear of old age, sickness, death, and misfortune." (LAL XV)

The king renewed his efforts to guard the prince from all sight of sorrow or suffering, but Siddhārtha had awakened from the dream of pleasure in the palace. Everywhere his gaze fell he saw suffering. He looked upon his charming companions entranced with their luxurious way of life and lamented:

"These ignorant ones die like prisoners who have been condemned to death. These ignorant ones throw themselves like moths into the burning flames. These ignorant ones are caught like fish in a net."

Refusing to concede that the inner meaning of life and death was beyond the range of human knowledge, Siddhārtha decided to depart from the palace on horseback and summoned his friend and charioteer Chandaka. Again and again, Chandaka pleaded with the prince to live the royal life and retire to the forest in his old age to meditate and seek wisdom. He reminded the prince of duty, of pleasure, of love, of family:

"Do you not see her on the couch, the beautiful one,
with eyes like the petals of the lotus in bloom . . .
how can you abandon it all?"

The prince explained that he had indeed experienced every possible pleasure and delight life could offer—not only in this life but in countless previous lives—without ever finding an end to suffering.

"I have already enjoyed the greatest prosperities
which could delight the heart . . .
and I was not satisfied.
All the more today—how could I be satisfied
by depending on these demeaning conditions?
In the wilderness of misery
and suffering, those ferocious emotions
always carry us away in despair and confusion.
In the darkness of ignorance and confusion,
there is no refuge and no protector."

Faced with Siddhārtha's unshakable resolve, Chandaka prepared the horses. They left the palace and made their way to the stupa of the former Buddha Kāśyapa, where the prince exchanged his royal garments for the tattered robes of a mendicant. Taking his sword, he cut off his long hair, the sign of his royal status, symbolically severing his connections to his former life. When the prince told Chandaka to return to the palace with the horses, Chandaka hesitated, unable to bear the suffering of the royal family. But Siddhārtha asked him to tell the family not to grieve—for when he attained enlightenment, he would return with teachings that would bring all suffering to an end.

Siddhārtha set forth in search of "the unborn, the undying, the unsorrowful, the stainless, the completely secure." (MN XXVI) For a time he lived alone on a mountaintop near Rājagṛha. Seeing him from afar, Bimbisāra, king of Magadha, determined to meet him, and fulfilled his resolve by climbing the mountain on foot. So impressed was the king that he offered Siddhārtha half of his kingdom if he would settle there. Having already renounced one kingdom, Siddhārtha had no need of another.

"O king and protector of the land,
the more one serves desire,
the more things to desire limitlessly appear . . .
finding no joy in the things of the world,
I renounced them to gain supreme enlightenment."

King Bimbisāra replied:

"Pray be patient in your heart with one
who desires to be free from all desire
and thus invites you here.
When you have attained enlightenment,
may you share your teachings with me,
O Master of Dharma." (LAL XVI)

At that time India was home to various systems of meditative practice and numerous speculative philosophies, including forms of theism, scepticism, materialism, hedonism, and fatalism. Siddhārtha proceeded to investigate them all. He sought out the wisest teachers in the land and quickly mastered their teachings. The prince had a very clear test for knowledge, which he applied to each tradition: Does the application of this teaching bring an end to frustration and suffering? While many approaches offered temporary happiness, he found none that led to the complete cessation of suffering. Followed by five ascetics attracted to his quest, Siddhārtha took leave of other teachers and continued the spiritual search on his own.

Siddhārtha lived in the wilderness and practiced the most strenuous austerities—at one point eating only one grain of rice a day—in order to gain complete control of body and mind. Through such practices he experienced very expansive but temporary levels of awareness and bliss and developed extraordinary powers of determination.

As his austerities grew more severe, his father sent messengers every day inquiring after his condition, and his mother appeared from the heaven realms, begging him to desist. But Siddhārtha consoled her and demonstrated his resolve:

"Do not fear; you shall have your son again . . . The renunciation of a Buddha is always fruitful . . . The earth could be torn in a thousand pieces, the peak of Mount Meru could be turned upside down, the multitude of stars could fall to the earth; yet should a single suffering being remain, I would not die! . . . The time is not far distant when you will see the enlightenment of a Buddha." (LAL XVII)

Conquering Māra and Attaining Enlightenment

For six years Siddhārtha assiduously practiced asceticism until he had thoroughly demonstrated that even this path, which was so highly respected in ancient India, would not yield the knowledge necessary to pass completely out of the realm of suffering, old age, and death. Siddhārtha recalled how his mind had traversed the stages of concentration when as a young boy he was meditating in the farmer's field.

"This is the path of enlightenment, which will lead to the disappearance of the miseries of birth, old age, sickness, and death. This was my thought." (LAL XVIII)

Compelled by compassion for suffering beings, he gave up the practice of austerities. When offered boiled milk and rice by a maiden, he accepted, knowing that the attainment of his purpose would require great physical stamina. His five followers left in disillusionment, not realizing why Siddhārtha had given up the ascetic way of life.

Siddhārtha proceeded alone to the bodhi tree several miles south of the village at Gayā. Taking his seat beneath the tree, he vowed not to arise until he had attained complete and perfect enlightenment.

"Here on this seat my body may shrivel up,
my skin, my bones, my flesh may dissolve,
but my body will not move from this very seat
until I have obtained enlightenment,
so difficult to obtain
in the course of many kalpas." (LAL XIX)

Now Māra, the lord of illusion, together with his retinue of fierce warriors and his loveliest daughters, advanced on Siddhārtha, attempting first to frighten and then to seduce him. But Māra's attacks failed, and the attempts at seduction went unheeded. At last Māra confronted the prince and demanded to know by what right Siddhārtha was worthy of enlightenment. Siddhārtha called the earth itself as witness to the innumerable deeds of compassion he had performed over countless aeons. Against such universal and constant goodness, Māra gave way, powerless to stop the momentum toward transformation, now close at hand.

That night, Siddhārtha understood the inner workings of samsara, the cycle of birth and death; he comprehended the past lives of all beings and observed karma in operation. He understood the patterns of suffering, their interlocking causes and conditions, and the way to bring them to an end. With the coming of dawn he broke through the most subtle obstacles to knowledge and passed beyond suffering to become a fully awakened Buddha.

For seven weeks, the Buddha remained in deep meditation, experiencing many different realms of existence. Brahmā, the highest of the gods, appeared before him, beseeching him to begin to teach. The Buddha hesitated, for the only antidote to suffering was perfect understanding of reality. He knew that few would be able to comprehend knowledge so deep and penetrating, so vast and subtle. Finally, moved by great compassion, the Buddha responded to Brahmā's request and agreed to teach.

Compassion: Turning the Wheel

The Enlightened One arose from beneath the bodhi tree and proceeded to the Deer Park in Vārāṇasī where his five former followers were residing. There the Buddha began the process of bringing truth into the world, setting in motion the wheel of the Dharma through his first teaching. Over the next forty-five years, the Buddha traveled widely, teaching the Dharma to hundreds of thousands of followers and liberating countless beings in other realms as well. It is said that he presented 84,000 teachings, only a fraction of which survive today.

Seated among his disciples, the Buddha was like a shining golden mountain encircled by a lake of lotuses in full bloom. His compassion was so deep that he radiated a subtle light that touched people's hearts; even his skin seemed to glow. The Lalitavistara tells us:

"He is known as the destroyer of dark ignorance; the one who sees distinctly with the great light of knowledge; the one free of conceptualization; the one illuminating an immeasurable domain with love, kindness, and great compassion; the one shining equally for each living being; the possessor of the maṇḍala difficult to envision, difficult to attain, and profound in transcendent wisdom." (LAL XXVI)

The Buddha's teachings were available to any who were able to hear them. His wisdom and compassion cleared away limited viewpoints, doubts, and confusions—his very presence awakened the seeds of wisdom in the hearts of those around him. During his lifetime, people from all walks of life dedicated themselves to following these teachings and many thousands of them attained enlightenment.

Liberation: The Parinirvāṇa

During the Lord Buddha's eightieth year, the time came for his final teaching. With his disciples gathered around him, the Buddha answered their last questions and presented anew his fundamental teachings. He urged his followers to seek out the truth for themselves and to hold fast to the truth as a lamp and a refuge. After pronouncing his final words, "Monks, decay is inherent in all compounded things," the Enlightened One passed through the highest stages of meditation and entered into parinirvāṇa, merging with the inconceivable all-pervasive Dharmakāya.

The Path of Knowledge

In his own years of seeking and in the way that he taught others, the Buddha demonstrated the importance of individual responsibility for knowledge. Once one recognizes the need for knowledge—both for one's own sake and to be of benefit to others—inspiration to pursue the quest for knowledge arises from within. The Buddha, having followed a way to complete understanding, compassionately offers guidance, innumerable techniques of transformation, and maps of consciousness that identify landmarks along the path. But it is up to each person to travel the path—each individual must develop his or her own motivation, experience, and conclusions. Hearing the teachings is only the beginning of knowledge. They must then be studied, reflected upon, and tested in experience. In this process of continuous refinement, the mind can be educated to see through all forms of self-deception and attain new dimensions of freedom.

The Buddha taught that if knowledge depends on the doctrines of another, or the experience of another, it is not ultimately satisfying and has little power to transform one's life. The belief that knowledge lies "elsewhere"—that we must believe in it rather than experience it—prevents knowledge from entering our lives. The human heart yearns to touch knowledge directly and to bring it to life. In the end, all that remains to guide us is living knowledge, that which we have deeply realized and put into practice.

THE TWELVE ACTS OF THE BUDDHA

1. Resolve to be born in the human realm
2. Descent from Tuṣita heaven
3. Entrance into the womb
4. Physical birth
5. Accomplishment in worldly arts
6. Life of pleasure
7. Departure from home
8. Ascetic practices
9. Conquest of Māra
10. Enlightenment
11. Turning the wheel of the Dharma
12. Passing into nirvana

The Twelve Acts

The historical Buddha emerges out of a past beyond reckoning. The jātaka texts explain that Siddhārtha had been a Bodhisattva for incalculable aeons, taking birth as human, god, or animal, in whatever form would most benefit others. Accumulating boundless wisdom and merit, he perfected six qualities: giving, self-discipline, patience, effort, concentration, and wisdom. When the time finally arrived to embody the truth of perfect realization, the Bodhisattva took his final birth in the world and completed the twelve acts of a Buddha.

The Mahāyāna Sūtras cast the achievements of the Buddha in a context that is even more profound. The Lalitavistara Sūtra explains that the twelve acts are a "great play," a beautiful and inspiring drama that unfolds to demonstrate to others the way to enlightenment.

The Mahāyāna Sūtras portray the Buddha on three levels at once. He is immutable and universal, enlightened since beginningless time. Yet he is also one who has accomplished immeasurable aeons of training as a Bodhisattva, moving in a visionary realm beyond ordinary understanding. And he is a human being whose knowledge is refined and developed through time. Even these three dimensions only suggest the true nature of enlightened being, which is manifold and inexpressible, inseparable from our own being. The Sūtras say that Manjuśrī, Bodhisattva of wisdom, could speak for a lifetime without being able to express fully the nature of the Awakened One.

Kāliyuga

According to the Buddha's teachings, the process of suffering is continuous and self-generating: Confusion and ignorance give rise to suffering, and that suffering engenders more confusion and more ignorance, a vicious circle that is known as samsara.

The signs around us clearly indicate that confusion and suffering are not diminishing in our time. Destructive and confused patterns of action have been reinforced for centuries. The reality of suffering is growing greater, even though modern medicine and technology provide relief for some physical miseries. Within the last few generations, life has become noticeably more stressful and more complex. As the pace of events quickens, time becomes pressured and demanding, bearing down upon us. While there is an explosion of information and technology, the most basic human problems have not been resolved.

The Buddhist tradition calls our time the kāliyuga, an era of increasing darkness, heaviness, disorder, and friction. In symbolic terms it is said that aeons ago, beings had bodies of light, but over time, their embodiment grew more material and more dense. In psychological terms, people feel constrained on all sides by limitations, obstacles, and obligations. Individual lives grow more painful and complicated; the sense of personal integrity weakens, and even simple honesty becomes a difficult practice. Manipulation and aggression rule the day, and society is beset with rules that attempt to restrain the increasingly selfish orientation of its members.

Trust in the basic goodness of humanity, compassion, enjoyment of life, and spiritual pursuits becomes extremely difficult in the kāliyuga. There is scarcely the time, inclination, or support for healing human suffering on any other than the most basic physical level. Pursuing a different, richer way of life based on harmony, cooperation, communication, and creative accomplishment without the struggle of competition seems a remote possibility indeed. In the midst of confusion and daily pressure, inquiring into alternatives seems almost a luxury. Yet without willingness to inquire into our situation, we cannot find a more meaningful way of life.

Complete Understanding of Samsara

The heritage of the Buddha's enlightenment belongs to all the world, not just to the civilizations of the East, and this heritage remains available today: the deepest, most complete understanding of the human situation ever envisioned. The path to lasting happiness and the achievements of those following that path are well documented in the Buddhist texts. The selfless purity and devotion of the great Buddhist masters, their meditative accomplishments and brilliant creative philosophy are convincing evidence that more knowledge is available to us than we may realize.

As the Buddha's teachings enter Western civilization with its technological expertise and its communication networks, we witness a rare occurrence in human history: the conjunction of ancient and modern knowledge, the meeting of East and West, and the opportunity for vast numbers of people to hear about the possibility of enlightenment. People in the West are coming to realize that the complexity and intensity of the difficulties we face today as individuals and as members of society cannot be resolved with the knowledge at our command. Understanding the limits of our present approach to knowledge may awaken us to the need for a more enlightened view. Now, more than ever before in history, the world needs the light of the Dharma. Though we live in a difficult era, we are fortunate indeed, for that light still shines.

CHAPTER TWO

Ancient Times and Sacred Places

In the Mahāparinibbāna Sutta, the Buddha names the four most important places of pilgrimage: where the Enlightened One was born, where he reached enlightenment, where he first set the wheel of the Dharma in motion, and where he attained parinirvāṇa. These locations, together with others associated with the Twelve Acts, are revered as holy sites by Buddhists around the world. Holy sites are said to arouse deep conviction, contentment, and commitment in the heart of one who approaches them in faith. For centuries pilgrims have braved the dangers of travel across oceans, deserts, and mountain peaks to visit these sacred places.

The Holy Sites

Born in Lumbinī, Siddhārtha Gautama led the princely life at the palace in Kapilavastu. After leaving home and pursuing ascetic practices, he attained enlightenment at Bodh Gayā. He then taught at the Deer Park in Sārnāth, in the Bamboo Grove and on the Vulture Peak Mountain at Rājagṛha, at Vaiśālī, and at Śrāvastī, where he spent most of his later years. At Saṁkāśya, he returned from the heavenly realms, where he had gone to teach his mother. The parinirvāṇa took place at Kuśinagara.

The Buddha taught in many locations throughout India, visiting Taxila, Oḍḍiyāna, Nāgarahāra, Mathurā, Orissa, Dravida, and other places. The Vinaya describes the teaching travels of the Buddha, and each of the Sūtras opens with a description of where the Buddha related that specific teaching.

"Thus have I heard at one time. The Lord Buddha was in residence in the garden of Āmrapālī in the city of Vaiśālī, attended by a great gathering."

—*Vimalakīrtinirdeśa Sūtra*

"Thus have I heard. The Blessed One once stayed in the Castle of Laṅka which is situated on the peak of Mount Malaya on the great ocean, and which is adorned with flowers made of jewels of various kinds."

—*Laṅkāvatāra Sūtra*

"Thus have I heard. At one time the Bhagavat dwelt in Rājagṛha on Vulture Peak with a large assembly of monks . . ."

—*Sukhāvatīvyūha Sūtra*

"Thus have I heard. At one time the Buddha was in the land of Magadha, in a state of purity at the site of the enlightenment (Bodh Gayā), having just realized true awareness . . . "

—*Avataṁsaka Sūtra*

"Thus have I heard. Once the Buddha was dwelling in the garden of Anāthapiṇḍada in the Jeta Grove near Śrāvastī. At that time, King Prasenajit and Queen Mallikā of Kosala had just had an initial realization of the Dharma. . ."

—*Śrīmālādevī Sūtra*

"Thus have I heard. Once the Lord was staying among the Kurus. There is a market-town of theirs called Kammāsadhamma. And there the Lord addressed the monks. . . "

—*Mahāsatipaṭṭhāna Sutta*

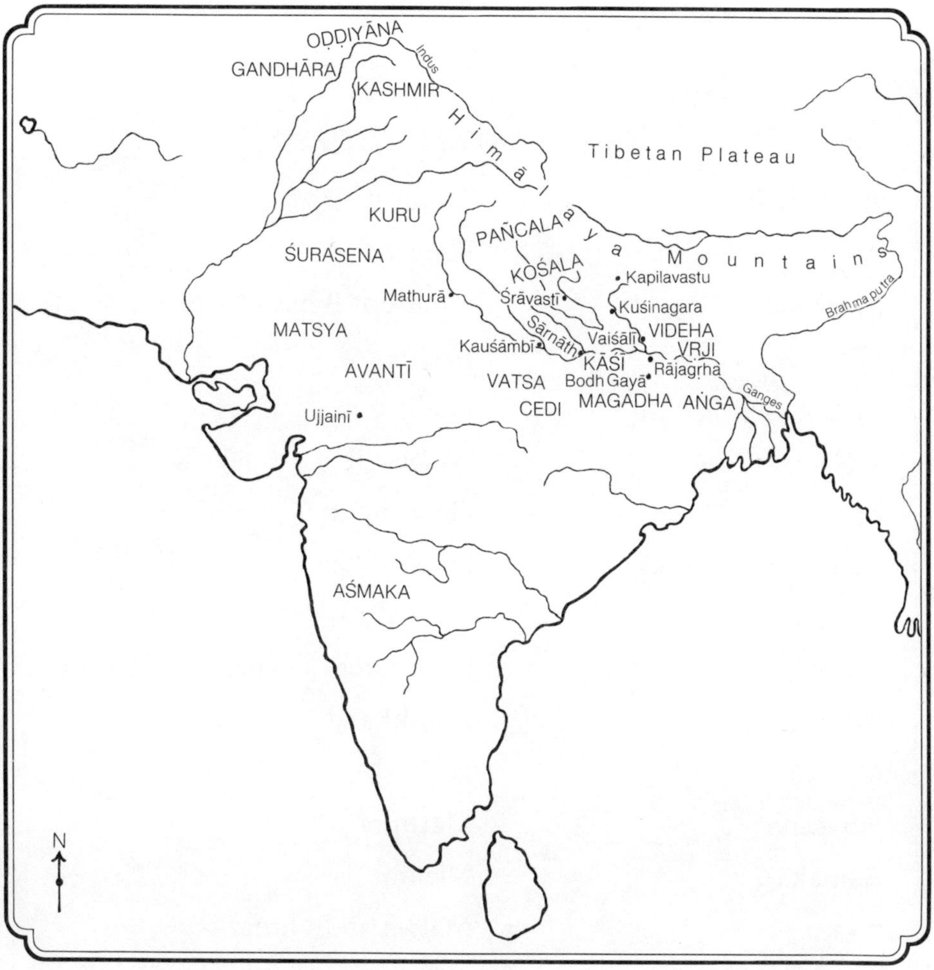

© 1984 Dharma Publishing Unauthorized reproduction is a violation of international copyright law.

India at the Time of the Buddha

India at the time of the Buddha was divided into sixteen kingdoms or great communities (mahājanapadas). These kingdoms are frequently mentioned in the Buddhist texts: Aṅga, Magadha, Kāśī, Kosala, Vṛji, Malla, Ceḍi, Vatsa, Kuru, Pañcāla, Matsya, Śūrasena, Aśmaka, Avanti, Gandhāra, and Kāmboja. In the early years of the Sangha, the rulers of two of these great communities were important patrons: King Bimbisāra, who ruled Magadha, and King Prasenajit, who reigned in Kosala. The kingdom of the Śākyas, with its capital at Kapilavastu, was a republic in the foothills of the Himalayas. It was ruled by King Śuddhodana, the father of Siddhārtha.

GREAT COMMUNITIES

Ancient Name	*Modern Area*
Aṅga	Bengal
Magadha	Southern Bihar
Kāsī	Benares
Kosala	Oudh
Vṛji	North Bihar
Malla	Gorakhpur
Ceḍi	Bundelkhand
Vatsa	Allahabad
Kuru	Delhi area, Thaneswar, Meerut
Pañcāla	Rohikhand
Matsya	Jaipur
Śūrasena	Mathura
Aśmaka	Nizam
Avanti	Malwa and Nimar
Gandhāra	Peshawar and Rawalpindi
Kamboja	Southwest Kashmir, Kafiristan

The Śākyas of Kapilavastu were known as the "Brave and Daring Ones." One of a number of republican clans in ancient India, they lived under an egalitarian form of self-government, with the king regarded as the first among equals. The Lalitavistara describes Kapilavastu as "the shining city," inhabited by powerful men excelling in archery and physical courage. Yet not one would harm another even to save himself, for the whole population observed religious precepts. When the Buddha returned to Kapilavastu after the enlightenment, his family and all the Śākyas became his disciples.

HOLY SITES

Benares Vārāṇasī, Bā-ra-ṅa-si. Capital of Kaśī, where the Buddha first preached at Sārnāth. HT II:44–61.

Deer Park Mṛgadāva (or Ṛṣipatana), Ri-dwags-kyi-gnas-drang-srong-lhung-ba. Pleasure garden in Sārnāth where the Buddha often taught. HT II:45.

Vaiśālī Vaiśālī, Yangs-pa-can. Capital of Vṛji, where the Buddha often taught. Modern Allahabad. HT II:66–76.

Rajgir Rājagṛha, rGyal-po'i-khab. Capital of Magadha, where the Buddha often taught. Residence of King Bimbisāra. HT II:165.

Bamboo Grove Veṇuvana, 'Od-ma'i-tshal. Park in Rājagṛha given to the Buddha by King Bimbisāra. HT II: 161, 165, 188.

Vulture Peak Gṛdhrakūṭa, Bya-rgod-phung-po'i-ri. Mountain near Rājagṛha where the Buddha taught the Prajñāpāramitā. HT II:152–153.

Kauśambī Kauśambī, mDzod-ldan. Capital of Vatsa, ruled by King Udayana. Modern Kosam. HT I:235-238.

Śrāvastī Śrāvastī, mNyan-yod. Capital of Kosala, ruled by King Prasenajit, where the Buddha spent many years. HT II:1–12.

Jeta's Grove Jetavana, rGyal-bu-rgyal-byed-kyi-tshal. Just south of Śrāvasti, where the Buddha often taught. HT II:4–5.

Bodhimaṇḍa Bodhimaṇḍa, Byang-chub-snying-po. The seat of enlightenment at Bodh Gayā. HT II:113–114.

Kapilavastu Kapilavastu, Ser-skya'i-gnas-kyi-grong-khyer. The early home of the Buddha, located in the Nepal foothills. HT II:13–25.

Lumbinī Lumbinī, Lu-mbi-nī. Grove near Kapilavastu where the Buddha was born. HT II:24–25.

Kuśinagara Kuśinagara, Ku-sha'i-grong-khyer. While traveling to Kuśinagara, the Buddha stopped at a sala grove where he entered parinirvāṅa. HT II:31–43.

A Summary of Chronologies

The chronology of the Buddha's life has been studied by Buddhist historians, who have traced the references in the canonical texts to when and where he taught after his enlightenment. Though accounts differ in details, the order of events is well established. Historians differ, however, in their views of when the Buddha lived.

The date of the Buddha's parinirvāṇa has been calculated by masters of all Buddhist traditions. The earliest date for the Buddha's parinirvāṇa was calculated by Sureśamati to be 2420 B.C.E. Three Tibetan sources also place the date in the third millenium B.C.E.: the Gyabod Yigtsang gives 2150 B.C.E., dBus-pa-blo-gsal gives 2146 B.C.E., and Sakya Paṇḍita calculated 2133 B.C.E. Atīśa, the Indian paṇḍita who worked for the Dharma in Tibet during the eleventh century, gives 2136 B.C.E.

Though these dates are quite different from those calculated by modern scholars, the Tibetan masters had compelling reasons for considering such distant dates. Predictions of how long the Dharma would last mentioned that the teachings would reach the "land of the red-faced men" (which was taken to mean Tibet) after 2,500 years. The first Tibetan Dharma King, Srongtsan Gampo, ruled in the seventh century, which would place the Buddha about 2000 B.C.E. Ancient records of when statues were placed in the temple in Bodh Gayā also indicate very early dates for the Buddha.

The Tibetan master Phukpa Lundrup calculated 962 B.C.E. as the Buddha's birthdate, placing the parinirvāṇa in 881 B.C.E.; this date is very close to the 878 B.C.E. given by Buton and Khedrupje, and the 876 B.C.E. calculated by Buton from the Kālacakra Tantra. Kamalaśīla, disciple of Śāntarakṣita, had previously arrived at 718 B.C.E. using this same source. The Tibetan masters of the Jonang tradition propose 835 B.C.E.

Basing his calculations on the history of the sandalwood Buddha, the Tibetan master Tshalpa Kunga Dorje calculated the date of the parinirvāṇa at 750 B.C.E. Orgyenpa arrived at a date of 651 B.C.E. The latest date related for the parinirvāṇa in the Tibetan tradition is 544/543 B.C.E., calculated by the fourteenth-

GREAT PERSONAGES

961 B.C.E. Birth of Buddha	558 B.C.E. Zoroaster begins teaching
c. 953 B.C.E. King Solomon dedicates temple	550 B.C.E. Cyrus the Great rules Persia
c. 860 B.C.E. Elijah the Prophet	527 B.C.E. Death of Mahāvīra
605? B.C.E. Birth of Lao-tzu	469–399 B.C.E. Socrates
582 B.C.E. Birth of Pythagoras	427–347 B.C.E. Plato

century Indian master Śākyaśrī, the last abbot of the monastic university of Vikramaśīla.

The Southern (Theravādin) tradition uniformly places the parinirvāṇa in 544 B.C.E. This dating relies on the "dotted record," which grew out of the tradition of placing a dot in the Vinaya scriptures at the conclusion of the early rainy season retreat. This date, however, is incompatible with the currently accepted chronology of the kings of Magadha. The Buddha was a contemporary of two historical kings of Magadha, Bimbisāra and Ajātaśatru, but their reigns are difficult to date. The chronology of ancient India is far from reliable, for written records are largely absent, and what literature survives focuses on legendary ages that are difficult to define. Thus the time of the Buddha in relation to historical events requires careful investigation.

Further Readings

Lalitavistara. *The Voice of the Buddha: The Beauty of Compassion,* 2 volumes. Life story of the Buddha.

Jātakamālā by Āryaśūra. *The Marvelous Companion.* Tales of the previous lives of the Buddha.

bsTan-pa'i-rnam-gzhag and Chos-'byung, by Dudjom Rinpoche. *The Nyingma School of Tibetan Buddhism,* book II, pp. 416–427. On the life of the Buddha.

Chos-'byung, by Bu-ston Rinpoche. *History of Buddhism,* part II, pp. 7–73.

"Prayer to Śākyamuni Buddha," by Lama Mipham. In *Footsteps on the Diamond Path* (Crystal Mirror I–III), pp. 144–147. On how to visualize the Buddha.

The Life of the Buddha as it Appears in the Pāli Canon, by Bhikkhu Ñāṇamoli.

The Life of the Buddha and the Early History of His Order, by W. Woodville Rockhill.

The Three Jewels and History of Dharma Transmission (Crystal Mirror VI), pp. 1–80. On the life of the Buddha.

Light of Liberation (Crystal Mirror VIII), pp. xx–xxv, 17–27, 37–148. On dates of the Buddha, lineages, and the life of the Buddha.

Holy Places of the Buddha (Crystal Mirror IX), forthcoming.

SECTION TWO

Dharma:
The Teaching of Freedom

CHAPTER THREE

The Three Turnings

The teachings that convey the view and the path to liberation are known as the Dharma. The comprehensive knowledge and deep inner peace of the Enlightened One evoked profound responses even from those who glimpsed him from afar or heard his words repeated by others. Kings and princes made obeisance to him, warriors laid down their arms before him, and famous philosophers discarded their views to embrace his teachings.

The way in which the Enlightened One taught surpasses ordinary understanding. According to the Sūtras, the form of the Buddha always seemed to face each listener, no matter how large the gathering; the voice of the Buddha reached each being in his or her own language; the inner meaning of the teachings was revealed directly to each person's heart. The Buddha conveyed enlightened knowledge in many ways: through silent transmission, through blessings, or through a multitude of languages. The Mahāyānasūtrālaṁkāra (MSA XII:9) relates that the speech of the Buddha possesses sixty special qualities. Omniscient and compassionate, the Buddha communicates the path of freedom to each individual in ways he or she can understand.

Shortly after the enlightenment, the Buddha began the process of bringing truth to living beings known as turning the wheel of the Dharma. The Enlightened One set the wheel of the Dharma in motion three times, each time displaying different aspects of enlightened knowledge suited to the capacities of his hearers.

The First Turning

Seven weeks after the enlightenment, the Buddha traveled through Vārāṇasī to the Deer Park of Sārnāth. There he gave the teachings fundamental to all schools of Buddhism: the four noble truths, the eightfold path, the three marks of existence, the four laws of the Dharma, and the twelve links of interdependent co-operation.

The teachings of the First Turning reveal the way in which sentient beings are conditioned by ignorance of the true nature of existence and so perpetuate suffering from one moment to the next, throughout endless cycles of birth and death. The primary cause of suffering is the belief in a self; thus, the cessation of suffering comes with the complete understanding that the self has no reality.

The Buddha presented the First Turning teachings to break through the veil of apparent enjoyment that masks the truth of suffering inherent in existence. Desiring to put an end to pain and sorrow, individuals who can hear these teachings abandon clinging to the cycles of delusion and suffering. Through mastering these teachings, they attain a limited form of nirvana: the cessation of suffering and the attainment of peace. These teachings are the basis for the ways to enlightenment known as the Śrāvakayāna and Pratyekabuddhayāna. The most extensive collections of First Turning teachings are preserved in the Pāli and Chinese canons.

The Second Turning

The teachings of the Second and Third Turnings, much more difficult to comprehend, provide the path to complete liberation. These teachings are the basis for the way of enlightenment known as the Bodhisattvayāna.

While the First Turning teachings reveal the emptiness of the self, the Second Turning teachings demonstrate the emptiness of all elements of reality, transcending all limits and extreme views. Revealing the Prajñāpāramitā, the transcendent wisdom that "crosses over" to fully enlightened knowledge, the Second Turning teachings proclaim that no thing, no phenomenon, no element of existence, exists in and of itself. All experience—from physical and material forms up to and including the most refined omniscience of the Buddha—is liberated as all-pervasive emptiness. The wisdom of emptiness and the compassion that responds to sentient beings arise together. Thus, there is no separation between relative and ultimate reality.

The teachings of the Second Turning are the Prajñāpāramitā Sūtras, which convey the Perfection of Wisdom in lengthy texts of 100,000, 25,000, 18,000, 10,000, and 8,000 lines. Shorter expressions of the Prajñāpāramitā teachings include the Diamond Sūtra and the Heart Sūtra.

The Buddha taught the profound teachings of the Second Turning at Vulture Peak near Rājagṛha to the great assembly of Bodhisattvas as well as to the four ordinary assemblies: Arhats and monks, nuns, laypeople, and beings of other realms.

The Third Turning

The Third Turning teachings were taught at Vaiśālī, Mount Malaya, Bodh Gayā, and other locations to an assembly of Bodhisattvas. The path toward realization of these teachings is said to be fully open only to those well-trained in wisdom, who have completely and one-pointedly directed their minds to enlightenment.

Expressing the expansive vision of the Enlightened Ones, Third Turning teachings reveal the vastness of the path, the purity of all experience, and the inexpressible wonder of being. They set forth the teachings of the Tathāgatagarbha, the potential for enlightenment within all sentient beings.

The Third Turning teachings ascertain the ultimate nature of reality by means of an analysis in terms of the three natures: the imaginary, the dependent, and the absolute. All elements of existence—from physical and material forms up to and including the most refined omniscience of the Buddha—are found to be utterly pure.

Sūtras of the Third Turning include the Avataṁsaka, the Saṁdhinirmocana, the Ratnakūṭa, the Laṅkāvatāra, and the Tathāgatagarbha Sūtras.

The Second and Third Turning teachings that have come down to us are just a portion of the original teachings, which are said to have been much more extensive. Hundreds of texts were lost, in part because of hostilities toward the Dharma, when monastic libraries were burned in the early centuries of the Christian era. Additional texts were lost in the later Muslim invasions of India. The Second and Third Turning texts that exist today were preserved in both the Tibetan and Chinese canons, while Sanskrit manuscripts of some works survive to the present day.

The Dharma Teachings

The teachings of the Buddha have a twofold nature: explanation and realization. The explanations are the transmission of the texts that express the meaning of the teaching; realization is the individual's understanding of the meaning. (AKB VIII:39a-b) The explanations include the twelve aṅgas, which were compiled into the three collections of Vinaya, Sūtra, and Abhidharma.

Twelve Aṅgas

On the day of the parinirvāṇa, the Buddha reminded his disciples that the Dharma teachings had been imparted in twelve aṅgas, or branches, each a means of evoking a different response and realization. (AS III)

Sūtra Discourses on a single topic. Seeing ten advantages of this type of teaching, the Tathāgata often taught in this way. Sūtra teachings are well-suited for presenting a single topic; they easily evoke the listener's response; they increase respect for the Dharma, supporting the rapid application of the teachings to one's life; they enable the teachings to penetrate deeply; they inspire serene joy based on faith in the Buddha, faith in the Dharma, and faith in the Sangha; they support supreme happiness even in this lifetime; they please the minds of the wise through exegesis; and they are recognized as extremely wise.

Geya Discourses in verse. These are the stanzas often found at the end or beginning of a Sūtra. Sometimes an idea not discussed within the Sūtra will be explicated in verse.

Vyākaraṇa Prophecies. These are discussions of the past lives and future possibilities of the assembly of the Sangha. They serve to clarify points presented in a Sūtra.

Gāthā Verse summaries. These teachings are given in metered verse within Sūtras. They recapitulate the main themes and are easy to remember.

Udāna Words spoken not to instruct particular individuals but to maintain the Dharma. These teachings are said to have been spoken by the Tathāgata with a very joyful heart.

Nidāna Explanations following a specific incident. In these teachings, the Buddha gives a principle or guideline and explains the reason for it.

Avadāna Life stories of Buddhas, Bodhisattvas, disciples, and various individuals.

Itivṛttaka Historical accounts such as geneologies.

Jātaka Accounts of previous lives of the Buddha.

Vaipulya Lengthy Sūtras with complex organization. These include the Sūtras of the Mahāyāna, with teachings that are especially profound and vast.

Adbhutadharma Accounts of wondrous accomplishments of the Buddha, the disciples, and the Bodhisattvas.

Upadeśa Topics of specific knowledge. These are exact, profound, and subtle instructions on the nature of reality.

CHAPTER FOUR

The Three Collections

The task of preserving the teachings of the Buddha for future generations was begun directly after the Buddha's parinirvāṇa. The Buddha had urged his disciples to gather together and recite all of his teachings as they had heard them, thereby affirming the teachings and ensuring their preservation. In the Pāsādika Sutta the Enlightened One says:

"Compare meaning with meaning, and phrase with phrase, in order that this pure religion may last long and be perpetuated, in order that it may continue to exist for the good and happiness of the great multitudes, out of love for the world, for the good, the profit, and the benefit of gods and human beings." (DN XXIX)

The First Council

Under the patronage of King Ajātaśatru, the Arhat Mahākāśyapa, who had been named the first patriarch of the Dharma by the Buddha, convened a council of five hundred Arhats to set forth the Buddha's teachings and guarantee the accuracy of the transmission.

The great Arhats assembled and sorted the twelve aṅgas into three collections (piṭaka)—Vinaya, Sūtra, and Abhidharma. Upāli recited the Vinaya, Ānanda recited the Sūtras, and Mahākāśyapa recited the mātṛka that formed the basis for the Abhidharma. The minds of these three great Arhats were perfectly composed and pure, clear of the emotional confusion that characterize ordinary minds. Having developed the capacity for perfect recall, these Arhats could describe where each teaching had been given, exactly who had been present, and what the questions and answers had been. The assembly of five hundred Arhats unanimously affirmed that the teachings had been recited just as the Buddha had spoken them.

At the same time that the first council was held at Rājagṛha, another council was convened at Mount Vimalasvabhāva, a short distance south of Rājagṛha, to recite the Mahāyāna teachings. Here the Bodhisattva Maitreya recited the Vinaya, the Bodhisattva Vajrapāṇi recited the Sūtras, and the Bodhisattva Mañjuśrī recited the Abhidharma of the Mahāyāna.

Vinaya or Dharma Training

The Vinaya is the reflection of the Buddha's quality of perfect conduct, the manifestation of the body of enlightenment. The word Vinaya is associated with making decisions, determining what actions of body, speech, and mind promote calm and clarity, and which lead to confusion and suffering. The Mahāyānasūtrālaṁkāra notes four purposes of the Vinaya teachings: identifying wrong action, identifying the causes of wrong action, redressing wrong action, and overcoming wrong action. (MSA XI:1–3)

The Vinaya gives rules of conduct and requirements for monastic life and ordination. In response to specific situations that raised questions about appropriate behavior, the Buddha gave guidelines on the basis of his deep understanding of karma, and his replies were codified into a body of ethical law. The Vinaya rules of conduct counter confusion and awaken mindfulness of the consequences of each thought, word, and action.

The Mahāyānasūtrālaṁkāra explains that the Vinaya is an antidote for extremes of behavior and counteracts the deleterious

THE THREE COLLECTIONS

Collection	*Training*	*Purpose*
Vinaya	moral discipline	protection
Sūtra	concentration	communication
Abhidharma	wisdom	investigation

As these lists were elucidated by disciples such as Śāriputra and Maudgalyāyana, there arose a collection of questions and answers on related themes from various teachings of the Buddha. For example, the Sangīti Suttanta in the Pāli canon gives long lists of study topics organized by number: by two's, by three's, and so forth "arranged for chanting in assembly." In this way the teachings known as Abhidharma began to develop. The Abhidharma contains the teachings classified as upadeśas in the aṅga system.

The Mahāyānasūtrālaṁkāra (MSA XI:1–3) explains that Abhidharma is a remedy for wrong views, for it clarifies the true nature of the Dharma. Abhidharma is associated with training in wisdom. Its treatises describe the constituents of experience, the functioning of the body and mind, the workings of karma and emotions, the stages of the path, and the obstacles along the path. Abhidharma analysis trains the mind in analytical thinking, opening the door to direct insight. Once insight is linked with meditative stability, it discloses knowledge that goes far beyond conventional frames of reference.

One who understands the Abhidharma will have unshakable faith in the Buddhadharma. Like scientists who fully comprehend the workings of nature, Abhidharma masters are fully conversant with the science of consciousness in all its depth and detail. Unconvinced by opinions, unswayed by belief systems, they do not rely on a set of rules or injunctions, for they know the basis for investigating truth. Understanding meanings and definitions, they discern correctly the nature of reality. Perceiving how the fundamental laws of karma operate in human life, in society at large, and in the universe, they understand the causes and consequences of action and can take responsibility for their words, thoughts, and deeds.

Tantra

The Tantras are variously considered a fourth collection or a part of the Sūtra collection, part of the Abhidharma collection, or as encompassing all three collections. The Tibetan canon contains over five hundred Tantras in thirty volumes, as well as more than two thousand commentaries and related texts. In addition, hundreds of esoteric Nyingma Tantras are contained in a collection known as the 100,000 Ancient Tantras. Tantric teachings are also preserved as terma texts, some of which are contained in the Rinchen Terzod and in the collected works of Nyingma masters.

Further Readings

Chos-'byung, by Bu-ston Rinpoche. *History of Buddhism,* part I, pp. 30–41. On the aṅga and the three collections.

bsTan-pa'i-rnam-gzhag and Chos-'byung, by Dudjom Rinpoche. *The Nyingma School of Tibetan Buddhism,* book I, part I, pp. 73–87; book II, part I, pp. 428–431. On transmission of Dharma teachings and the councils.

The Eternal Legacy, An Introduction to the Canonical Literature of Buddhism, by Sangharakshita, pp. 9–19. On the oral tradition and the aṅgas.

The Life of the Buddha and the Early History of his Order, by W. Woodville Rockhill, chapter V, pp. 148–180. On the first council and the formation of the canon.

The Three Jewels and History of Dharma Transmission (Crystal Mirror VI), pp. 27–36, 50–52. On the three turnings.

Buddha, Dharma, Sangha in Historical Perspective (Crystal Mirror VII), pp. 38–41. On the first council.

Light of Liberation (Crystal Mirror VIII), pp. 156–165. On the first council.

SECTION THREE

Sangha: Bridge to Enlightenment

CHAPTER FIVE

Followers of the Buddha

Touched by the greatness of the Buddha's love, knowledge, and power, thousands of individuals turned toward the Dharma and dedicated their lives to attaining knowledge and liberation. Thus the Sangha, the community of those who have taken refuge in the Three Jewels—the Buddha, Dharma, and Sangha—came into being.

The Sangha embraced individuals of all backgrounds and stages of development: kings and commoners, monks and nuns, Arhats and other liberated ones, and the great gathering of Bodhisattvas, some dwelling in the ordinary world of suffering and others abiding in pure realms. Beings everywhere responded to the truth of the Buddha's teachings. The Sūtras describe rays of light spreading throughout immense world-systems, turning hearts and minds toward enlightenment. Transformations took place in the land wherever the Buddha taught: Even spirits of the mountains, rivers, and forests were soothed and uplifted by the sound of the Buddha's voice.

The Vinaya texts describe eight types of Sangha: ordained monks, ordained nuns, male novices, female novices, laymen, laywomen, laymen and laywomen taking temporary vows, and beginners not yet of age. Historically, the Buddhist traditions have strongly emphasized the ordained Sangha as the way of life most suited to spiritual development, but the Buddha did not discriminate in terms of class, caste, sex, or race. The Dharma is open to everyone, and anyone can benefit from it to whatever degree he or she can develop understanding. Nāgārjuna has said that even householders living in the lap of luxury can ford the river of emotional confusion if they possess knowledge of the Dharma. (SL 115) The Mahāyāna tradition, which emphasizes compassion and tolerance, has always encouraged laypeople to study and to meditate. Laypeople in turn materially support the members of the Sangha, who can then focus completely on the work of the Dharma.

Purposes of the Sangha

Manifesting the results of the way of the Buddha, the Sangha demonstrates the truth of the teachings and inspires emulation. Members of the Sangha, being present within the world and yet beyond the confusion of the world, form a bridge between ordinary individuals and the Enlightened Ones. Worthy of respect and admiration, they are a focus for the devotion of those who wish to practice the Dharma. Truly embodying the virtue of the Dharma, they are able to accumulate merit, which they can bestow upon all beings. They hold the lineage of the teachings and are therefore the best counselors and guides for others. They possess the power to teach, to grant blessings, and to remove suffering. Wherever there is a Sangha, the Dharma is alive and the Buddha is present.

For the Dharma practitioner, the monastic Sangha offers support, encouragement, and inspiration. The Sangha can be relied upon by the ordinary person, who participates in the lay Sangha as he or she develops confidence in the Buddha, the Dharma, and the Sangha. When trust deepens into wholehearted devotion, the individual comes into contact with the inner Sangha of those far advanced on the path. These great Arhats and Bodhisattvas, whose wisdom and compassion transcend the boundaries of

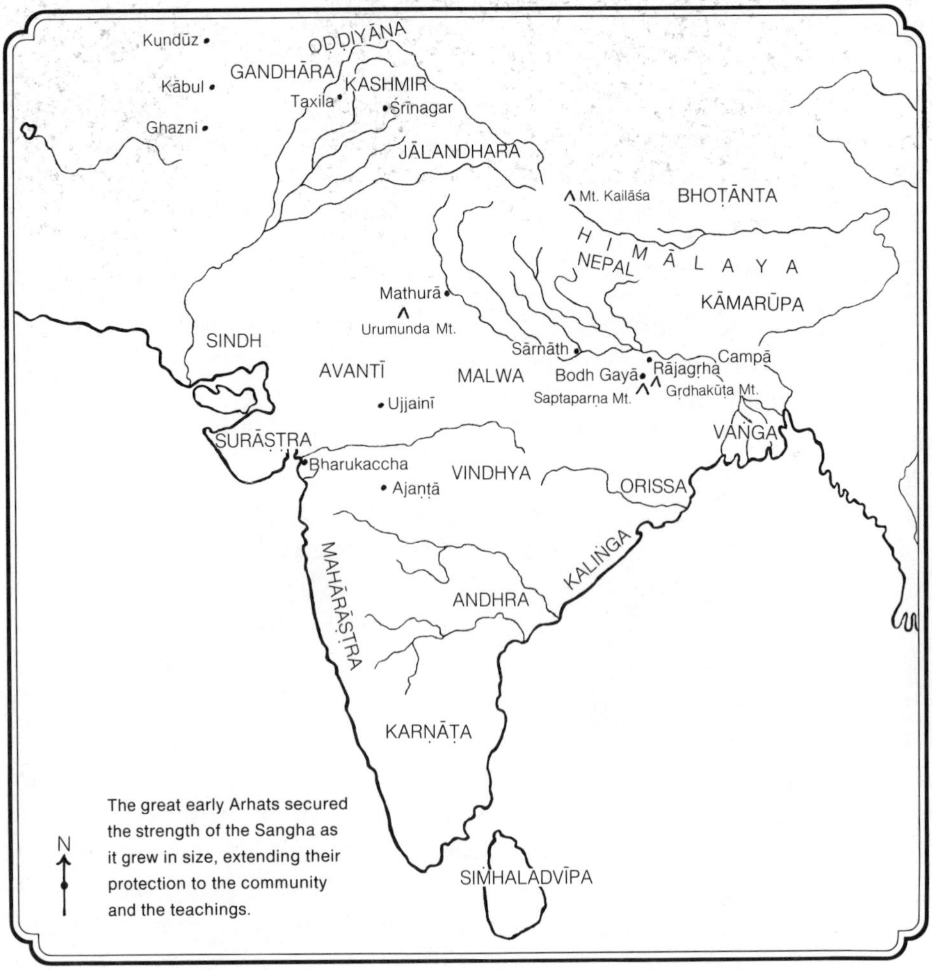

The great early Arhats secured the strength of the Sangha as it grew in size, extending their protection to the community and the teachings.

© 1984 DHARMA PUBLISHING Unauthorized reproduction is a violation of international copyright law.

space and time, are always available to those who devotedly invoke their guidance and blessings.

The Seven Patriarchs

Entrusted with maintaining the Dharma after the Buddha's passing from this world, Mahākāśyapa was the first in a lineage of patriarchs who guarded the purity of the Dharma and extended the benefits of the teachings to new lands. When the first council came to an end and the transmission of the teachings was assured, Mahākāśyapa in turn entrusted the Dharma to Ānanda, the second patriarch, as the Buddha had requested.

Ānanda worked for the Dharma for forty years, during which he led ten thousand monks and five hundred sages to the stage of Arhat. His presentation of the teaching was so powerful that he was able to lead people to the truth in seven days.

The third patriarch, Śānavāsika, first taught the Dharma in Śrāvastī to a thousand monks who soon became Arhats. Highly respected by the various noble families, he ordained hundreds of royal officers and attendants. He preached in six of the great communities of northern India, where he was well known among the common people for his ability to offer protection against dangers such as epidemics. Spending the rainy seasons in the formidable cemetery of Chilly Grove at Śītavana, he once invited his followers to practice there with him to purify their minds of desire, and hundreds achieved realization.

Śānavāsika ordained the son of an incense seller, Upagupta, who attained realization in a single week. After entrusting the Buddha's doctrine to Upagupta, Śānavāsika passed into nirvana at Campā in eastern India. The Buddha had predicted that no one would surpass Upagupta in compassion for living beings. Upagupta taught in Videha and then at Mathurā, where the residents begged him to remain. His preaching attracted so many thousands of people that it is said that Māra, lord of illusion, began making magical displays to distract the listeners. Upagupta engaged Māra in magical contests, defeating him completely. The great reverence that this victory produced in Upagupta's followers allowed them to listen all night to the teachings, and in the morning hundreds achieved realization.

Upagupta spent his final years in Mathurā, taking up residence in a cave. From there he issued a set of seven precise instructions to guide his followers to increasing understanding. Using wooden counters, Upagupta kept track as each one reached the state of an Arhat, and eventually these counters filled his entire cave.

Upagupta was succeeded by Dhītika, the son of a wealthy Brahmin in Ujjain. After becoming a monk, Dhītika went to Mathurā where he met Upagupta. Having received the sevenfold instructions from Upagupta, he attained the state of an Arhat. Dhītika traveled throughout six of the great communities of India, carrying the Dharma as far as Tokharia in central Asia. Preaching to kings and commoners all across northern India, he turned the populace away from nature worship, black magic, and animal sacrifices.

Kṛṣṇa, the sixth patriarch, was entrusted with the Dharma by Dhītika, who then entered nirvana at Ujjain. Together with five hundred followers, Kṛṣṇa expounded the Dharma in Siṁhaladvīpa (Śrī Laṅka) at the request of the king. Kṛṣṇa entrusted the teachings to the Arhat Sudarśana. Sudarśana also made efforts to end animal sacrifices and tamed wild places in the west of India. He traveled extensively in the south, even to island kingdoms, as well as in the north along the borders of China. After Sudarśana's passing, as the Dharma spread across India and Asia, the Sangha was led by various convocations of Arhats and other realized masters.

Councils and Schools

The early Arhats convened councils on three occasions: the first immediately after the parinirvāṇa of the Buddha, the second about a hundred years later, and the third four hundred years after the parinirvāṇa. Each of these councils served to guarantee the transmission of the Dharma and preserve the integrity of the expanding Sangha.

At the first council, five hundred Arhats recited the teachings of the Buddha and compiled the twelve aṅgas into the three collections. At the second council, seven hundred Arhats resolved questions of conduct. As the Sangha became established across India, each community had to determine the extent of the influence of local customs on monastic guidelines. Having established a clear consensus on how to interpret the Vinaya rules, the convocation of Arhats recited the teachings once again in their entirety.

Shortly after the second council, two distinct traditions began to emerge. The Sthaviras emphasized a monastic Sangha, while the Mahāsāṁghikas took a wider view of Sangha. By the time of King Aśoka, India's great Dharma king, there were eighteen schools of Buddhist thought and practice, each emphasizing particular doctrines and approaches. The rise of the eighteen schools was predicted long ago by the previous Buddha Kāśyapa. When

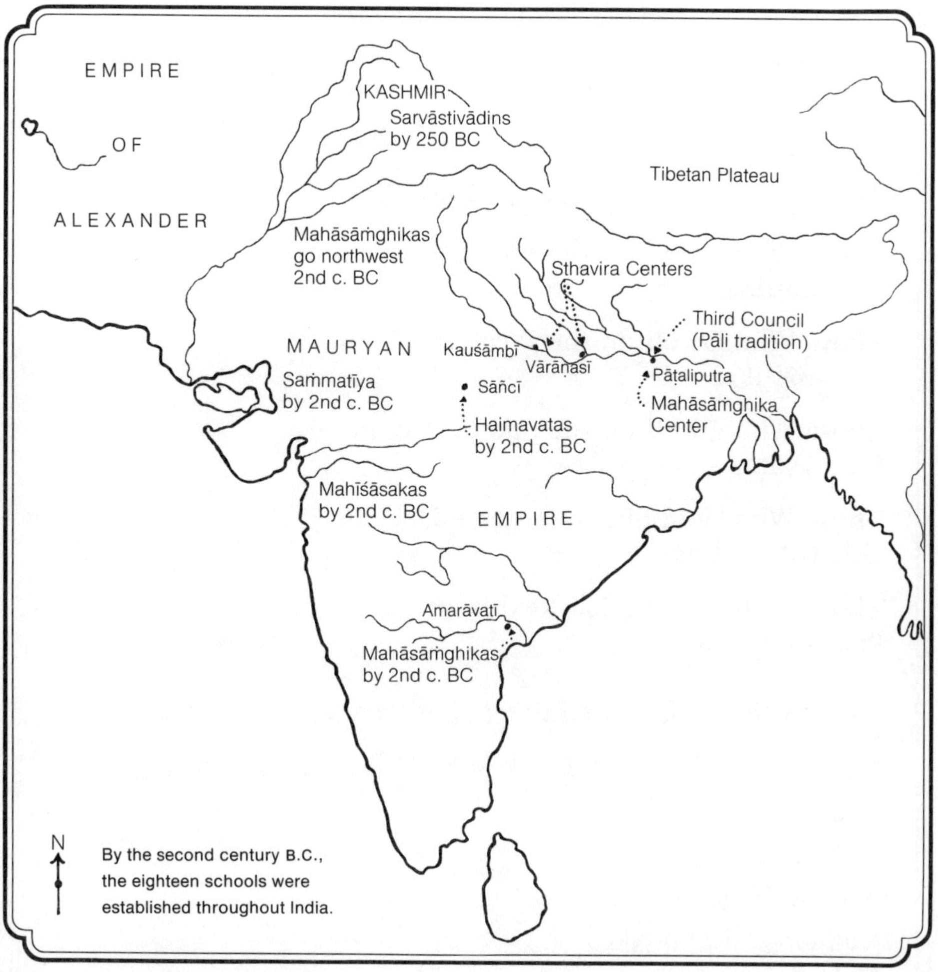

By the second century B.C., the eighteen schools were established throughout India.

© 1984 Dharma Publishing Unauthorized reproduction is a violation of international copyright law.

King Kṛkin sought his advice about a dream in which eighteen men were pulling at a single robe, the Buddha explained that the dream foretold the time of the future Buddha Śākyamuni: His teachings would give rise to eighteen schools, yet the Dharma would remain whole.

King Kaniṣka sponsored the third council in the period when the Buddhadharma entered central Asia. Kaniṣka ruled an empire that included western central Asia, the far northwestern reaches of India, the Punjab, and portions of central India. Noting that there were differences in the teachings among different schools, and deeply interested in the unity of the Sangha, King Kaniṣka convened the council to clarify the true teachings of the Buddha. The account most well known in Tibet describes how five hundred Arhats, five hundred Bodhisattvas, and hundreds of paṇḍitas

EIGHTEEN SCHOOLS*

The Great Assembly: Mahāsāṁghikas

Those Who Dwell on the Eastern Mountain
Pūrvaśailikas

Those Who Dwell on the Western Mountain
Aparaśailikas

Those Who Dwell on the Snowy Mountain
Haimavatas

Those Who Hold Supramundane Doctrines
Lokottaravādins

Those Who Distinguish Real from Fictitious
Prajñaptivādins

Those Who Hold that Everything Exists: Sarvāstivādins

The Root Tradition of Those Who Hold that Everything Exists
Mūlasarvāstivādins

Followers of Kāśyapa
Kāśyapīya

Followers of Mahīśaka
Mahīśāsaka

Followers of Dharmagupta
Dharmaguptaka

gathered together in Kashmir. The council examined the doctrines propounded by all the schools and determined that all were true to the teachings of the Buddha.

Languages of the Dharma

The Buddha's teachings were transmitted orally for many centuries, spoken in the languages of the disciples. Then, as now, India was a land of diverse peoples and cultures. As the Sangha developed and monks traveled widely, they expressed the Dharma

EIGHTEEN SCHOOLS

Broadly Learned Ones
Bahuśrutīya

Followers of Tāmraśata
Tāmraśāṭīya

Those Who Make Distinctions
Vibhajyavāda

The Elders: Sthaviras

Those Who Reside at Jeta Grove
Jetavanīya

Those Who Reside at Mount Abhaya
Abhayagirivāsins

Residing at the Great Temple
Mahāvihāravāsins

Followers of Saṁmita: Saṁmitīya

Kaurukullaka
Kaurukullaka

Protectors
Avantaka

Followers of Vātsīputra
Vātsīputrīya

*Following Vinītadeva

in local languages and dialects. Certain languages came to be associated with specific traditions. The eighth-century Buddhist scholar Vinītadeva recorded that the eighteen schools could be grouped into four major traditions, each associated with a different language or dialect:

Sarvāstivādins, associated with Sanskrit
Sthaviras, associated with Pāli
Mahāsāṁghikas, associated with Prākrit
Saṁmatīyas, associated with Apabhraṁsa

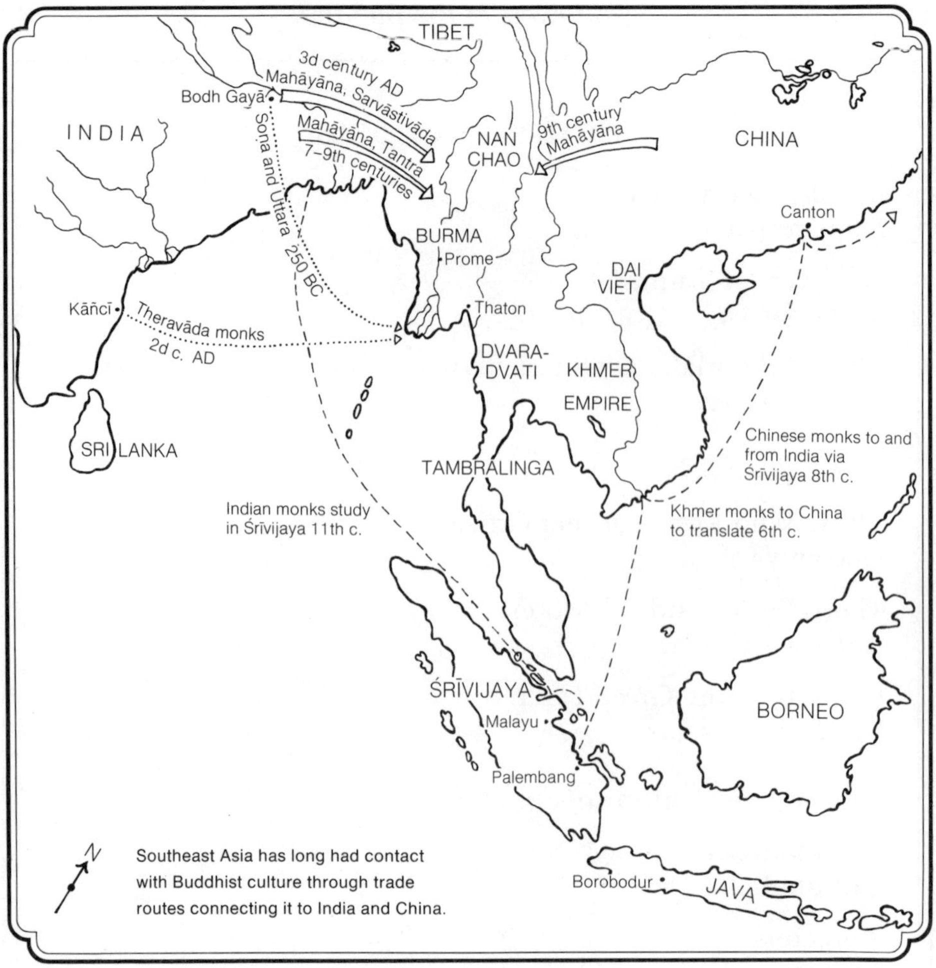

Southeast Asia has long had contact with Buddhist culture through trade routes connecting it to India and China.

© 1984 Dharma Publishing Unauthorized reproduction is a violation of international copyright law.

Northern and Southern Traditions

Taken to Śrī Laṅkā by the son of King Aśoka a century after the Buddha's parinirvāṇa, the three collections of the Sthavira (Theravādin) school were transmitted in an oral tradition until a few generations before the common era when they were written down in Pāli. The Pāli texts form the canon for the southern tradition.

At the third council, convened during the reign of King Kaniṣka, the masters of the northern schools wrote down the Vinaya collection, as well as any texts of the Sūtra and Abhidharma collections that had not been previously committed to writing.

SOUTHERN TRADITIONS

3rd Century B.C.E.
Sthavira school to Śrī Laṅkā

2nd–5th Centuries C.E.
Mahāyana and Theravāda
Dharma centers in Burma, Cambodia, Vietnam

7th–10th Centuries C.E.
Vajrayāna to Burma and Indonesia

11th Century C.E.
Burma adopts Theravāda

13th Century C.E.
Cambodia and Thailand adopt Theravāda

14th–15th Century C.E.
Theravāda into Laos
Dharma disappears from Indonesia

All of these texts belonged to the First Turning. The Second and Third Turning teachings were just emerging into view about the time of the third council, previously having been transmitted in secret by the Bodhisattvas.

Abhidharma doctrines of the Śrāvaka schools have been preserved in the Mahāvibhāṣa, an encyclopedic Abhidharma compendium written at the time of the third council and still extant in Chinese translation. The Vinaya collections remain for six of the Śrāvaka schools, including the Sarvāstivādin Vinaya lineages preserved within the Tibetan tradition. Some of the views of two philosophical traditions that branched off from the Mūlasarvāstivādins, the Vaibhāṣika and the Sautrāntika, are preserved in the Abhidharmakoṣabhāṣya and other sources. Many other texts have been lost.

CHAPTER SIX

Mahāyāna Traditions

After the parinirvāṇa of the Enlightened One, the Mahāyāna teachings were preserved by the Mahābodhisattvas for centuries and transmitted in secret until the time when their deep meaning could be comprehended. According to the Tibetan historian Tāranātha, these teachings were reintroduced in Orissa in eastern India. A monk (said to be Mañjuśrī himself) taught Mahāyāna doctrines to Candrarakṣita, the king of Orissa, and left a text in the royal palace. Tāranātha places this event before the third council.

At the time of the third council, the Mahāyāna texts began to become known and taught, although not extensively. Eight great masters, including Kamalagarbha and Ghanasa, were teaching the Madhyama, the Middle Way, and three masters of Yogācāra—Nanda, Paramasena, and Samyaksatya—were composing treatises. These three became known as the Early Yogācārins. The Early Yogācārins focused on an esoteric meditative practice, using special methods that resembled tantric techniques: visualization, mantra, rituals, and dhāraṇis. The Later Yogācārins followed the works of Maitreya and Asaṅga.

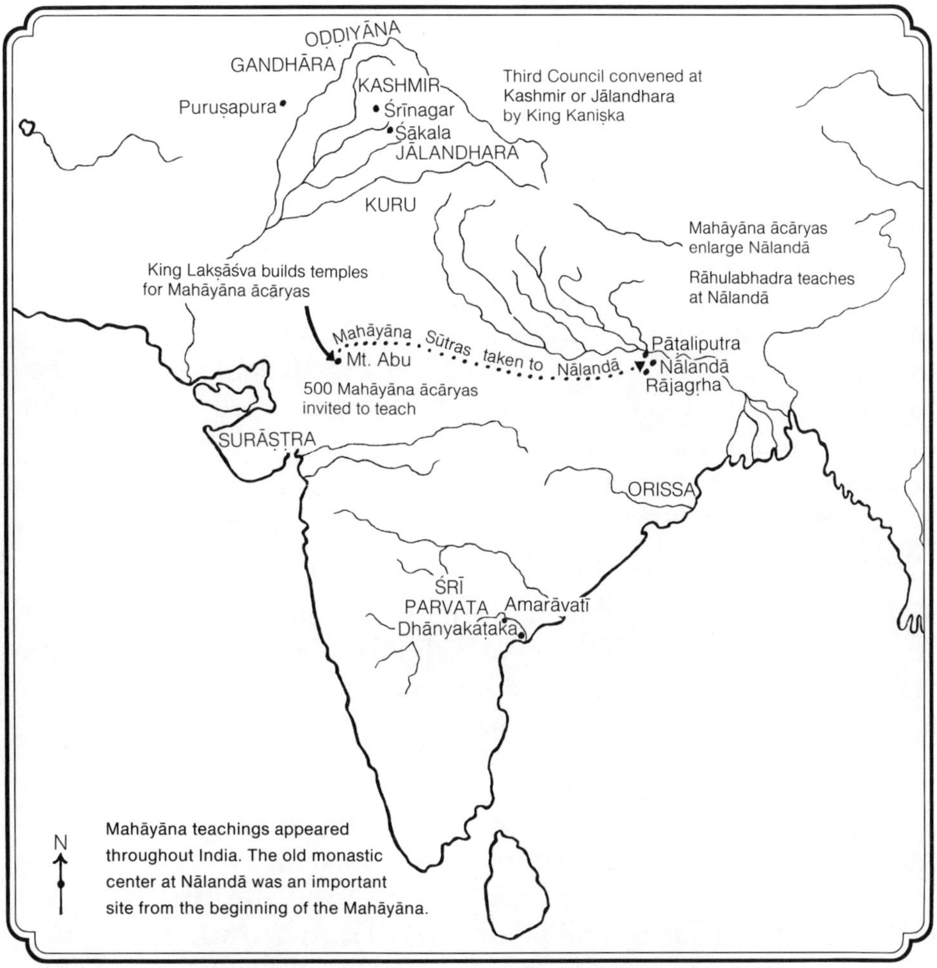

© 1984 Dharma Publishing Unauthorized reproduction is a violation of international copyright law.

Mount Ābu and Nālandā

In Surāṣṭra in western India, shortly after the third council, a layman whose activities were predicted by the Buddha greatly admired the Mahāyāna doctrines and began inviting teachers to come to his land to explicate them. According to Tāranātha, teachers of the Mahāyāna suddenly appeared everywhere. Hundreds of masters emerged, holders of the Bodhisattva lineage transmitted by Mañjuśrī, Avalokiteśvara, Vajrapāṇi, Maitreya, and others of the eight great Bodhisattvas. Among them was Avitarka, who taught Mahāyāna doctrines to Rāhulabhadra.

The ruler of the region, King Lakṣāśva, began to support the propagation of the Mahāyāna teachings and invited five hundred masters to teach at Mount Ābu. There he built each teacher a temple and offered his own ministers and attendants as disciples.

At the behest of King Lakṣāśva, Mahāyāna texts were collected and copied; later these texts were taken to Nālandā, an ancient holy site that had been the birthplace of Śāriputra, the Buddha's disciple who was foremost in Abhidharma. King Aśoka had built the first temple at Nālandā, and now two brothers who were outstanding Dharma scholars built eight temples there and provided support for five hundred Mahāyāna monks. The Mahāyāna master Rāhulabhadra taught numerous disciples at Nālandā, including the great philosopher Nāgārjuna. Supported by lineages of outstanding masters, the Mahāyāna teachings spread widely from Nālandā throughout India.

Followers of the Mahāyāna originally belonged to one or another of the eighteen Śrāvaka schools. Ordained within the Mahāsaṁghika or Sarvāstivādin tradition, for example, the Mahāyāna practitioner lived in the same monastery with the Śrāvaka monks.

Though at first only a few among many thousands of followers of the First Turning teachings, the masters of the Mahāyana began to embody a new, vaster vision of the spiritual path presented in the Sūtras of the Second and Third Turnings. Teachers of the Mahāyāna soon were explicating these Sūtras to large gatherings of disciples, stimulating a remarkable period of inquiry and spiritual accomplishment.

Two Commentarial Traditions

The Second and Third Turning teachings were explicated by two traditions of commentary (śāstra). The first, known as the tradition of inquiry in depth, was inspired by the Bodhisattva Mañjuśrī and was transmitted through Nāgārjuna. Nāgārjuna's works laid the foundation for the Mādhyamika school. The second, known as the tradition of vast perspective, originated with the Bodhisattva Maitreya, who will be the next Buddha after Śākyamuni. Maitreya transmitted the root teachings to Asaṅga, who transcribed them as the Five Treatises of Maitreya. Together with Asaṅga's own commentaries, these texts became the basis for the system known as Yogācāra or Cittamātra. A third master, Dignāga, developed the tools of logic and epistemology, protecting the teachings against misunderstanding and misinterpretations by Buddhists and non-Buddhists.

These three masters each had an outstanding commentator: Āryadeva, disciple of Nāgārjuna; Vasubandhu, brother and disciple of Asaṅga; and Dharmakīrti, holder of Dignāga's teachings. Together these six masters are known as the Six Ornaments. When Nāgārjuna and Asaṅga are honored separately as the Two Charioteers or the Two Supreme Ones, the Vinaya masters Guṇaprabha and Śākyaprabha are included in the Six Ornaments.

Five Subjects of Dharma Study

In Tibet the works of these masters form the curriculum of five subjects essential for Dharma study: Vinaya, Abhidharma, Prajñāpāramitā, Mādhyamika, and Logic. The works of Indian masters of these subjects are explicated by Tibetan scholars in learned commentaries, which are also studied intensively.

Masters of Vinaya Guṇaprabha is a major explicator of the Vinaya; he also composed texts on Abhidharma and on the Bodhisattva path.

Masters of Abhidharma Vasubandhu, Asaṅga, and Sthiramati are the major masters of the Mahāyāna Abhidharma. Their Abhidharma works comprise the foundation for the study of Abhidharma.

Masters of Prajñāpāramitā Haribhadra and his disciple Vimuktasena are the foremost explicators of the Prajnāpāramitā.

Masters of Mādhyamika Nāgārjuna, Āryadeva, Bhāvaviveka, Buddhapālita, Śāntideva, Candrakīrti, Śāntarakṣita, and Kamalaśīla are the major Mādhyamika masters. Their works are the basis of the Mādhyamika philosophical tradition.

Masters of Logic The works of Dignāga and Dharmakīrti are the essential texts for the study of logic.

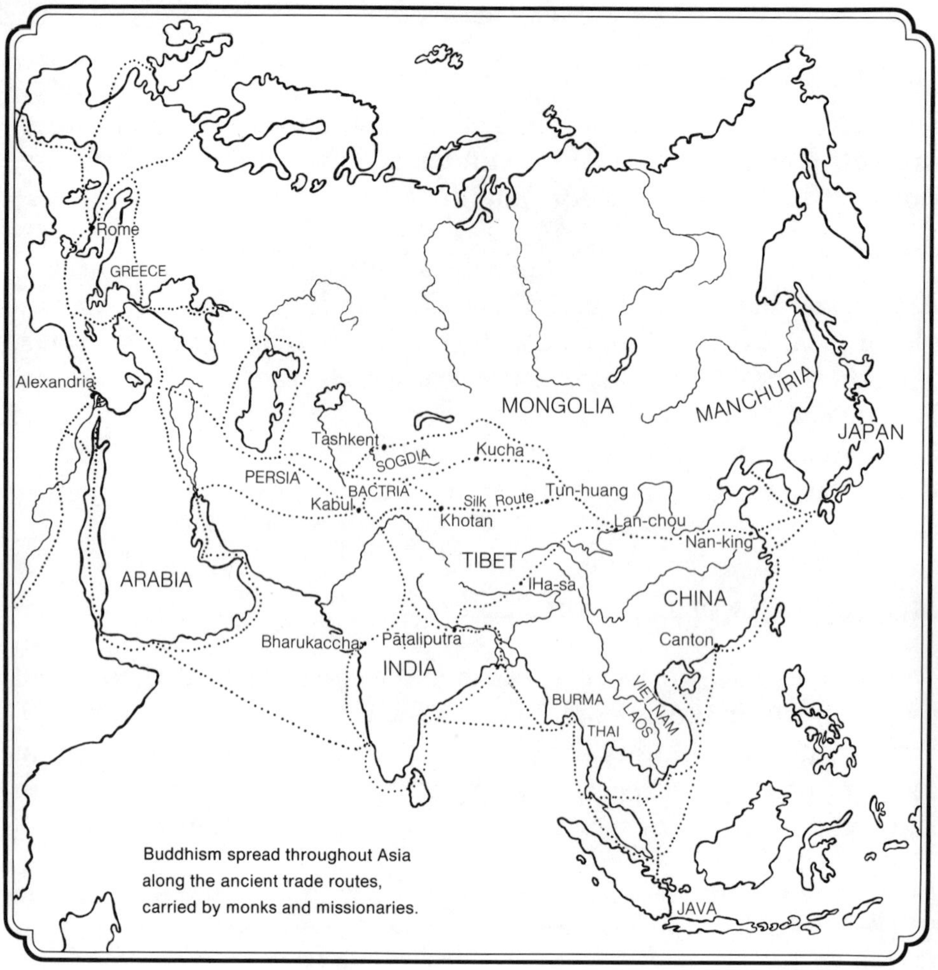

Buddhism spread throughout Asia along the ancient trade routes, carried by monks and missionaries.

© 1984 DHARMA PUBLISHING Unauthorized reproduction is a violation of international copyright law.

Spread of the Mahāyāna

Beginning in the first centuries of the common era, the Mahāyāna lineages were carried throughout India and then spread across Asia. By the third century, monks had established monasteries in central Asia along the Silk Route that linked the Far East with the Near East. By the eighth century, the teachings of the way of the Bodhisattva had reached China, Korea, and Japan in the far east; Tibet and Khotan in central Asia; and all of southeast Asia including Java and Indonesia. By the thirteenth century, the Mongol khans were interested in the Dharma, and in the seventeenth and eighteenth centuries the Manchus printed Tibetan, Chinese, Mongolian, and Manchu canons.

NORTHERN TRADITIONS

Century C.E.	
	Central Asia
1st	Monasteries established along Silk Route.
3rd	Khotan centers flourish and monks travel to China.
7th	Mahāyāna and Sarvāstivādin centers well-established
8th–9th	Turks and Uighurs become Buddhists.
10th–11th	Muslim Turks rule Central Asian kingdoms.
	China
2nd–3rd	Central Asian translators in China
4th	First catalogue of Sūtra translations
5th–6th	Schools established based on Madhyamaka, Abhidharma, Cittamātra, Lotus Sūtra established; Ch'an and Pure Land schools established.
7th	Hua-yen and Fa-hsiang schools established.
9th	After persecution of Sangha, only Ch'an and Pure Land survive.
10th–11th	Sung dynasty supports modest revival of Buddhism; Chinese canon printed.
13th	Mongol court supports Buddhism.
	Korea and Japan
4th–5th	Buddhism enters Korea.
6th–7th	Buddhism enters Japan; Golden Age of Korean Buddhism; Pure Land flourishes in Korea.
	Ch'an teachings introduced to Korea.

NORTHERN TRADITIONS (continued)

8th–9th	Buddhism becomes state religion in Japan. Nine Ch'an lineages (Nine Mountain School) flourish in Korea.
9th–11th	Shingon tantric school and Tendai Lotus school established in Japan; Amitābha practices flourish. Kōryō dynasty in Korea supports Dharma.
11th–13th	Pure Land and Zen (Ch'an) flourish and Nichiren Shōshu founded in Japan; Chinese canon printed in Korea.

Tibet and Mongolia

4th	Buddhist influences first enter Tibet.
7th	Tibetan Dharma Kings actively support Buddhism.
8th	Guru Padmasambhava, Abbot Śāntarakṣita, and Tibetan King Trisong Detsen found Samye monastery; first monks ordained; extensive translations made; Nyingma lineages established.
10th–11th	Beginnings of new Tibetan schools: Kadampa, Kagyudpa, and Sakyapa. Era of Atīśa and Dromton, Marpa and Milarepa, Virūpa and Drogmi Lotsawa.
12th–14th	Tibetan canon established; terma masters active. Era of Longchenpa, Sakya Paṇḍita, Dolpoba, Buton Rinpoche, Karmapa Rangjung Dorje, and Siddha Orgyenpa.
14th–16th	Gelugpa school established by Tsongkhapa; Mongols convert to Buddhism; first Dalai Lamas recognized.
17th–18th	Tibetan and Mongolian canons printed. Era of Fifth Dalai Lama, Terdag Lingpa.

The Eight Tibetan Practice Lineages

The transmission of the Buddhadharma into Tibet occurred in eight distinct teaching lineages: Nyingma, Kadampa, Sakyapa, Kagyudpa, Shangpa, Pacification of Suffering, Six-limbed Yoga, and Orgyenpa's Lineage. The teachings of these original eight are continued today within four remaining schools: Nyingma, Kagyudpa, Sakyapa, and Gelugpa.

The distinctive approach of each school can be studied in the writings of its major authors. The following recommendations provide a good starting point for developing a basic understanding of the Tibetan Buddhist schools.

For Nyingma studies, see the works of Rongzom Mahāpaṇḍita, Kunkyen Longchenpa, Terdag Lingpa, Minling Lochen Dharmaśrī, Lama Mipham, and Khyentse Wangpo.

For Sakya studies, see the works of Sakya Paṇḍita, Gorampa, Rongton, and Sakya Chogden.

For Kagyudpa studies, see authors in the Karmapa lineage, for example Rangjung Dorje and Mikyo Dorje, as well as Drigung Kyopa, Drugpa Padma Karpo, Tsuglag Trengwa, and Kongtrul Lodro Taiyay.

For Gelugpa studies, see the works of Je Tsongkhapa, Gyaltsabje and Khedrubje, together with the four famous Gelugpa textual guides (yig-cha).

Commentators may emphasize the perspective of one of the four philosophical schools, such as the Prāsaṅgika Mādhyamika or the Yogācāra. Interpretations may rely closely on quotations from the Sūtras and śāstras; they may follow logic and experiential methods, or emphasize the living realization passed down by the lineage masters.

The points of view of the major commentators have inspired generations of scholars and practitioners. Presented as formal discourses or debates, the key issues are of deep import to the follower of the way of the Buddha: the relationship of the two truths, the inner nature of reality, the essentials of practice, the definition of the stages of the path, and the process of purification and transformation of the obscurations.

THIRTEEN GREAT TEXTS
gZhung-chen bcu-gsum

Prātimokṣa Sūtra

Vinaya Sūtra, by Guṇaprabha

Abhidharmakoṣabhāṣya, by Vasubandhu

Abhidharmasamuccaya, by Asaṅga

Mūlamadhyamakakārikā, by Nāgārjuna

Catuḥśatakaśāstra, by Āryadeva

Bodhicaryāvatāra, by Śāntideva

Abhisamayālaṁkāra, by Maitreya

Mahāyānasūtrālaṁkāra, by Maitreya

Madhyāntavibhaṅga, by Maitreya

Dharmadharmatāvibhaṅga, by Maitreya

Mahāyānottaratantra, by Maitreya

Each school of Tibetan Buddhism focuses on a specific set of Mahāyāna texts, though there are a number studied by all schools. The Nyingma tradition includes the curriculum of six great monasteries: Katog, Palyul, Dzogchen, Dorjedrag, Mindroling, and Zechen.

The nineteenth-century Nyingma master Zhenpen Chokyi Nangwa composed commentaries on thirteen essential Mahāyāna texts. Scholars and students of all the Tibetan schools revered and studied these commentaries, which were made according to the Indian śāstra tradition rather than reflecting the viewpoint of any particular Tibetan school.

This study guide frequently cites these thirteen texts to familiarize Dharma students with their contents and to lay the foundation for Nyingma education.

CHAPTER SEVEN

The Canons

Three major canonical traditions have endured to the present time: the Pāli canon of the southern Theravādin school and the Chinese and Tibetan canons based on the Sanskrit texts of the northern Mahāyāna schools. Several other canons are based on either the Tibetan or Chinese; for example, the Mongolian relies on the Tibetan and the Manchu on the Chinese.

The Theravādin schools of southeast Asia traditionally rely on the Pāli canon, while the Mahāyāna schools of Japan, Korea, and China base their study and practice on the Chinese canon. The Chinese canon includes the entire Sarvāstivādin Tripiṭaka (the three collections), the Mahāyāna Sūtras, and a large number of Mahāyāna śāstras.

The Tibetan canon, with its extensive collection of Tantras and śāstras, represents the most complete collection of Mahāyāna texts extant today. The Tibetan canon is divided into two sections, the words of the Buddha (Kanjur) and the words of the great masters (Tanjur). Three major editions include the Narthang edition compiled in the fourteenth century, the Peking edition compiled in the seventeenth century, and the Derge

DIVISIONS OF THE PĀLI CANON

Vinayapiṭaka	*Suttapiṭaka*	*Abhidhammapiṭaka*
Suttavibhaṅga	Dīgha Nikāya	Dhammasaṅgaṇī
Khandhaka	Majjhima Nikāya	Vibhaṅga
Parivāra	Saṁyutta Nikāya	Dhātukathā
	Aṅguttara Nikāya	Puggalapaññati
	Khuddaka Nikāya	Kathāvatthu
		Yamaka
		Paṭṭhāna

DIVISIONS OF THE CHINESE CANON

Vinaya Piṭaka	*Sūtra Piṭaka*	*Abhidharma Piṭaka*
Vinayas of six early schools:	Sūtras of the Mahāyāna:	Mahāyāna Abhidharma
Dharmaguptaka	Prajñāpāramitā	Hīnayāna Abhidharma
Mahīśāsaka	Ratnakūṭa	
Mahāsāṁghika	Mahāsannipāta	
Sarvāstivādin	Avataṁsaka	
Mūlasarvāstivādin	Nirvana Class	
	Sūtras of the Hīnayāna:	*Miscellaneous*
Kāśyapīya		Indian works
	Āgama	Chinese works

Based on Nanjio's Catalogue

edition compiled in the eighteenth century. The Nyingma Edition, a reprint of the Derge with supplementary texts from other editions, is the most comprehensive collection of canonical texts in the Tibetan language.

The Three Collections and the Canons

Vinaya texts of all known traditions are similar. The Tibetan Buddhist schools follow the Vinaya of the Mūlasarvāstivādins, one of the eighteen early schools. These texts were preserved first in Sanskrit, and then translated into Tibetan and Chinese.

Sūtra Collections

The Sūtras of the First Turning were transmitted in Sanskrit (āgamas) and Pāli (nikāyas). While the Pāli nikāyas are preserved in the Pāli canon, the Sanskrit texts survive completely only in Chinese translation. Some of the First Turning Sanskrit Sūtras were translated into Tibetan and preserved in the Sūtra section (mDo-sde) of the bKa'-'gyur. Sūtras of the Second and Third Turning, originally transmitted in Sanskrit and related dialects, survive today primarily in Tibetan and Chinese.

Although many Sūtra teachings have been lost, hundreds have been preserved in the Pāli, Chinese, and Tibetan canons. The Nyingma Edition of the Tibetan Canon contains 352 Sūtras in twenty-two volumes.

Abhidharma Collections

The Abhidharma collections of the northern and southern traditions, systematized by the Buddha's disciples, developed differently. The Abhidharma of the southern tradition is preserved in seven Pāli texts. The Abhidharma of the northern tradition was developed and written down in seven Sanskrit texts.

The Tibetan tradition makes a sharp distinction between the words of the Buddha and the words of the disciples. Therefore, the essential topics of the Abhidharma given by the Buddha (mātṛka) are found together with the Sūtras in the Tibetan Kanjur. The works of the disciples were placed in the Tanjur. However, six of the seven early Abhidharma texts are not found

DIVISIONS OF THE TIBETAN CANON

Kanjur (bKa'-'gyur)

Vinaya	Vinaya 'Dul-ba NE 1–7A
Perfection of Wisdom Sūtras	Prajñāpāramitā Sher-phyin NE 8–43
Flower Ornament Sūtra	Avataṁsaka Phal-chen NE 44
Jewel Heap Sūtras	Ratnakūṭa dKon-brtsegs NE 45–93
Sūtra Section includes Abhidharma	Sūtra mDo-sde NE 94–359A
Tantras	Tantra rGyud NE 360–827
Ancient Tantras	Pratantra rNying-rgyud NE 828–844
Wheel of Time	Kālacakra Dus-'khor NE 845
Dhāraṇī	Dhāraṇī gZungs-'dus NE 846–1108

DIVISIONS OF THE TIBETAN CANON

Tanjur (bsTan-'gyur)

Eulogies	Stotra bsTod-tshogs NE 1109–1179
Tantra	Tantra rGyud NE 1180–3785
Perfection of Wisdom	Prājnāpāramitā Sher-phyin NE 3786–3823
Middle Way	Madhyamaka dBu-ma NE 3824–3980
Sūtra Commentaries	Sūtra mDo-'grel NE 3981–4019
Mind-Only	Cittamātra Sems-tsam NE 4020–4085
Abhidharma	Abhidharma mNgon-pa NE 4086–4103
Vinaya	Vinaya 'Dul-ba NE 4104–4149
Birth Stories	Jātaka sKyes-rabs NE 4150–4157

DIVISIONS OF THE TIBETAN CANON

Tanjur continued

Letters and Accounts	Lekha/Parikathā sPring-yig NE 4158-4202
Logic	Pramāṇa Tshad-ma NE 4203–4268
Language Studies	Śabdavidyā sGra-mdo NE 4269–4305
Medicine	Cikitsāvidyā gSo-ba-rig-pa NE 4306–4312
Sacred Art	Śilpavidyā bZo-ba-rig-pa NE 4313–4327
Worldly Conduct	Nītiśāstra Lugs-kyi-bstan-bcos NE 4328–4345
Miscellaneous Texts by Tibetan Masters Bhāvanopadeśa Prayers and Blessings Later Additions to the Canon	Viśvavidyā sNa-tshogs NE 4346–4364
Indexes	Sūcilipi dKar-chag NE 4465–4466

in the Tanjur and survive only in Chinese translation. The seventh, the Prajñaptiśāstra, survives in full in Tibetan translation and can be found in the Abhidharma section of the Tanjur. (The Chinese version is incomplete.)

Further Readings

Chos-'byung, by Bu-ston Rinpoche. *History of Buddhism,* part II, pp. 73–180, 181–223. On the development of the Dharma in India and Tibet.

Deb-ther-sngon-po, by 'Gos Lo-tsā-ba. *The Blue Annals,* pp. 22–35, 35–47. On councils, the eighteen schools, and Dharma transmission to Tibet.

rGya-gar-chos-'byung, by Tāranātha. *History of Buddhism in India.*

The Opening of the Dharma, by 'Jam-dbyangs mKhyen-brtse'i Chos-kyi-blo-gros. On the origin of the Tibetan schools.

Record of Buddhistic Kingdoms: An Account of His Travels in India and Ceylon (A.D. 399–414), by Fa-hien.

Buddhist Records of the Western World, by Hsüan-tsang. On seventh-century Buddhism in Central Asia and India.

A Record of the Buddhist Religion as Practiced in India and the Malay Archipelago (A.D. 671–695), by I-tsing.

Mahāvaṁsa (The Great Chronicle of Ceylon).

The Three Jewels and History of Dharma Transmission (Crystal Mirror VI), pp. 52–179. On contents of texts and the history of Buddhism in India, Asia, and Tibet.

Buddha, Dharma, Sangha in Historical Perspective (Crystal Mirror VII). On Dharma history in Asia and the written tradition, with a bibliography of Buddhist texts.

Light of Liberation (Crystal Mirror VIII), pp. 149–413. On the growth of the Sangha and the rise of the Mahāyāna.

On the Diffusion of Buddhism

Buddhism in China, by Kenneth Ch'en.

The Buddhist Conquest of China, by E. Zurcher.

Zen and Japanese Culture, by D. T. Suzuki.

The Foundation of Japanese Buddhism, by Daigan and Alicia Matsunaga.

Lives of Eminent Korean Monks, translated by Peter H. Lee.

The Indianized States of Southeast Asia, by G. Coedès.

Tibetan Civilization, by R. A. Stein.

Tibet in Pictures, by Li Gotami Govinda. 2 volumes.

Ancient Tibet, by the Yeshe De Research Project.

SECTION FOUR

Fundamental Awakening

CHAPTER EIGHT

Basic Perspectives

O monks, when the Tathāgata became a perfect Buddha, the darkness and the shadows disappeared . . . the character of all beings was known, the conduct of all beings was understood. The remedy for the sickness of the world was well understood . . . (LAL XXII)

On the night of the enlightenment, the Buddha discerned the root causes and understood the fundamental patterns that give rise to samsara. When the Enlightened One first began to teach, he expressed his profound understanding in four noble truths:

The truth of suffering
The truth of the origin of suffering
The truth of the cessation of suffering
The truth of the path that leads to cessation

Essential Principles of Inquiry

The four truths set forth essential principles of inquiry in a meaningful order. First, we need to understand our basic human situation. Once we know clearly what that situation is, we can begin an inquiry into the causes that have given rise to that situation. Having understood the causes of our situation, we can comprehend the possibility of alternatives arising from different causes. Fourth, we can then trace out the path that actualizes those new possibilities.

Without knowledge of the four truths, we assume that the causes of problems are either external—such as social, political, or historical conditions—or internal—such as psychological or biological conditions—or some combination of the two. Study of the four truths reveals the more fundamental causes of our difficulties; it places in our hands the master keys that can free us from endless cycles of suffering. The root of suffering is ignorance, the shadow of not-knowing that obscures the truth. This ignorance permits the arising of all the mechanisms of samsara.

Because the root cause of samsara is ignorance, efforts to refine knowledge by study and practice make a significant difference in our ability to set ourselves free. Each of us must discover and apply this knowledge for ourselves, but we have the Buddha and other spiritual friends to rely on for guidance. Following in the footsteps of the Buddha, individuals in the past discovered for themselves the knowledge required for this transformation, put it into practice, and obtained the results: enlightened awareness and complete freedom from suffering. In century after century these liberated ones have explicated the path of the Buddha in the language and manner of their time and place so that future generations would have access to enlightened knowledge.

Living Body of Knowledge

All Buddhist traditions accept and practice the teachings of the four noble truths, the two truths, the eightfold path, and interdependent co-operation. These fundamental teachings on suffering, karma, and liberation are the gateway to the Mahāyāna teachings on śūnyatā and Tathāgatagarbha that completely transcend duality, causality, and all forms of self.

Deeply interconnected, these essential teachings form a living body of knowledge, a unified vision that arises from within enlightened awareness. The truth of suffering, the truth of origination of suffering, and the truth of the path are associated with relative truth, while the truth of the cessation of suffering is associated with ultimate truth. The cause and effect relationship described by interdependent co-operation sets forth the full explanation of the second truth, the cause of samsara and its suffering, and provides the basis for the fourth truth, the truth of the path that transforms the workings of samsara.

Śāriputra once explained the perfect view of the Buddha to a group of monks at Śrāvastī as recorded in the Discourse on Perfect View (Sammādiṭṭhisutta). One way to wisdom, he says, is to comprehend and remove the three poisons: attachment, aversion, and confusion. When the monks inquire if there might be yet another way, Śāriputra explains that the eightfold noble path is such a way. Again, the monks ask if there exists any other way; this time the great Arhat Śāriputra teaches the four noble truths. When they inquire yet again, he describes the twelve links of interdependent co-operation. In short, all these teachings explicate the perfect view of a Buddha.

The Mahāyāna śāstras, especially those associated with Nāgārjuna's Mūlamadhyamakakārikā, give detailed explanations as to how these teachings are interwoven with one another.

View, Practice, and Conduct

Just as a student of science studies theory, practices basic experimental procedure, and develops the orientation of a scientifically trained individual, students of human nature need to prepare themselves properly. One wishing to investigate the human situation must have a fundamental viewpoint that guides the inquiry, know the basic practices to take up in the laboratory of experience, and develop a way of life that supports the ongoing exploration.

Only when investigation becomes disciplined and precise can the results be reliable. The process of disciplined exploration opens the door to possibilities that we may have glimpsed, without knowing where they lead or how to pursue them. The support of view, practice, and conduct are essential if new understanding is to be brought into everyday life where it can effectively inspire the process of transformation.

Texts that focus on the view of the Dharma set forth the explanations of the nature of existence, the nature of human being, and the kinds of transformation possible. These teachings lay the groundwork for practice. Texts that focus on the meditative practice set forth the various contemplative techniques, the practice instructions, the stages of practice, the structure of the path, and the signs of progress. Texts that focus on ways of conduct describe attitudes, orientations, and ways of behaving that form an integral part of the path or manifest the results of following the path. For example, the treatises of Nāgārjuna demonstrate the view of the Bodhisattva, while Śāntideva's Bodhicaryāvatāra describes the conduct of a Bodhisattva. Each of the four philosophical schools studied in the Tibetan tradition (the Vaibhāṣika, the Sautrāntika, the Yogācāra, and the Mādhyamika) developed its own distinctive views, practices, and ways of conduct.

CHAPTER NINE

The Four Noble Truths

During the night of the enlightenment, the Buddha perceived how individuals are propelled by the force of their actions to repeat those patterns binding them to endless cycles of birth and death. Seeing the life experiences of all beings throughout endless reaches of time, the Buddha perceived the full extent of suffering and its manifestations not only within the human and animal world, but throughout all possible realms of existence.

The Enlightened One saw that everything that forms our reality is in a state of continuous flux. All of existence—from individuals, nations, and cultures to the very earth we stand on—is subject to change. The fortunes of individuals wax and wane, empires rise and fall, whole civilizations develop and vanish in the course of time.

The Truth of Suffering

For us as human beings, the full significance of such all-pervading impermanence is deep and unending suffering. The Buddha enumerated eight categories of suffering, four of which are related to physical realities and four to emotional discomforts. The first four are known as the four great rivers of suffering:

1. Birth is a source of suffering: It produces pain and shocks the body and psyche, establishing the conditions for the torments of hunger, thirst, and myriad other discomforts.

2. Old age is a source of suffering: We perceive our life and body disintegrating; our ability to enjoy life wanes; friends and family fall away; and we approach the end of our days torn between yearning for death and terror of what death might bring.

3. Sickness is a source of suffering: When illness arises, we are helpless and unpleasant to be near. Vitality and enthusiasm decline, and we are tormented by physical pain; our distress is intensified by fears and anxieties about what this pain indicates and where it may lead.

4. Death is a source of suffering: In death, we face the unknown utterly alone. Moreover, we may be confronted with this ultimate unknown at any moment, whether we are prepared or not.

The Four Additional Sufferings

5. Suffering arises from association with that which we dislike or find unpleasant. There is always the possibility of having to associate with people we dislike, of encountering enemies, or having to perform unpleasant tasks. No matter what wealth we acquire or how carefully we arrange our lives, we have no guarantee that we will not be subject to undesirable conditions.

6. Suffering arises from separation from that which we like and want to be close to. No matter how happy our family life or friendships, circumstances or eventually death will bring them to an end. With passionate or romantic love comes the suffering of jealousy; with attachment to one's children comes the pain of constant anxiety. When we are successful, friends hover close by, but when our fortune diminishes, they are difficult to find.

7. Suffering arises from not obtaining our desires as well as from obtaining them. Everyone wishes for peace, comfort, and happiness. If we lack these qualities, we suffer; if we have them, we fear that we will lose them. In the end we shall lose them, for no one

save the Enlightened Ones abides in enduring peace, comfort, and happiness. No matter how much effort we put forth, we cannot guarantee our own happiness.

8. Suffering arises from conditioned existence. This type of suffering refers to the operation of experience in a wholly self-oriented and fictitious way. The limitations of this manner of experiencing are severe, but ordinarily, this suffering escapes our attention. The Abhidharmakoṣabhāṣya explains that only the Noble Ones are aware of this suffering because noticing it requires refined awareness and sensitivity. The sensitivity of a Noble One is like the surface of the eye compared to the sensitivity of an ordinary individual, which is like the calloused palm of the hand:

"A hair placed on the palm of the hand is not even perceived, but if the same hair were to enter the eye, it would cause suffering and injury." (AKB VI:3)

While only those advanced on the path recognize the limitations of conditioned existence for what they are, we may glimpse these limitations when a moment of appreciation opens briefly, only to be closed down by the constraints of our more ordinary and automatic perceptions.

Three Kinds of Suffering

These eight kinds of suffering can also be categorized into three kinds of suffering: the suffering of suffering, the suffering of transience, and the suffering of the conditioned. The suffering of suffering results from being subject to what is unpleasant: birth, old age, sickness, and death, association with what we do not like, separation from what we like, and not obtaining what we want. These are readily comprehensible forms of mental and physical misery.

"Old age and suffering, disease and death,
terrible they come, accompanied by terror . . ." (LAL XIII)

The suffering of transience results from pleasant things. All that gives pleasure is a source of suffering because it is unstable and unreliable. Transitory pleasures delude and tantalize the mind, like the unreachable mirage-lake in the desert that leads us on and on, but never satisfies our thirst.

". . . Like the flame of a lamp,
they quickly shift and change;
like the wind, they die away;
like a spray of sea foam,
they are evanescent and insubstantial." (LAL XIII)

The suffering of the conditioned (the eighth suffering mentioned above) is the most subtle of all. Everything we do is associated with suffering in one way or another. Our well-being and enjoyment, our nonsuffering, is purchased at the cost of the suffering of others: insects, birds, animals, and other human beings.

"The food we eat, the clothing we wear,
our houses, wealth, and ornaments;
the feasts we offer are all sources of misery . . . " (KZLZ I:III)

Like a dye, the suffering of the conditioned permeates the entire fabric of experience. The Buddha explains in the Lalitavistara Sūtra:

"But even were there no old age,
no sickness, and no death,
great suffering would still arise,
based on the five skandhas, the elements of existence." (LAL XIV)

Knowing that we each will experience suffering, how can we be complacent? Understanding the truth of suffering and knowing with certainty that enduring happiness cannot be found in the ordinary world awakens a sense of urgency and inspires the determination to find the cause of suffering.

The Truth of the Cause

If we could clearly determine the causes of suffering, then we could see how these causes might be removed or transformed. The Buddha pointed out the causes; the Dharma invites us to investigate our experience to trace the operation of these causes; and the Sangha exemplifies the teachings, demonstrating that the causes of suffering can be removed.

Ignorance

The fundamental cause of suffering is ignorance. The Daśabhūmika Sūtra says of samsara that we are "entering into a deep forest on a wrong road." But the direction is already established, and we follow a well-traveled path. Even though we may wonder whether the path we are on leads in the direction we want to go, we find it easier to follow a familiar path than to strike out into the woods to explore alternative ways. This ignoring and unwillingness to inquire are the basic characteristics of our way of life.

Karma and Kleśa

The clarity and energy that we need to question and explore are not readily available, having already been diverted into emotional patterns. Emotions create highly motivated activity that deeply hypnotizes mind and body. Fully occupied by emotionality, consciousness is caught up in a moving network of fantasy, fascination, craving, grasping, and anxiety.

The action arising from the momentum of emotions is impulsive and compulsive. We are thrust into activity without full knowledge of its consequences and without a complete perspective on the situation. Operating on the basis of ignorance and confusion, we do not get the results we expect. The resulting frustration generates further emotional reactions which prompt further action.

In this way, emotion promotes ignorance and confusion, while actions we perform based on ignorance and confusion give rise to suffering and further emotional reactions. In blindly stimulating emotion, beings cultivate, reinforce, and hold on to suffering. This deep emotionality dominates the functioning of body, speech, and mind.

The Abhidharmakoṣabhāṣya explains that our world is created by actions (karma), while emotions (kleśas) are the roots of action (AKB V:1a). Foremost among the emotions are attachment, aversion, and confusion.

The ordinary person does not see through the patterns created by emotion and actions based on emotion. No longer informed by awareness, thoughts and actions flow along the currents established by emotion, taking on a disorderly, chaotic quality that generates confusion. Confusion attracts and binds the energy of mind like a magnet; basic intelligence—the ability to question or to make good decisions—is deactivated. Yet the senses continue to operate and present thoughts and perceptions to the mind. Confused, the mind believes that these thoughts and perceptions arise from "I."

Self-Orientation

Here is the fundamental confusion: No such thing as a unified, stable, permanent self exists. Our true identity is not what we believe it to be. Yet our whole world revolves around this illusory self.

Insecure and uncertain, the self must secretly reconstruct and reaffirm itself, while insisting on its importance and reality. The demands of the self can be glimpsed at the base of our emotional reactivity, in the "want" and "don't want" of the self. These demands come to rule our lives so completely that it is hard to know how to separate from them. We have not been trained to penetrate the illusion of the self or to work with the underlying confusion that surfaces when the self is challenged.

The reality of suffering, however, proves that our self-orientation is somehow faulty. Unless we simply give up the possibility of happiness and decide human life is meaningless, we must conclude that the way we are conducting our lives is mistaken; the self-orientation does not bring satisfying results, and questioning it is entirely legitimate.

Questioning the basis of self-oriented experience is the heart of the Buddhist path. The Buddha revealed clearly that the self is completely fabricated and that the inability to perceive that the self has no real existence is the source of all suffering.

The Abhidharma texts describe in detail how this illusion is established, activated, and reinforced. Meditation practice refines the faculties that can see how the structure of the self is set up, how it operates, and how to transcend it. With this training, we can identify the causes of suffering, learn to remove the darkness of confusion, and choose not to suffer. This education begins to develop knowledge that has the power to transform the self-oriented view.

The Truth of Cessation

The Buddha demonstrated that transformed consciousness can transcend samsaric patterns. If the erroneous belief in a self is completely transcended, body and mind dwell in samādhi in a nonconditioned state where no entity can be located or identified.

The Arhat's Nirvana

When the practitioner has completely disengaged from the cause and effect cycle of karma and the emotional affliction of kleśa, ignorance is transcended. This is the way of the Arhat, the victor, the conquerer of emotionality and confusion, the one free from false identity. The emotional afflictions disappear, for the self as possessor or enjoyer is no more. The Sūtras express this as the fire of the passions going out for lack of fuel.

The Arhat transcends the causes and conditions of personal identity and identification; all notions of self as agent or recipient of experience come to an end. The path to this great freedom produces peace, the "coolness" of equanimity as the heat of passion dies down, and liberation from karma and samsara.

The Arhat accomplishes what he sets out to achieve: release from samsara. Fully liberated from the entanglements of emotion and the ignorance that propels the flow of karma, he will never return to the arena of suffering. This nonreturning ensures that the Arhat will enter nirvana in this his final lifetime. Entry into nirvana is the purpose and result of the Arhat's path.

The Bodhisattva's Enlightenment

The Mahāyāna teachings, however, emphasize that further transformation is necessary. The limitless compassion, wisdom, and power of complete enlightenment can only arise when all the obscurations are cleared away. To attain complete, perfect enlightenment, the Arhat must move to the Bodhisattva path.

For the Bodhisattva, the goal is not release from samsara for himself alone. For the sake of helping all other beings, he aims at the perfect enlightenment of the Buddha that transcends both samsara and nirvana. The way to complete enlightenment is expressed in the teachings of wisdom and compassion: the profound wisdom of the two kinds of selflessness and the great compassion of the thought of enlightenment. Transcending not only all belief in a personal self but also all concepts of an essence or self-nature in any aspect of experience, the Bodhisattva moves in a realm of boundless freedom. All experience becomes useful on the path; nothing need be rejected or accepted. Transforming barriers to great knowledge, great love, and great power, the Bodhisattva willingly remains engaged in the world until all sentient beings are enlightened.

The Truth of the Path

The Buddha taught that the way to liberation from the endless round of samsara lay through following the eightfold noble path: genuinely pure view, genuinely pure thought, genuinely pure speech, genuinely pure conduct, genuinely pure livelihood, genuinely pure effort, genuinely pure mindfulness, and genuinely pure meditative concentration.

The Eightfold Noble Path

"Genuinely pure" (samyak) means that which transcends self-orientation and promotes liberation from suffering. Recognizing "self" as a delusion, we learn to see purely. The path of pure thought, speech, conduct, livelihood, effort, mindfulness, and meditative concentration comes forth from seeing the self as illusory. Developing the ability to act with a genuinely pure view and to live life free from self-centered concerns is the practice of the path.

In the "Garland of White Lotus Flowers," Lama Mipham notes that the path is called noble because by means of it what must be relinquished is given up and freedom is attained. He summarizes the path in this way: "The genuinely pure view is perfect understanding; the genuinely pure thought allows others to understand; genuinely pure speech, conduct, and livelihood inspire others with confidence; and genuinely pure effort, mindfulness, and meditative concentration remove the obscurations to wisdom." (GZ)

A fuller explanation is given in the Mahāsatipaṭṭhāna Sutta: "Genuinely pure view is the understanding of the four noble truths. Genuinely pure thought is the aspiration towards renunciation, benevolence, and kindness. Genuinely pure speech is free from lying, slander, abuse, and idle talk. Genuinely pure conduct is abstaining from killing, stealing, and wrong sexual conduct. Genuinely pure livelihood is to desist from any wrong livelihood. Genuinely pure effort is stirring up energy to support all that is virtuous and to set aside all that is nonvirtuous. Genuinely pure mindfulness is to be ardent, self-possessed, and mindful with regard to body, feelings, thoughts, and dharmas, having overcome both the yearning and the dejection so common in the world. Genuinely pure meditative concentration progresses through the four stages of dhyāna to achieve complete purity of mindfulness and equanimity." (DN XXII)

Embodying Wisdom

The eight branches of the path express the full range of activities of body, speech, and mind within the three trainings. Genuinely pure speech, conduct, and livelihood develop from training in moral discipline; genuinely pure mindfulness and meditative concentration develop from training in meditation; and genuinely pure view, thought, and effort develop from training in wisdom.

The Abhidharmakoṣabhāṣya explains (AKB VI:71a–b) that until view, thought, speech, and the rest are genuinely pure, they are not the noble path. Although the complete practice of this path is the accomplishment of the perfected Sangha who have come to embody the wisdom of the Buddha, the example of the eightfold path inspires the steps along the path from beginning to end.

CHAPTER TEN

Four Laws of the Dharma

Closely associated with the four truths are the three marks and the four laws of the Dharma. The three marks describe the nature of all compounded, conditioned things: impermanent, associated with suffering, and without self.

"Whether the Buddhas appear in the world or whether the Buddhas do not appear in the world, it remains a fact, an unalterable condition of existence and an eternal law that all compounded things are impermanent . . . subject to suffering . . . and without a self." (AN III)

The Dhammapada describes the three marks in this way:

"All conditioned things are impermanent. When you truly comprehend this, you will no longer be afflicted by suffering. This is the path of purity.

"All conditioned things are suffering. When you truly comprehend this, you will no longer be afflicted by suffering. This is the path of purity.

"All dharmas are selfless. When you truly comprehend this, you will no longer be afflicted by suffering. This is the path of purity." (DP XX:5–7)

The four laws of the Dharma state: All that is compounded is impermanent. All that is corrupt is suffering. All things are without self. And nirvana is peace. (AS II)

Pointing Out Compoundedness

Compounded means composite, produced or assembled. The Abhidharmakoṣabhāṣya explains: "The term saṁskṛta, conditioned, is explained as that which has been created (kṛta) by causes in conjunction and combination. No dharma is engendered by a single cause." (AKB I:7a–b)

It can be shown that all compounded things are impermanent. Since all compounded things have arisen in dependence on causes and conditions, they may also be reduced to parts and are thus subject to disintegration and decay. With the passing of time, what appears to be whole is revealed as composite, holding together only so long as certain conditions hold together. This includes everything in ordinary experience: youth and beauty, wealth and fame, friends and partnerships. Physical bodies as well as mountains and oceans do not last forever but eventually disintegrate into their component parts.

Pointing Out Corruptedness

It can be shown that all that is corrupt is suffering. Corrupt (śāsrava) is sometimes translated into English as contaminated or impure. It means associated with or related to the emotions. The Abhidharmakoṣabhāṣya explains that impure conditioned things are qualified as impure or possessing impurity because the emotional afflictions adhere to them. (AKB I:4d,8a–b)

The six basic emotions are desire, anger, pride, ignorance, false views, and doubt. When experience is characterized by agitation, when the mind and body are troubled or disturbed, emotion is known to be present. (AS II) The second truth states that all suffering can be traced to emotion (kleśa) and action based on emotion (karma).

Whatever supports the emotions or offers a place where emotions can adhere or grow is termed corrupt. All conditioned things except the knowledge and virtues associated with the advanced stages of the path are considered corrupt. Noncorrupt things are called pure, calm, and excellent. (AKB I:5a–b,VII:2c–d,V:16c)

Pointing out Selflessness

It can be shown that all things are without self; whether pure or impure, conditioned or nonconditioned, all things are without self, and none of them together or in any combination constitute a self. But the notion of self pervades ordinary experience. The Madhyāntavibhaṅga gives a list of various forms of belief in a self.

1. We imagine that the self is unitary.
2. We imagine that the self is the one who causes action.
3. We imagine that the self is the enjoyer of experience.
4. We imagine that the self is the creator or doer.
5. We imagine that the self is an autonomous power.
6. We imagine that the self is the one possessing control.
7. We imagine that the self is enduring through time.
8. We imagine that the self is the one defiled or purified by following the path.
9. We imagine that the self is the subject engaged in meditation.
10. We imagine that the self is the one who was formerly bound but now is freed. (MAV III:15–16).

In the "Wheel of Analytic Meditation" (in *Calm and Clear*), Lama Mipham teaches the procedure for meditative analysis of experience in the light of the three marks. After giving the basic instructions, he points out the fundamental awakening that takes place when the true nature of experience is seen:

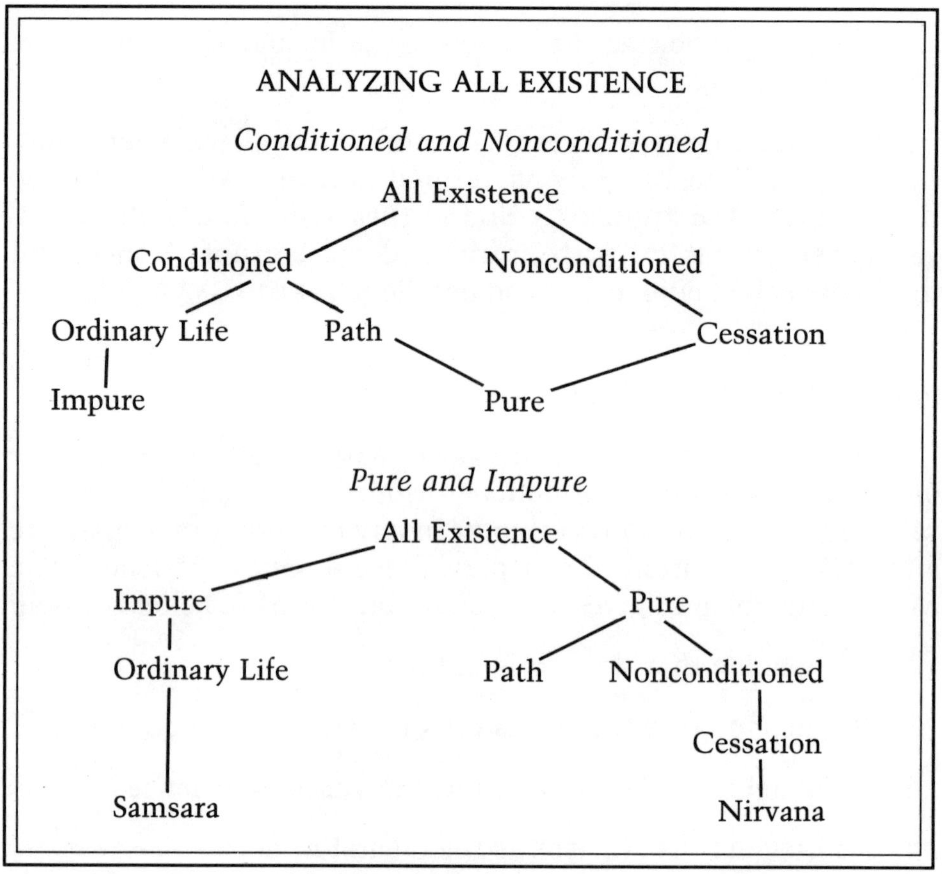

According to the Abhidharma of the Sarvāstivādins

"Having become accustomed to this practice,
deeply impress upon your mind that
all conditioned existence and the whole body of experience
belonging to oneself and to others
is characterized by compoundedness, impermanence,
suffering, and no-self. . .

"When this understanding develops into penetrating insight,
it is called the way of initiation,
the common door to the three vehicles." (CC 29,32)

The Ten Topics of Expert Knowledge

The ten topics of Lama Mipham's Khenjug are associated with ten views of self. Each topic counters one of the mistaken ways

TEN TOPICS AS ANTIDOTES TO BELIEF IN A SELF

Topics	*Belief in Self*
1. skandhas	as unitary
2. dhātus	as cause
3. āyatanas	as enjoyer of experience
4. interdependent co-operation	as creator
5. possible and impossible	as autonomous power
6. indriyas	as controlling tendencies toward defilement and purification
7. temporality	as eternal
8. four truths	as the ground of defilement and purity
9. ways to enlightenment	as experiencer of meditative states
10. conditioned and nonconditioned	as one to be bound or liberated

of imagining a self, revealing the reality of selflessness. The skillful knowledge that overturns these ten wrong views evolves as one becomes knowledgeable in the ten topics. (MAV III:15–16, KJ 2a.2, KJD)

Further Readings

Lalitavistara Sūtra. *The Voice of the Buddha: The Beauty of Compassion,* chapters XXII, XXVI.

Sacca-vibhaṅga-sutta. Majjhima Nikāya, CXLI. Discourse on the analysis of the truths.

Suhṛllekha, by Nāgārjuna. In *Golden Zephyr.* A letter of spiritual advice on practicing Dharma in everyday life.

Chos-bzhi-rin-chen-phreng-ba, by Klong-chen-pa. "Four-Themed Precious Garland," chapter I, in *Footsteps on the Diamond Path* (Crystal Mirror I–III), pp. 92–97. On orienting the mind toward the teachings.

Rin-chen-them-skas, by sMin-gling gTer-chen 'Gyur-med-rdo-rje. *The Jewel Ladder, A Preliminary Nyingma Lamrim.*

Ngal-gso-skor-gsum, by Klong-chen-pa. *Kindly Bent to Ease Us,* volume I, chapters II, III. On impermanence and suffering.

Kun-bzang-bla-ma-zhal-lung, transcribed by dPal-sprul Rinpoche. *Kun-zang La-may Zhal-lung,* part I, chapters II, III.

Sems-dpyod-rnam-sbyong, by Lama Mi-pham. "Wheel of Analytic Meditation," in *Calm and Clear.*

Padma-dkar-po-phreng-ba, by Lama Mi-pham. "Garland of White Lotus Flowers," in *Golden Zephyr.* Mi-pham's commentary on the Suhṛllekha.

Footsteps on the Diamond Path (Crystal Mirror I–III), pp. 260–266. On the relation between the inner teacher and the external teacher.

SECTION FIVE

Training for Freedom

CHAPTER ELEVEN

Three Trainings of the Path

Because they lead to genuine liberation from the suffering inherent in the ordinary world, the Buddha's teachings are known as the path to complete freedom. Today we often associate freedom with a lack of external restrictions, a perspective that overlooks the possibility that the individual could take responsibility for his or her own inner freedom. According to the Dharma, inner freedom is developed through a process that depends on a fundamental choice made by the individual: to engage or disengage from a self-oriented way of life.

Nāgārjuna says in the Suhṛllekha: "As far as liberation is concerned, this depends on oneself; there is no one else who can be a friend." (SL 52)

Genuine Freedom

At every moment, choice presents itself, for actions and reactions of body, speech, and mind are continually taking place. Impulses are constantly arising; some lead in neurotic, destructive directions reinforcing a deluded self-centered orientation; others lead in more positive directions, promoting a lighter, freer consciousness not circumscribed by the self. Genuine freedom depends upon two major factors: knowledge and power. First, it is necessary to ascertain which direction is wholesome and which unwholesome, and to discern correctly which actions of body, speech, and mind lead in each direction. Secondly, it is necessary to develop the power to transform these actions. Equipped with such knowledge and power, we are no longer trapped in the self-oriented way of seeing and being, but become capable of embodying real freedom.

Though it has the potential for enlightenment, the ordinary mind is so deeply involved with complex samsaric patterns that it cannot see the way to freedom or develop the power to follow such a way. Ordinary mind tends to identify with whatever arises, believing that each thought and perception "belongs to me." Without special training, the myriad forms of self-oriented experience are difficult even to recognize as unwholesome.

Rongzom Mahāpaṇḍita explains in his commentary on Man-ngag-lta-ba'i-phreng-ba that mind (sems) is basically naive, simply accepting appearance at face value. Sentient being (sems-can) means one possessing such a gullible mind. Ordinary mind (sems), however, can be transformed into awakened mind (byang-chub-sems) when wisdom and compassion are inseparably present.

Three kinds of training can transform emotion and confusion and clear away the network of karmic patterns: śīla, discipline of body, speech, and mind; samādhi, meditative concentration that can open access to higher levels of consciousness; and sophisticated analysis that leads to prajñā or wisdom, the direct perception of reality. A penetrating meditative analysis can demonstrate the nonexistence of the self. But analysis alone is not enough to completely penetrate the illusion or change the patterning: In order to transform self-oriented experience, disciplined action and meditative concentration must be joined with analysis that leads to insight.

Modern Western education does not support these three trainings. Higher forms of self-discipline are reserved for certain fields of endeavor and are not generally applied to all of one's life.

Concentration is not taught as a subject at all, and rarely even as a technique. Instead of learning how to observe and analyze direct experience, one learns only to think about thoughts, emotions, feelings, etc. For many today, the distinction between meditative analysis and thinking is very vague.

Neither does the restless, stressful modern way of life support the three trainings. Competitiveness and busyness, together with the rapid pace of life, foster anxiety and nervousness. The heart closes tightly with fear, the body is barraged with sensory stimulation, and the mind is filled with dialogues and concepts. Unable to find peace and silence within ourselves, we lose touch with the nature of our being. In this state, we cannot even begin to train ourselves.

Learning to relax the body, breath, and mind is a first step toward developing the three trainings. Once body, breath, and mind are relaxed and joined harmoniously, we can exercise and refine a whole range of human capacities.

Śrāvaka and Bodhisattva Training

The Visuddhimagga states: "When a wise man, established well in virtue, develops mind and understanding, then, as an ardent and sagacious monk, he succeeds in disentangling this tangle." (VM I:1)

Virtue means moral discipline, mind (citta) refers to training in concentration, and understanding means wisdom. The tangle is the network of craving, while the one who succeeds in disentangling himself from the network of craving is one who is trained in the three trainings. Ardent means possessing energy and commitment powerful enough to burn up the tangled branches of emotionality that are as impenetrable as a dense thicket. This is the way of the Śrāvaka, who focuses especially on the harmful and dangerous nature of the emotions and regards them as enemies to be conquered or thorns to be removed.

The Mahāyāna Sūtras present a different perspective on the emotions. The Daśabhūmika Sūtra describes working with the emotions as a process of refinement and likens the stages of the Bodhisattva path to the refining of gold. With repeated refinement, impurities are removed; the gold becomes bright and shining and its nature workable and useful. It can then be shaped by a master craftsman into a royal crown studded with jewels. In order to assist all beings, the Bodhisattva will make unending efforts to perfect the threefold training.

Training in Moral Discipline

The Sanskrit term śīla means habit, custom, conduct, disposition, character, and moral conduct. The Visuddhimagga says śīla means "compose" in the sense of coordinating and upholding. Coordinating body, speech, and mind brings about consistency. Deeds match words, and action and intention are in harmony. Upholding refers to being a basis for virtue, a foundation for beneficial states. (VM I:19) The nature of discipline is to promote virtue and abandon nonvirtue.

The basis for all virtue is two positive mental events: self-respect or conscience and the sense of propriety or shame. (VM I:22) The goal of moral discipline is, above all else, lack of remorse, a greatly beneficial attitude that results from disciplined conduct and prevents agitation, guilt, worry, self-hatred, and many other disturbing emotions. Moral discipline leads toward integration and balance, giving rise to the capacity for deep concentration.

There are five general benefits of moral discipline: diligence, good reputation, fearlessness, lack of confusion at death, and rebirths in the higher realms.

Moral discipline is the foundation for the other two trainings. The Saddharmasaṁgaha explains: "Discipline is for the purpose of restraint, which is for the purpose of lack of remorse, which is for the purpose of gladness, which is for the purpose of rapture, which is for the purpose of repose, which is for the purpose of bliss, which is for the purpose of concentration, which is for the purpose of knowing and seeing the truth, which is for the purpose of renouncing the world, which is for the purpose of dispassion, which is for the purpose of liberation, which is for the purpose of knowing and seeing liberation, which is for the purpose of nirvana." (SDS VI)

The focus of moral discipline is first on taming the actions of body and speech, which are easier to govern than the array of mental actions. Following the guidelines given in the Vinaya, with continued practice one is able to recognize unhealthy action. The next step is to apply antidotes, a process that begins to build confidence in self-discipline. Eventually one can firmly establish this discipline, which will completely overcome all unhealthy tendencies.

Training in Concentration

Concentration is called "the profitable unification of the mind" in the Visuddhimagga. Concentration is the centering of consciousness, the balancing of mind and mental events evenly on a single object, which is called one-pointedness of mind. Concentration means this state of being focused and calm, unscattered and undistracted. (VM III:2)

Meditative concentration increases the capacity of the mind to see directly how the self operates, how "I" and emotions arise. Deep concentration penetrates to the level of consciousness where these emotions originate and develops stability that does not waver as emotions surface. This stability is essential for clear observation and for generating the confidence to disengage from harmful patterns.

The ultimate purpose of concentration is to achieve full contemplation that transcends the emotions. When the mind is completely stable, it cannot be agitated by disturbing emotion. Concentration eliminates distraction and manifests as unwavering stillness. Its cause is said to be bliss, for when the mind is blissful, it settles naturally. (VM III:2–4)

The practitioner develops the second training by calming the restless activity of mind through the practice of śamatha. Śamatha techniques include focusing practices, breathing practices, relaxation practices, and practices that open the senses. The focus of concentration may include, for example, any one of forty different subjects given in the Visuddhimagga. (VM III:104)

One-pointedness is developed in stages, first settling the mind, then stabilizing it, and strengthening concentration until

FACTORS OF DHYĀNA

Dhyāna	*Factors*
4th	one-pointedness
3rd	bliss/one-pointedness
2nd	happiness/bliss/one-pointedness
1st	investigation/analysis/happiness/bliss/one-pointedness

one can maintain unwavering one-pointedness. Mahāyāna texts have set forth nine such stages.

Once one-pointedness is attained, the practitioner can traverse the four stages of meditation (dhyāna) and four formless absorptions. The first dhyāna is characterized by one-pointedness, investigation, analysis, mental happiness, and bliss. In the second dhyāna, investigation and analysis have ceased, and only mental happiness and bliss remain together with one-pointedness. In the third dhyāna, mental happiness ceases; in the fourth dhyāna, only one-pointedness and equanimity remain.

Each of these five factors is an antidote to emotional agitations of different kinds. Investigation counteracts doubt, analysis counteracts torpor, mental happiness counteracts aversion, bliss counteracts agitation and worry, and one-pointedness counteracts attachment. (VM IV:86)

Investigation is like the hand that firmly grips a vase and analysis is like the hand that polishes it. Investigation is a coarse operation that intervenes or takes up an inquiry. It is like a bird spreading and forcefully flapping its wings in order to take off from the ground. Analysis follows investigation. Quiet and subtle, it is like the small adjustments a soaring bird makes to sustain and direct flight. (VM IV:89–91)

Mental happiness is like sighting water in crossing the desert, while bliss is like actually satisfying one's thirst. Mental happiness and bliss arise naturally as disturbing emotions settle down and concentration develops. In turn, happiness and bliss intensify concentration by integrating body and mind. Together, they refresh and uplift the body and mind and eventually pervade them, like an ocean wave completely floods a cavern on the shore. When mature, happiness perfects tranquility, and when tranquility matures, it perfects bliss. When bliss is matured, it perfects concentration. (VM IV:94–99)

Nāgārjuna explains the progression in this way: "Bliss (bde-ba) means to be free from the traces of emotionality. A blissful mind is tranquil; a tranquil mind is not confused; being free from confusion is to understand truth. By understanding truth, one obtains liberation." (BCV 69–70)

Training in Wisdom

The characteristic of wisdom is distinguishing the nature of reality. Its function is to abolish the darkness of delusion and it manifests as nondelusion. Its cause is said to be samādhi: One who is concentrated knows and sees correctly. (VM XIV:7)

The purpose of wisdom is to develop full understanding of the path of liberation. The Prajñāpāramitā teachings state: "Knowing the nature of reality by means of wisdom, one becomes fully liberated from the three realms."

Penetrating the illusion of self, wisdom cuts through the ignorance that is at the root of all the emotionality and karmic activity that perpetuate samsara. The First Turning teachings focus on dispelling the illusion of self in individual things and persons, while the Second and Third Turning teachings demonstrate that all elements of reality are without self-nature.

As the Abhidharmakoṣabhāṣya explains, one who wishes to see the four truths should first of all keep the precepts. Then one listens to the teachings; having heard, one reflects and having reflected, one cultivates meditation. In this way the teachings of the Buddha can be verified in one's own experience. (AKB VI:5a–b, VM XIV:14)

Listening, reflecting, and meditating are the three sources of prajñā or wisdom. Progressing from listening to reflecting to meditating, wisdom becomes more direct and experiential. Wisdom based on listening arises from first understanding the words that are being spoken or words written in the texts. With these words in mind, one progresses to understanding the meaning, which is wisdom based on reflection using logic and reasoning that one personally applies. Having grasped the meaning, one meditates on it to develop wisdom from experiential contemplation.

Each of these three kinds of wisdom possesses certainty. The certainty that arises from listening to the teachings is due to relying on a qualified person or authoritative text; the certainty that arises from reflection is due to rational examination; the certainty that arises from meditation is due to concentrated practice. (AK VI:5c-d)

Wisdom begins with analysis and observation that lead to direct understanding. Learning to categorize events within experience based on listening to the teachings sharpens the effectiveness of observation. Once these categories are clear and events are recognized, then the healthy and unhealthy consequences of different events can be traced and analyzed. This analysis reveals how the cycles of samsara are established.

Through this process, wisdom clarifies the way that the mind manufactures emotion and karma, and finally penetrates the illusion of self. Just as though one were investigating how a magician created his display of illusions, one studies mental events to understand the conditions and causes that support the operation of ordinary self-oriented experience. One first understands the root emotions as the basis for samsara, then studies the workings of the associated emotions and how each one manifests a distinctive character. Gradually, the manner in which the self supports emotion and emotion supports the sense of self becomes clear. Self and emotion are seen as relying on and reinforcing each other's existence. Understanding how this collusion gives rise to the whole range of samsaric delusion liberates the mind from all forms of deception.

Order of the Three Trainings

The Visuddhimagga explains that one begins with virtue, continues with concentration, and concludes with wisdom. (VM I:10)

THE THREE TRAININGS

Training	*Development*
Moral Discipline	recognizing faults applying antidotes establishing virtue practicing discipline overcoming emotion conquering completely
Meditative Concentration	focusing the mind continuous focusing re-focusing close focusing disciplining pacifying completely pacifying making one-pointed mental stabilization
Wisdom	listening based on words spoken by respected authority reflecting based on meaning reached through reasoning meditating based on direct experiential contemplation

Training in discipline is the entryway to the teaching and concentration is the basis for wisdom. Yet all three trainings operate in varying degrees at every stage of the path. In order to recognize healthy and unhealthy actions, one must listen and reflect on the teachings and learn to categorize events. In order to observe experience, the mind must be calm and focused. The practice of moral discipline thus requires concentration and wisdom, while the result of moral discipline is psychological integration and peacefulness essential for concentration. Once the water of a lake grows calm, the depths can be clearly seen; in the same way, a calm and concentrated mind is necessary for the penetrating clarity of wisdom to arise.

TRAINING DYNAMICS

Training	*Way of Abandoning*	*Prevention*
Moral Discipline	substitution of opposites	misconduct
Meditative Concentration	controlling arising of emotion	obsession with emotion
Wisdom	cutting through the root of emotion	false views habitual tendencies

Dynamic Interactions

All three trainings support the clearing away of emotional afflictions, but each does so in a distinctive way. Through the exercise of moral discipline, one replaces emotional reactions with healthy attitudes and good qualities. This is called removing the defilements by the substitution of opposites. By applying concentration, one controls the arising of emotional reactions. This is called removing the defilements by controlling. By employing wisdom, one sees through the illusion of self and removes the defilements at their root. This is called removing defilements by cutting through.

Training in moral discipline prevents misconduct and transgressions; training in concentration purifies craving and prevents obsession with emotionality; and training in wisdom purifies false views and transforms habitual tendencies. (VM I:12–13)

The way of the Buddha is the only path that contains all three trainings and the only path that possesses the training in wisdom. Each training alone brings only limited benefits; all three are necessary to ensure complete liberation.

The Abhidharmakoṣabhāṣya says: "Essentially, moral discipline has [rebirth in] heavenly states as its result; meditation has disconnection from the kleśas as its result." (AKB IV:124a–b)

OPERATION OF THE THREE TRAININGS

Training	*Definition*	*Nature*	*Purpose*
Moral Discipline	training in conduct	promoting preventing	manifest example of Buddha
Meditative Concentration	training of mind	calming focusing controlling	transcending emotion
Wisdom	training in knowledge	observing categorizing analyzing penetrating	understanding path of liberation

Moral discipline alone leads to good rebirths and even to heavenly experiences; one ceases to perform those actions that cause suffering and life becomes smooth and joyful. But without samādhi and prajñā there can be no complete liberation from suffering. While samādhi can lead to heavenly realms and experiences of bliss that temporarily protect one from suffering, it cannot lead to complete cessation of suffering. Only through insight into the four noble truths can one definitively escape from suffering.

The three trainings of the Buddhist path bring freedom so complete that those who follow this path are said to travel unseen even by Māra, the lord of illusion and death. The Dhammapada tells us: "Māra does not know the path of those who abide in perfect conduct, meditative mindfulness, and genuine wisdom." (DP IV:14)

As the Enlightened One says in the Mahāsīhanāda Sutta: "Kassapa, there is nothing further or more perfect than this perfection of morality, this perfection of the mind and heart, and this perfection of wisdom." (DN VIII)

CHAPTER TWELVE

Three Trainings, Turnings, and Collections

Each of the three trainings is associated with the three turnings and the three collections. The three trainings as practiced by the Śrāvaka followers of the First Turning teachings are expanded and deepened by the practices of the followers of the Second and Third Turning teachings.

The Bodhisattva's moral discipline is threefold: It abstains from nonvirtue, cultivates virtue, and brings benefit to others. Guided by compassion, the Bodhisattva may even act in ways forbidden to the Śrāvaka monk. While the practice of the Śrāvaka focuses especially on disciplining body and speech, the moral discipline of the Bodhisattva focuses especially on disciplining intention.

The training in meditative concentration that leads to samādhi is the basis for the development of knowledge and supernatural power. The Bodhisattva practice brings forth supernatural powers used for the benefit of all beings. Moreover, the power of vows, determination, and confidence supports his efforts to overcome all obstacles and never to abandon beings. The special actions of the samādhis of the Bodhisattva are said to include the cultivation of virtue, the teaching of others, the creation of a Buddha field, and developing the innumerable qualities of the Buddha. (MSG VII:12)

The training in wisdom begins with analytical knowledge that is initially dependent on language, but moves on toward nonconceptual nondual wisdom (MSG VIII). For the Bodhisattva, wisdom includes not only comprehending the selflessness of individual things and persons, but also thoroughly understanding the selflessness of all elements of reality. Although the difference in the wisdom realized by Śrāvakas and Bodhisattvas is described in various ways, all Mahāyāna masters agree that the perfected Bodhisattva fully comprehends reality. Practicing the perfection of wisdom that transcends all limitations, the Bodhisattva reaches the complete omniscience of the Enlightened One.

Vinaya and the First Training

The Vinaya is especially associated with the first training in moral discipline that guides the activities of body, speech, and mind, and with the second training in concentration that integrates body, speech, and mind. In the Vinaya teachings, the Buddha points out clearly which attitudes and actions intensify suffering and confusion and which promote clarity, peacefulness, and joy. These guidelines form the basis and starting point of the path to liberation.

The Vinaya teachings of the First Turning emphasize the importance of abandoning nonvirtuous behavior and adopting virtuous behavior. The path revealed in the First Turning teachings is characterized by a deep respect for the Vinaya and a love of self-discipline, moderation, and simplicity.

Most of the First Turning Vinaya teachings were given by the Buddha in Rājagṛha and Śrāvastī. Within the Vinaya are contained the precepts for monks and nuns, rules for admission to the order, procedures for ordination, the manner of making confession, special rules for daily life, and rules guiding the functioning of the community.

The Vinaya teachings within the Second Turning focus on the Bodhisattva vow. The Bodhisattva path is characterized by a deep commitment to compassion and love that extends to all beings. The Bodhisattva discipline of abandoning nonvirtue and cultivating virtue is thus dedicated to the purpose of benefitting others.

The Vinaya teachings within the Third Turning emphasize ways of subduing emotionality and confusion that augment the Bodhisattva path with skillful means such as visualizations. Not focusing on the method of antidotes, not regarding the emotions as enemies, this approach directly transforms the energy of emotions into energy directed toward realization.

Sūtra and the Second Training

The second training in meditative concentration is closely connected with study and practice based on the Sūtras, though the Sūtras support all three trainings. The Sūtras promote deep concentration that integrates body and mind with the direct realization of the Buddha. Listening to the teachings awakens intuition and evokes the heartfelt resolve to pursue the highest human values. Hearing of the qualities of the Buddha, we can envision the perfect balance of body, speech, and mind; we sense the possibility of integrating our deepest aspirations with our lived reality. This focus of the heart is the seed of meditative concentration that is natural and unforced, based on interest, willingness, and appreciation.

Sūtra teachings of the First Turning contain numerous discourses on mindfulness and concentration, and ways of controlling and guiding action. These teachings especially promote contemplation, the stages of dhyāna (meditation), and purity of action. The training of samādhi is closely associated with promoting the ten virtuous actions (three of body, four of speech, and three of mind) and practicing the eight stages of concentration and absorption.

The Sūtra teachings of the Second Turning reveal the profound and vast contemplations of the Bodhisattva traversing the ten stages of the path. In the Bhadrakalpika Sūtra, when the Bodhisattva Pramuditarāja asks the Buddha how to practice, the

Enlightened One describes at length the samādhi called "Showing the Way of All Dharmas" and mentions eighty-four thousand samādhis practiced by the Bodhisattvas.

Sūtra teachings of the Third Turning evoke complete realization of the fundamental knowledge of the body of reality, the realm of Buddhahood. The Bodhisattvas who practice these teachings move in the spheres of knowledge and action of the Fully Enlightened Ones.

Abhidharma and the Third Training

Associated with the training in wisdom, Abhidharma refines intelligence for the purpose of seeing the true nature not only of body, speech, and mind, but of all reality. As Vinaya practice calms the heat of the passions, and concentration practice develops integrity and mental stability, the study of Abhidharma develops prajñā. Abhidharma teachings demonstrate the four truths and show clearly how to apply the three trainings.

The Abhidharma of the First Turning analyzes mind and body; it teaches how to recognize which actions of body, speech, and mind predispose one to suffering and which promote the calmness and clarity essential for bringing suffering to an end. This knowledge makes it possible to follow the Vinaya rules effectively and derive the greatest benefit from them.

With this knowledge, backed by discipline and powerful concentration, body, speech, and mind can be transformed. Unhealthy patterns can be countered with antidotes, and healthy ones can be encouraged, improving the entire environment of the mind. As prajñā and samādhi begin to defuse emotional reactivity, the causes of samsaric sufferings are clearly seen and removed.

The Abhidharma of the Second Turning adds extensive analyses of the stages of the Bodhisattva Path and its various levels of knowledge, purity, and powers. The Second Turning teachings do not emphasize accepting and rejecting, but focus on profoundly reeducating the mind. Penetrating beyond the distinction of self and other, the practitioner cultivates wisdom that transcends concepts and duality.

THE THREE TURNINGS

First Turning
Vinaya Perspective

Emphasizes training in moral discipline.

Possesses fundamental teachings followed by all schools.

Presents few interpretations.

Second Turning
Sūtra Perspective

Emphasizes training of concentration.

Possesses more profound teachings.

Presents special circumstances and richer meanings.

Third Turning
Abhidharma Perspective

Emphasizes training of wisdom.

Possesses very subtle teachings.

Presents full elaboration serving more purposes.

The Abhidharma of the Third Turning analyzes the nature of consciousness, enlightenment, and Buddha activity, providing a map for advanced stages of the path. It includes the Abhidharma of the Vidyādharas, which teaches how to transcend all traces of the three poisons of attachment, aversion, and confusion.

Three Collections as Antidotes

The Mahāyānasūtrālaṁkāra explains that Vinaya is an antidote to the extreme of indulging in desires and the extreme of self-mortification. The Sūtra teachings are antidotes to doubt, giving the definitive solutions to difficult questions, while Abhidharma teachings are antidotes to false views. (MSA XI:1)

Viewed as a whole, the teachings of the three collections can be seen as antidotes that overcome the three poisons of attachment, aversion, and confusion. The Vinaya teachings, originally classified into 100,000 topics, are antidotes to the mind of desire and attachment; the 100,000 topics of Sūtra are antidotes to the mind of egoism and aversion; and the 100,000 topics of Abhidharma are antidotes to the mind of ignorance and confusion.

The 100,000 topics of the inner Vajrayāna practices of the Tantra are considered antidotes for all three poisons in all of their forms. The Master Āryadeva calls the Tantras a fourth collection. The Paṇḍita Vimalamitra includes the Tantras within the Abhidharma collection, and the Mahāsiddha Śāntipa assigns the Tantras to the Sūtra collection.

All the guidelines for self-development are included within the three trainings. Nāgārjuna summarizes the path in the Suhṛllekha: "Always train yourself in moral discipline, meditative concentration, and wisdom. All the one hundred and fifty-one trainings are included within these three." (SL 53) And further: "By means of moral discipline, meditative concentration, and wisdom, strive to attain the pure and powerful state of nirvana, which has nothing to do with old age or death, and which is free from earth, fire, wind, sun, and moon." (SL 105)

Further Readings

Subha Sutta, Digha Nikāya X. Discourse on moral discipline, concentration, and wisdom.

Visuddhimagga, by Buddhaghosa. *The Path of Purification,* chapters I, III, IV, XIV. On discipline, concentration, and wisdom.

Mahayānasaṁgraha, by Asaṅga, chapters VI, VII, VIII. On the three trainings.

Chos-'byung, Bu-ston. *History of Buddhism,* part I, pp. 34–42.

bsTan-pa'i-rnam-gzhag and Chos-'byung, by Dudjom Rinpoche. *The Nyingma School of Tibetan Buddhism,* book I, part I, ch. IV, and book II, part I, ch. I. On the three turnings and the three trainings.

Gesture of Balance, by Tarthang Tulku, part II, Relaxation.

Kum Nye Relaxation, by Tarthang Tulku. 2 volumes. Exercises to balance body and mind.

SECTION SIX

Ways to Enlightenment

CHAPTER THIRTEEN

The Three Vehicles

The Buddha appeared in this world to provide the opportunity for others to realize the wisdom of complete awakening. Toward this purpose, the Enlightened One taught differently to different audiences. Thus there arose three vehicles for liberation: the Śrāvakayāna, the Pratyekabuddhayāna, and the Bodhisattvayāna. The first two together are sometimes called the smaller vehicle, or Hīnayāna, while the Bodhisattvayāna is also known as the great vehicle, or the Mahāyāna. Within the Mahāyāna is included the Vajrayāna, the diamond vehicle.

Historical Viewpoint

The various teachings of the Enlightened One were not all made widely available at the same time. From an historical perspective, Hīnayāna, Mahāyāna, and Vajrayāna follow one another in succession as more practitioners became able to hear the refined and subtle teachings. The eighteen early Śrāvaka schools, represented today by the Theravādin tradition, were established in early centuries after the Buddha's parinirvāṇa. The Mahāyāna schools arose later as the Second and Third Turning teachings

THE THREE YĀNAS		
Hīnayāna	Śrāvakayāna	
	Pratyekabuddhayāna	
Mahāyāna	Bodhisattvayāna	Sūtrayāna Mantrayāna

were studied and practiced by more and more individuals. As this foundation was established, the Vajrayāna teachings were transmitted by the great siddhas.

Geographical Viewpoint

The various ways to enlightenment have developed distinctive patterns in space as well as time. The Hīnayāna schools took root strongly in Śrī Laṅkā and southeast Asia, although the Mahāyāna had earlier flowered in Burma, Thailand, and Śrī Laṅkā. The Mahāyāna developed vigorously in the north, throughout India, central Asia, China, Vietnam, Japan, Tibet, Korea, Mongolia, and Manchuria.

Śrāvakayāna

Quiet is the mind,
quiet the body and speech.
Completely freed by genuine knowing,
such a being is truly at peace.

—*Dhammapada*

The followers of the Śrāvakayāna (vehicle of the listeners) are those who have understood the teachings of the First Turning. Relying on what has been heard, they set out to liberate themselves from suffering and gain lasting peace, the goal of an Arhat. Śāriputra, Maudgalyāyana, Rāhula, Ānanda, and other great Arhats possessed the direct transmission of these teachings.

The Śrāvaka lives a life of purity, peacefulness, and renunciation. Applying antidotes to attachment, aversion, and confusion, practicing the path that leads toward deliverance from all suffering, the Śrāvaka strives over many lifetimes to attain the state of an Arhat. All efforts, study, practice, and discipline are directed toward this goal. The Śrāvakas are said to be the speech sons of the Buddha, embodying the Buddha's communication and explications of the inner workings of samsara.

Pratyekabuddhayāna

The Pratyekabuddha realizes enlightenment without relying upon a teacher. Practicing for numerous lifetimes, the Pratyekabuddha accumulates knowledge and meritorious action to the extent that he is able to reach deliverance independently. In his final lifetime, he is born into a period when no Buddhas or Śrāvakas appear and ardently sets out to discover for himself the laws that govern existence. Relying on First Turning teachings, as does the Śrāvaka, the Pratyekabuddha focuses on interdependent co-operation, thereby realizing that the self is a fiction.

Having freed himself from the illusion of the self and the suffering inherent in this illusion, a Pratyekabuddha teaches others by signs, but not through discourse. Still in the world, he is no longer of this world. His days are spent moving from place to place like clouds or like water. Alone or in the company of others of his kind, he wanders freely until he chooses to enter nirvana.

Bodhisattvayāna

"Clinging to nothing, but aspiring to compassion
like a bird in the clear sky
gliding fearlessly through life,
the Bodhisattva, offspring of the Buddha,
reaches the highest planes."

—*Lama Mipham*

The way of the Bodhisattva is inspired by the Second and Third Turning teachings that bring forth a fuller understanding of the nature of enlightenment, of human being, and of all existence. Based on a long-range vision of the stages of complete human development, the Bodhisattva path culminates in a nearly unimaginable goal: to assist all beings in attaining the full enlightenment of the Buddha. The realization that such a goal could be possible rests on insight into complete reality and unshakable confidence in the enlightened potential of human being.

Those on the Bodhisattva path aspire to great wisdom and great compassion, for the benefit of themselves and others. The Bodhisattvas are said to be the heart sons of the Buddha, embodying the love of the Buddha for all beings. Within the Bodhisattvayāna are two ways of practicing: according to the Sūtras and according to the Tantras.

Sūtrayāna Practice

The path of the Sūtrayāna emphasizes wisdom and compassion and the practice of the six perfections: giving, discipline, patience, effort, meditative concentration, and wisdom. The perfection of wisdom or prajñā is the most powerful antidote to ignorance and confusion, transcending the very root of samsara. This living realization develops not only through the practice of meditation, but also through understanding that becomes completely integrated into daily life. The development of the perfections is not accidental. Arising from the accumulation of meritorious actions and the growth of understanding, it is clearly defined and predictable. The Prajñāpāramitā Sūtras, the Abhisamayālaṁkāra, the Daśabhūmika, and the Mahāyānasūtrālaṁkāra, among other texts, set forth the details of specific stages and the dynamics of development from the initial levels of practice to the most advanced realizations.

Mantrayāna Practice

The Tantras encompass a vast number of texts and teachings, commentaries, and explanations that present a vision even broader than the vision of the Sūtras. The path based on the teachings of the Tantras, known as the Mantrayāna, emphasizes the practice of sādhana, the development and completion stages of meditation, and the skillful use of a great array of transformational techniques. Mantrayāna practice is elaborately structured in stages: preliminary practices, study of commentaries, formal initations, and receiving profound oral instructions. Essential to these studies and practices is a qualified teacher who possesses the full realization lineage and the level of consciousness necessary to guide others through the advanced practices.

To traverse the way of the Bodhisattva and fulfill the vision of awakening proclaimed in the Sūtrayāna in a single lifetime requires the skillful knowledge uniquely transmitted within the Mantrayāna. Many of the Sūtrayāna masters also studied, practiced, and taught the Mantrayāna. The Mantrayāna is also known as the Vajrayāna or diamond vehicle, a name symbolizing indestructibility.

Hetuyāna and Phalayāna

While both the Sūtrayāna and Mantrayāna are identical in purpose, they differ in their methods for attaining Buddhahood. The teachings of the Sūtrayāna are known as the Hetuyāna or the vehicle based on cause and effect, for they guide the follower along a progressive path of development in much the same way as favorable causes and conditions enable a sprout to emerge from a seed. The practitioner follows a path where virtues are cultivated and understanding is refined, an approach that steadily increases merit and wisdom and culminates in complete and perfect enlightenment.

From the perspective of the Mantrayāna, complete awakened reality abides primordially and intrinsically. This is the ground, humanity's spiritual potential, as pervasive as the sky. It is also the path that brings about recognition and removal of the apparent clouds of emotions and ignorance. And it is the result because it is the recognition and actualization of the ground. Relying on this perspective, the Mantrayāna is the vehicle based on the result, the advanced transcendental vehicle called the Phalayāna.

CHAPTER FOURTEEN

Unity of Ways

Although the Mahāyāna scriptures explain that the way of the Bodhisattva is greater than the way of the Śrāvaka in its orientation, practice, wisdom, effort, skillfulness, accomplishment, and activity, the way of the Śrāvaka is seen as the foundation for further study and practice that opens the gateways to the Mahāyāna.

The Heritage

The heritage of the Śrāvaka tradition lives on in the teachings of the Theravādin schools. These fundamental teachings were also transmitted for centuries within the Vinaya lineages of the Mahāyāna schools of India, Tibet, and China. The Mahāyāna tradition preserved and continued the eight types of Sangha described in the Vinaya, and Mahāyāna practitioners adhered to the Vinaya discipline as they followed the expansive and profound philosophical vision of the Mahāyāna. The greatest Mahāyāna masters were often at once renunciate monks, learned scholars, and tantric siddhas, as can be seen from the lives of Nāgārjuna, Śāntideva, and many others.

The Vinaya lineage that passed through Rāhula, the Buddha's son, was transmitted in an unbroken succession through Sarvāstivādin masters to the abbot Śāntarakṣita. Śāntarakṣita brought this Vinaya lineage to Tibet in the eighth century, ordaining the first Tibetan monks according to the Prātimokṣa rules and rituals. The Tibetan monks also took up the Bodhisattva vows and practices transmitted from the Buddha through Ācārya Nāgārjuna and Bhavya to Śāntarakṣita. Shortly thereafter, Padmasambhava initiated these monks and others into the practices of the Mantrayāna. Thus the Tibetan tradition upholds three types of discipline: the Prātimokṣa monastic or lay vows, the Bodhisattva's vows, and the vows of the Vajrayāna adept. All the Tibetan schools transmit these three types of religious practice, and practitioners may take three kinds of vows.

Very advanced and accomplished practitioners are able to understand the perfect unity of the three ways as a living pattern of knowledge. Their external practice follows the Śrāvakayāna; their internal practice follows the general Mahāyāna; and their esoteric practice follows the Vajrayāna. Longchenpa explains the external, internal, and esoteric practices in terms of preliminary practices associated with each:

"Awareness of impermanence and disgust with samsara are the external preliminaries.

"Compassion and the thought of enlightenment are the special preliminaries. They bring everything into the Mahāyāna path.

"Therefore at the beginning activate these two preliminaries. Thereafter comes the most sublime preliminaries (of the Vajrayāna)." (KB II:III)

The most beautiful and profound aspects of each vehicle are uplifted within the next most advanced vehicle, where they are preserved and yet transformed. Inspired by the compassion and wisdom of the Mahāyāna, the practitioner of the Bodhisattvayāna takes up practices of the Hīnayāna, but without being bound by limited views or goals.

Śāntideva explains that higher teachings reveal the limitations of teachings that are lower and enable the practitioner to transcend those limitations. Whereas the Mahāyāna encompasses the Hīnayāna, the Hīnayāna cannot encompass the profound vision and practices of the Mahāyāna. Likewise, the Vajrayāna embraces the complete Mahāyāna teachings, while presenting the broader vision and effective means conveyed in the Tantras.

Orientation

The Abhidharmasamuccaya explains that there are different vehicles for enlightenment because individuals differ in their abilities, in their ways of practicing, in their motivations, and in the scriptures upon which they rely. (AS IV) Depending on these various conditions, one is able to understand one kind of teaching better than another.

The Śrāvaka schools take a particular view of the spiritual path that emphasizes subjugating, removing, or controlling the obstacles to enlightenment. The Mahāyāna takes the view that the path is a matter of spiritual reeducation; by purifying one's way of understanding and developing compassion toward oneself and others, one works at refining body, speech, and mind. The Mantrayāna regards the spiritual path as an alchemical process, a transmutation or transformation.

Although the Mantrayāna and the Sūtrayāna both adopt the ten stages of the Bodhisattva path, the Mantrayāna has the means to complete this path in one lifetime, while the Sūtrayāna pursues a longer path extending over numerous lifetimes. By the power of initiations, extraordinary vision, and skillful techniques, the properly prepared Mantrayāna practitioner can pass through the ten stages very quickly.

Individual Consciousness

Based on particular views, practices, and conduct set forth in the teachings of the Enlightened One, one is able to attain a certain degree of freedom by following any one of the vehicles of enlightened realization.

Hīnayāna Motivation

The motivation of the Hīnayāna practitioner is basically centered on one's own liberation. One first recognizes the problem of suffering in all its severity, and then fully determines to be rid of the problem. Samsara is regarded as contaminated and the samsaric mind as toxic and poisoned, lacking any redeeming qualities. The only solution is to remove oneself from samsara as quickly as possible. By taking vows and following a disciplined way of life, one gives up all attachments and desires, which are regarded as addicting, fraudulent, and deceitful, leading inevitably to deeper immersion in samsara and further suffering.

Recognizing the insubstantial, heartless quality of the samsaric way of life, the Hīnayāna practitioner renounces it completely. One lives in the manner of a perfect monk or nun, developing a consciousness that is pure, free of desire, guilt, anxiety, and fear. The First Turning scriptures reinforce this way of understanding and support the emphasis on the training in moral discipline.

The pure light left to the Sangha by the Enlightened One guides beings through the darkness of samsara, and the Sangha must take responsibility for preserving and transmitting this lamp of virtue. The beauty of the renunciate's way is sparklingly pure and refreshing, like a cool fragrant breeze that soothes the passionate sufferings of samsara.

Mahāyāna Motivation

The motivation of the Mahāyāna practitioner is oriented toward the liberation of others. One has seen suffering everywhere; all beings endure life after life of difficulty, confusion, frustration, pain, and fear. Like bees shut in a jar, they try furiously to escape, but can only circle round and round. The desperate lack of solutions draws forth the Bodhisattva's love, sympathy, and compassion. Other beings are as dear as one's own family, and the Bodhisattva's concern for them steadily grows until it completely surpasses all self-centered concerns. The Second and Third Turning scriptures strongly reinforce this perspective.

The Bodhisattva's vision is more acute than the vision of the Śrāvaka follower. Like the Śrāvaka, he sees that ignorance of selflessness and the endless dualities that arise from this not-knowing are the causes of the suffering of samsara. Recognizing how the illusion of self and other ensnares the mind, the Mahāyāna practitioner focuses on awakening from illusion, using wisdom and compassion. The Bodhisattva trains especially for the sake of others, compassionately developing his practice so that he can manifest as friend, helper, teacher, or in any form in which he can lead others to freedom. The fully developed power of compassion allows the Bodhisattva to descend even into hell to save others. Fearless and as free as the wind, he goes immediately wherever he is needed. Having completely transcended all forms of duality, the Bodhisattva neither abides in nirvana nor rejects samsara.

Fully engaged in this way of life, the follower of the Bodhisattvayāna acts without thought for personal salvation, dedicating his time and energy to the urgent need to rescue others. Willing and able to exchange himself for others, he will accept any suffering: So great is his love that he does not consider the pain; so great is his understanding of selflessness that suffering cannot engage him.

Mantrayāna Motivation

The follower of the Mantrayāna knows that samsara can be transformed and that extraordinary beauty can be realized. Seeing no enemies and no ultimate barriers, this practitioner perceives the enlightened nature of all existence. First recognizing that the mind is the cause of all samsaric suffering, the Mantrayāna adept analyzes and penetrates fully the nature of mind. Completely transformed through realization, mind becomes the perfect peace of samādhi, great compassion, and Dharmakāya. The Mantrayāna adept recognizes that mind is utterly groundless, lacking all foundation whatsoever.

Longchenpa expresses this recognition as magical wonderment: "Mind is like the sky independent of affirmation and negation. Clouds may appear and disappear in the sky, but the sky's magic remains not-two and pure. So also it is with primordial

Buddhanature—spotless, uncreate, spontaneously present meaningfulness." (KB I:X)

Penetrating all layers of consciousness, the practitioner understands, realizes, and completely awakens to the nature of mind, which can manifest either as samsara or as nirvana. Awakening to this direct realization, the practitioner is released from suffering. According to the Mantrayāna, mind is what must be understood, carefully seen, tracked, and transformed. Mantra means instrument (tra) for transformation of mind (man). With skillful techniques and precise knowledge, the agitation of mind, its thoughts, feelings, echoes, and reflections can be completely transmuted.

From this perspective, the mindfulness and careful discipline of the Hīnayāna are not sufficient; even the compassion and wisdom of the Sūtrayāna are not powerful enough to effect transformation. To transform mind from moment to moment, without positioning, without projections—this is the peerless way of the Mantrayāna.

Further Readings

Visuddhimagga, by Buddhaghosa. *The Path of Purification,* chapter II. On the ascetic conduct of the Śrāvaka.

Dhammapada. *Dhammapada.* On the attitude and conduct of the Śrāvaka.

Vajracchedikā Prajñāpāramitā. *Diamond Sūtra.* On the perspective of the Bodhisattva.

Bodhicaryāvatāra, by Śāntideva. *Entering the Path of Enlightenment,* chapters I, III. On the attitude and conduct of the Bodhisattva.

Yid-bzhin-mdzod-kyi-grub-mtha'-bsdus-pa, by Lama Mi-pham. In *Buddhist Philosophy in Theory and Practice,* pp. 25–30; 87–89. On Śrāvaka and Pratyekabuddha.

Introduction, by Tarthang Tulku. In *Footsteps on the Diamond Path* (Crystal Mirror I–III), pp. xiv–xviii. On the Vajrayāna path.

SECTION SEVEN

Relying on Dharma

CHAPTER FIFTEEN

Faith in the Dharma

The idea persists that faith is a remnant of an ancient way of life, a way of knowing that asks for unthinking acceptance of a belief system or adherence to specific dogma. This may be the case for some spiritual traditions, but the Buddha insisted that his disciples investigate his teachings with the powers of reason, test them in the inner laboratory of meditation, and build their faith on a firm foundation of knowledge. As a result, faith in the Dharma implies faith in one's ability to recognize truth when it presents itself and to take responsibility for verifying it through analysis and meditative experience.

Traditionally, knowledge of the Dharma is introduced in an orderly progression that clears away uncertainties as they arise, so that knowledge and faith grow together step by step. In the West, where the teachings of enlightenment are new, accurate and orderly knowledge of the Buddha, Dharma, and Sangha is not easy to find, and doubts are thus more difficult to resolve. Many different kinds of teachings suited to individuals at various levels of understanding are readily available. Students choose what is interesting or appealing to them without necessarily knowing how to lay the groundwork for effective study and practice.

Confidence Based on Personal Experience

In the beginning, the basis for following the Dharma is not direct knowledge of reality, but personal experience of the teachings. Such experience, although limited, gives sufficient confidence to study and practice. This confidence or faith is itself a form of knowledge that reveals deeper knowledge.

The beginner's confidence is based on personal experience of each of the three trainings. By taking up the practice of virtuous conduct (śīla), one begins to see the beneficial results of positive healthy action. By engaging in meditation (samādhi), one experiences the benefits of concentration and begins also to see the need for stabilizing the mind. By making efforts to read, study, and observe experience, one begins the development of wisdom (prajñā) and sees how the teachings apply directly to one's own life. These experiences develop and nourish a dynamic and vital understanding of the Dharma.

Confidence in the Lineage

Further levels of confidence develop through meeting living teachers and studying Dharma histories and biographies to understand the accomplishments of the great masters of the past. Becoming acquainted with the lineage in this way, one begins to appreciate the purity of the Dharma transmission. Accomplished masters who investigate and realize the teachings through study and practice preserve the power of the teachings within their own experience. The transmission of this living realization is what is meant by lineage.

The most admirable accomplishments of a lineage holder are teaching, writing, debating, and research. These activities extend the Dharma to others and clear away doubts and confusion. Through their writings, the masters of the lineage express their understanding in ways suited to their time and place.

The Nyingma school emphasizes the oral lineage transmitted directly from master to disciple. The inner esoteric teachings can be transmitted only to one who is wholly devoted to the Dharma and properly prepared, one with abilities well developed through practice and study over a long period of time. Selflessly serving the Dharma, uninterested in worldly gain and loss, power or possessions, magical or psychic powers, such a pure vessel is fit to receive the highest teachings.

The Qualities of the Student

Three qualities are essential in a student of the Dharma: devotion to the teacher and to the Dharma; zeal, which is the willingness to strive vigorously for understanding; and intelligence. The Mahāyānasūtrālaṁkāra explains that the marks of the follower of the Bodhisattva teachings are compassion, faith, patience, and the ability to accomplish good. Compassion means a loving heart toward others; faith means confidence in the Mahāyāna teachings; patience means enduring whatever is necessary by developing the strength that can sustain one through difficulties; and accomplishment is achieved through the practice of the perfections. (MSA III:5)

Equipped with these qualities, one follows the teachings and begins to deepen one's understanding. As understanding grows, one practices more and more from direct knowledge. Since direct knowledge opens fully only in advanced stages of the path, the way of faith is traveled for a long time.

Three Motivations

The type of faith that can develop depends on the nature of the motivation. The Mahāyānasūtrālaṁkāra describes the three weakest motivations as those rooted in needs for personal gratification, in unwillingness to inquire, and in fear.

"In those possessed by desire, faith is like a dog; in those involved in mundane practices, faith is like a tortoise; in those focused on themselves, faith is like a nervous servant. But in one who is oriented toward others, faith is like a king." (MSA X:9–10)

The faith of the dog is based on hungry pursuit of whatever appears to benefit oneself. The faith of the tortoise is based on a wish for security that accommodates the dominant culture without individual inquiry and decision. The faith of the servant is based on anxious adherence to what we believe will remove our fears. Depending on various combinations of desire, fear, and guilt, individuals in different cultures are more or less susceptible to these three substitutes for faith.

Faith based on these weak motivations is like a contract between two individuals. It lasts as long as both sides keep an implicit agreement; when it fails to meet conditions and expectations, we "lose faith," often with devastating effects.

The faith necessary to support growth in the Dharma is not temporary or blind; it does not depend on a particular belief, a person, a teacher, an organization, or a specific interpretation of reality. Faith that we can rely on is directly connected with open inquiry and leads inevitably to greater knowledge.

There are three kinds of faith described in the Abhidharma: the admiring faith that is inspired by knowing about the accomplishments of the great masters and Bodhisattvas; the longing faith that is highly motivated to follow the path and achieve the results; and the trusting faith that arises from seeing the truth of the teachings in one's own experience. A fourth type of faith is irreversible faith, which arises at the beginning of the Bodhisattva path, upon the first glimpse of enlightenment. (KZLZ II:I)

Opinion and Knowledge

The Western scholastic tradition tends to view knowledge as an individual matter, a type of personal property. This view easily confuses knowledge with personal opinion, which masquerades as knowledge but in actuality cuts off its growth.

The Abhidharma texts describe opinionatedness as an emotion. The intellectual content of opinions differs, but opinions all share the same emotional quality: They are strongly adhered to as positions. Having established a position, we accept what matches our position and find reasons to reject what does not match it. Holding to our own opinions may appear to be "independent thinking," but it prevents us from questioning these views. The emotion of opinionatedness convinces us that our established views are valid, making them "feel right" because "they are mine."

Doubt and Inquiry

While doubt and a questioning, inquiring mind are commonly equated, doubt and inquiry are distinctly different. Whereas questioning and inquiry arise from wanting to know and heighten receptivity to knowledge, doubt is rooted in fear and insecurity.

Doubt reinforces opinion and belief and undermines efforts to develop faith. Doubt is oriented toward conflict and strategy; once doubt rules, it perpetuates itself, attacking faith from every conceivable angle, insisting on one more "verification," no matter how well known the subject is.

The Abhidharmasamuccaya explains: "Doubt is uncertainty about the truth and its function is to serve as a basis of not becoming involved with what is positive." (AS I) Doubt continually divides the mind into opposing purposes and views, preventing resolution. With mental energies fragmented, we are unable to "make up our mind;" faith cannot develop and deeper knowledge cannot emerge. Once doubt establishes its hold, it erodes the ability to generate faith. The student will doubt the teachings, the teacher, and eventually even himself.

The faith that supports progress in the Dharma is steady, free from the shifting realm of likes and dislikes. It opens and surrenders to truth with no expectation and no conditions, based on knowledge that truth is deeply precious and worth the time and effort necessary to develop and protect it. Absolute truth, the Lord Buddha explained to Ānanda, can only be understood through faith that becomes heartfelt certainty.

For the fearful, doubting mind that wants "its own way," surrendering expectations and conditions seems an utterly irrational choice and an impossible risk of losing personal identity and control. The fear of loss that stimulates doubt is based on a sense of the self that Dharma teaches to be delusion. We have "put our faith" in the wrong thing: in the self's logic based on the distinction between self and not-self, and in the self's emotions based on personal likes and dislikes. Appearing rational and objective, this logic is not concerned with discerning truth but rather with ensuring that the self is protected. It accomplishes this by convincing us that we are right, justified, and unblamable.

Faith and Logic

While doubt is always dualistic and tends to fragment knowledge, faith is inherently nondualistic and expands knowledge. When we awaken faith in the Dharma, this faith is not opposed to faith in ourselves. If we understand that faith is a unifying force, the basis for doubt and fear disappears, and the gates to knowledge open of their own accord.

We cannot create faith from logic alone, but neither are faith and logic contradictory. Logic is a tool of the mind that can be used to prove or disprove almost anything, depending on what assumptions one begins with. Faith is a faculty, almost like one of the senses. It allows us to see through the elaborate network of self, to perceive the potential for greater knowledge, and to awaken our ability to attain it. Faith opens a new channel of receptivity, so that teachings, teacher, and one being taught are recognized as a continuum.

Like an advance guard, faith goes before us, encouraging us to enter an ever broader realm of experience and knowledge. Once we have reached this broader realm, we see from our new perspective that we were guided along this unknown path by a beautiful and multifaceted logic. Through such experience and insights, we learn to trust the teachings of the Dharma and become more willing to pass beyond the boundaries enforced by doubts, fears, and emotionality.

Surrender and Faith

The Visuddhimagga speaks of faith in several ways:

"The function of faith is to clarify, like a gemstone that clears muddy water.

"The function of faith is 'to enter into', like setting forth to cross a flooded river.

"Faith manifests as nonfogginess and as resolve. Its cause is something to have faith in—the Dharma.

"Faith is like a hand, because it takes hold of what is profitable. It is like a seed, the beginnings of all good. (VM XIV:140)

When life is lived in faith, the quality of life grows rich and creative. Abandoning doubt and opinionatedness allows the mind to settle into deepening certainty. Based in certainty, we become strong and confident, standing for what we know, and experience becomes meaningful and joyful. We are able to give ourselves openly and completely to what we love, which guarantees that we will accomplish something of value.

Such confident love supports inner realization that moves toward higher consciousness and the highest goals of completion. The deep certainty of the spiritual path is unknown to us until we are completely in love, surrendering our heart to truth. Longchenpa expresses the importance of faith as the ground or basis of all virtue and accomplishment:

"When the soil of faith, which is the pure mind,
is well watered by the rain of merit and wisdom,
virtue springs forth and grows,
and the harvest of the excellent Buddha qualities ripens."(KB I:VI)

If we refuse to surrender to truth, we travel the opposite direction toward unending uncertainty and doubt. Standing for nothing of lasting value, we are bereft of joy and unable to accomplish much. Our many questions bring no answers; our many efforts bring few results. Even our desire to learn produces little of benefit because our intention is not oriented toward truth. Our lack of accomplishment further undermines faith in ourselves, and increases the skepticism that is corrupting the mind. Eventually, we find nothing worthwhile or meaningful, and life becomes mechanical.

The speed and pressure of the modern world foster a restless, superficial way of life that promotes doubt and drifts inexorably toward the mechanical. When we begin to realize how crucial the Dharma is for the future of humanity, we acknowledge a priority higher than the self, and faith begins to flourish. When we are moved to act, despite personal hardships or sacrifices, love and compassion gain ascendancy, empowering us to escape from the illusory and limiting cage of the self.

CHAPTER SIXTEEN

Refuge in the Three Jewels

There is no higher refuge and no greater protection than the Three Jewels, for the Buddha, the Dharma, and the Sangha have the power to resolve the fundamental problems we face on the human level.

"Rely on the noble, the spiritual, the steady, the learned, the prudent, the wise. One wise enough to follow such beings is like the moon on the path of the stars." (DP XV:12)

The rGyud-bla-ma explains the basis for faith in the Three Jewels as a deepening understanding of their value: "The refuges (of Buddha, Dharma, and Sangha) are called jewels because they are rare, immaculate, possessed of power, the ornaments of the world, the most excellent, and immutable." (GL 22)

The body of knowledge encompassed by the Three Jewels is extraordinary, for it includes the knowledge of how samsara operates: the functioning of emotion, perception, thoughts, memory, and consciousness throughout the past, present, and future. It includes as well the knowledge of how enlightenment manifests: the qualities of the Bodhisattvas and Buddhas and the activities of enlightened body, speech, and mind. Because the scope of ordinary knowledge simply does not extend this deep or this far, the knowledge of the Dharma is called "most excellent."

Opening the Heart

Learning about the Three Jewels and appreciating the qualities of the Buddha, Dharma, and Sangha, we begin to develop admiring faith. If we believe it possible that we ourselves could develop the knowledge and qualities of the Three Jewels, we turn toward the teachings with an open mind and let them speak to us directly and personally. Realizing that we need this knowledge and wishing to approach it, we open our hearts to the Dharma. This is the beginning of longing faith.

Opening the heart is prayer that asks only to see the light of truth. Rather than asking for anything or searching for anything, we simply open to truth. This is the beginning of trusting faith.

Patrul Rinpoche tells us that if we have trusting faith, the compassionate light of the Buddha immediately enters our lives. Openness brings tranquility, and as thoughts and questions settle, we no longer follow the guidance of inner dialogues, projections, memories, and emotional habits. We have found another guide, a deeper knowing. (KZLZ II:I)

Although we may not yet fully know this perfect guide, nourished by faith and knowledge, we begin to surrender to truth. Opening the heart to the Three Jewels, we touch a confidence that clears away fear, doubts, and conflicting emotions. Again and again we surrender, gradually healing all the polarities and judgments of the samsaric mind. In their place arise the warmth and beauty of compassion for ourselves and others.

Patrul Rinpoche explains the deep connections between human being and the Three Jewels. The blessing of the Three Jewels enters one's mind because of the power of faith. This blessing gives birth to perfect knowing that allows one to see the meaning of truth. Seeing truth in turn gives rise to ever deeper faith in the Three Jewels. Nourished by faith and knowledge, the enlightened nature of being shines forth. (KZLZ II:I)

Discovering that we are part of the enlightened family, the royal lineage of the Buddha, we realize that the potential of human being embraces an enlightened field of knowledge and pure qualities that are utterly reliable. Protected and uplifted by faith, we are able to manifest a more enlightened way of being. We accomplish our aims and face obstacles without fear. A deep peace of mind surrounds us, like a halo around the shining moon: We have touched the faith that is hidden within the human heart and found the unfailing experience of truth.

Further Readings

Sampasādanīya Sutta. Digha Nikāya XXVIII. On serene faith.

rGyud-bla-ma. *The Sublime Science of the Great Vehicle,* verses 1–22. On the Three Jewels.

Jo-mo-la-gdams-pa'i-chos-skor, Padmasambhava's oral instructions to Ye-shes-mtsho-rgyal. *Dakini Teachings,* pp. 1–28. On ways of taking refuge.

Dam-chos-yid-bzhin-nor-bu-thar-pa-rin-po-che'i-rgyan, by sGam-po-pa. *The Jewel Ornament of Liberation,* chapters I, III, and VIII. On motivation, spiritual teachers, and taking refuge.

Ngal-gso-skor-gsum, by Klong-chen-pa. *Kindly Bent to Ease Us,* volume I, chapters V and VI. On spiritual guidance and taking refuge.

Chos-'byung, by Bu-ston Rinpoche. *History of Buddhism,* part I, pp. 80–82. On the definition of a Dharma student.

Kun-bzang-bla-ma'i-zhal-lung, transcribed by dPal-sprul Rinpoche. *Kun-zang La-may Zhal-lung,* part I, chapter VI. On following a spiritual teacher.

SECTION EIGHT

Body of Knowledge

CHAPTER SEVENTEEN

Abhidharma Analysis

The teachings of the Buddha demonstrate that the self is fabricated and that our inability to perceive this truth is the primary source of suffering. The Mahāyānasūtrālaṁkāra uses a common set of eight similes to describe the self. It is: "Like an illusion, a dream, a mirage, a shadow, a magical display, an echo, a reflection of the moon in water, an apparition . . ." (MSA XI:30)

How is such an illusion created? In ancient India there were magicians who could conjure up illusory horses by pronouncing spells over rocks. If the self is an illusion produced by pure wizardry, then what is the rock and what is the spell? Who is the magician?

Questioning the Self

Our sense of self establishes the self as something that obviously exists; its existence is beyond doubt, truly unquestionable. It seems self-evident that sense experience, feelings, impulses, thoughts, and memories belong to somebody or originate from some lasting source. There must be an owner, an origin, or at least a creator of our experience.

Since there is sensing, there must be someone performing the action. Seeing is interpreted as "I see." Qualities and attributes are also possessed: Anger is interpreted as "I am angry." Once "I" possesses the emotion or thought or perception, then "I" must respond, make distinctions, and judge whatever arises: "I like this and I don't like that." "I desire to be close to this person, and I do not want to be near that one." "I" reaches out to relish what is desired and to ward off what is not desired. Through these actions, "I" establishes what constitutes "my personal happiness and my personal suffering." Our life stories revolve around these two poles, developing and proliferating year after year.

If we look more closely into the structure of this self, we see that the belief in a self divides our world into subject and object: objects "outside" this self are identified as distinct and separate from the subject, which is "inside."

Once there is perception of an object, there must be one to perceive it. Identifying the object confirms the existence of the subject. If one asks, "Who recognizes, who accepts this object?" the answer must be "I," the owner of the perception. The witnessing created by perception, logic, and identification is very convincing. We do not notice the circularity: "I" creates the story that attributes the witnessing to an authoritative self-existent "I." This self-existent "I" is considered identical with itself over time; on some level, it is always "the same one." Moreover, self-existent "I" is considered central to experience, the necessary and subtle sensor within the senses.

The self is recognized also as an inner object, "me", and this recognition firmly establishes the inner recognizer-self as subject "I" and the object "me." The self-existent "I" is clearly possessed as "mine." The self does not belong to anyone else. That self is "mine." "Me" belongs to "I," but now my life belongs to it. It commands my being; it demands obedience, and I follow its commands without asking where it is leading. Our whole world is built around the meanings and stories of the self, its hopes and fears, its victories and defeats. If we were to inquire closely into the nature of this self, we might discover that apart from it, we do not really know who we are.

If the sense of self is, as the Buddha teaches, an illusion that one can penetrate, then the ordinary understanding of how experience arises and develops around a central self is completely misleading. Instead of accepting the self and the experience of the self as an intrinsic part of life, one can question: What is the nature of what I call the self? What is the nature of experience?

Abhidharma Explorations

Abhidharma study is training in wisdom, which develops through observing, categorizing, analyzing, and penetrating the true nature of experience. To begin the process of observation, we need an overview that guides the inquiry and a map of the territory we are about to explore. The Abhidharma provides maps created by those who have explored the breadth and depth of experience, with the aim of demonstrating to others the way to liberation from confusion and illusion.

Our understanding is confused in four particular ways known as the four errors:

1. We mistake what is impermanent for permanent.
2. We mistake what is full of suffering for a source of happiness.
3. We mistake what is impure for pure.
4. We mistake what is not self for self. (AKB V:9a–b, SL 48)

By observing, categorizing, analyzing, and finally penetrating the depths of experience, we will be able to clear away the confusion these errors create.

Learning how to observe moments of experience directly is the first step. Our attention is ordinarily attracted so strongly to experience that we are instantaneously involved and thus unable to observe how experience arises and develops. To be able to observe, we must develop mindfulness, which is not-forgetting to look, "to face the object." (VM XIV:141) Arising naturally from the intention to explore, mindfulness brings observation to bear directly on experience as part of the experiencing process.

Once in mindful contact with the flow of experience, we can begin to categorize moments as distinct nameable events: "This is the sensation of breathing." "This is a moment of anger." "This is a pleasant feeling." Having studied the categories of the Abhidharma, we begin to notice that experience is much richer than we had realized. Each moment there are new experiences, and these experiences are very changeable. Feelings shift, perceptions flicker rapidly from sense to sense, motivations are unstable. Thus observation and categorization introduce us directly to impermanence.

We discover how we mistake a source of suffering for a source of happiness when we become able to analyze events more extensively. When we can identify "anger" or "pride" or "faith," we are able to see what follows in the wake of each and to question where each leads us. What appears to be desirable may not actually bring pleasant or desirable results. What appears to be of little importance—a lack of attention, a little laziness, a tendency to be jealous—may make a substantial difference in the outcome of our efforts.

Likewise, by categorizing and analyzing, we begin to see that external objects, ideas, or mental events we consider beautiful and pure have an impure side we ordinarily ignore. The impurity may be physical, such as the naturally unclean aspects of the body that we deliberately ignore. Or the impurity may be emotional; what we believe is pure love or compassion turns out on closer inspection to be "contaminated" with self-interest.

The capacity to see how mistaken views of self arise is developed by the analysis of twenty possibilities. (These twenty are four ways of regarding the five skandhas in relation to the self. This analysis enables us to see through untested beliefs and vague assumptions. See chapter 22.)

As we learn to observe closely and consistently, to recognize distinct mental events, and to analyze results, we are less easily deceived by untested beliefs and more open to the direct evidence before us. In this way we begin to perceive the nature of different states of mind and to test the validity of our belief in the self.

Dharmas

Abhidharma studies begin by examining dharmas. The term dharma is derived from the root "dhṛ," which means to hold, and it has ten traditional definitions: that which is knowable, the path, nirvana, an object of mind, merit, lifespan, scriptures, material objects, rules or ways of conduct, and doctrinal traditions. (VY I)

In this context, dharma means a knowable object: experiential data that can be distinguished, named, and categorized. The correct discernment of dharmas in one's direct experience is called prajñā or wisdom.

The Abhidharmakoṣabhāṣya says: "Without dharma analysis, how can there be any means for extinguishing emotionality, this emotionality that causes the world to wander in the great ocean of existence?" (AKB I:3)

Once dharmas are recognized, they can be classified in terms of the four errors and in terms of the various purposes of the path to liberation. For example, dharmas can be categorized as pure or impure, as leading to suffering, as supporting specific aspects of the path, and as being necessary to remove or transform.

What are the types and numbers of dharmas? Experience is categorized into dharmas depending on a complex analysis that varies from school to school. The Theravādins noted eighty-two, while the Sarvāstivādins enumerated seventy-five dharmas.

Five Knowables

Dharmas are also sorted out according to various larger categories of analysis. The Sarvāstivādins defined five categories of all knowable things: four categories of the conditional—form, mind, events associated with mind, and events not associated with mind or with form—and one category of the nonconditioned. The seventy-five dharmas could be sorted into these five larger categories.

FIVE KNOWABLES

Conditioned	*Nonconditioned*
Form	Nonconditioned
Mind	
Mental events	
Nonassociated	

SEVENTY-FIVE DHARMAS

Form	11 dharmas
Mind	1 dharma
Mental events	46 dharmas
Nonassociated	14 dharmas
Nonconditioned	3 dharmas

Tools For Inquiry

"The things classified as skandhas, āyatanas, and dhātus, indriyas, truths, and interdependent co-operation, etc. are the basis for wisdom . . ." (VM XIV:32)

In the Sūtras, the Buddha described how experience could be categorized into the five skandhas, twelve āyatanas, and eighteen dhātus. The Madhyāntavibhāṅga (MAV III:15) explains how these three ways of analyzing experience break the hold of the belief in the self as unitary, the self as the causal agent, and the self as the enjoyer of experience. These analyses require that we suspend the ordinary divisions of experience into "self" and "other," "inside" and "outside," "body" and "mind," and observe instead from the perspective of dynamic fields of sensory experience.

Bringing this radically different view to bear from moment to moment is a highly effective tool for unravelling the sense of self.

Experience is revealed as a series of subtle but knowable interactions, while the basis for the illusory self is seen to be a mistaken apprehension of some combination of these interactions.

The Abhidharmakoṣabhāṣya says: "There are three teachings—skandhas, āyatanas, and dhātus—because there are three kinds of confusion, abilities, and interests." (AKB I:20c–d) Vasubandhu explains that this means that individuals make three different types of errors about the nature of the self, have three different levels of intelligence, and respond best to three different kinds of teachings.

Teachings on the skandhas are intended for those with sharp faculties who mistake mental phenomena for a self, and who enjoy and can work with a brief explanation. The teaching of āyatanas is for those with middling faculties, who mistake the body and material forms for a self, and who relate best to a medium-length explanation. The teaching of dhātus is for those with duller faculties who mistake a combination of material forms and mental phenomena for a self, and who work best with a lengthy explanation. It is helpful, however, to study and work with all three systems of analysis, for each system offers a different perspective.

Lama Mipham encourages Dharma students to analyze experience methodically until they begin to see in a new and different way. In the "Wheel of Analytic Meditation," he presents analysis by skandhas and assures us that the most beneficial and liberating practice is to recognize the impermanence, emptiness, and selflessness of experience for even a mere snap of a finger. Fully developing the practice of analytic meditation, the mind moves toward joyful serenity and refined clarity until "all trace of delusion vanishes into emptiness." (CC)

CHAPTER EIGHTEEN

Skandha of Form

Lama Mipham explains: "Study of the five skandhas develops expert knowledge of the conditioned dharmas and counteracts holding to the self as unified and single." (KJD 4a:3)

The Sanskrit "skandha" or Tibetan "phung-po" literally means "heap" or "pile". An analysis by skandhas sorts all compounded conditioned experience into five different "heaps." These five are form, feeling, perception, motivational factors, and consciousness. Together these five form the "body of experience," the basis for suffering which is taken up, appropriated, imagined, held on to, and believed in as a self (upādāna-skandha).

Recognizing Form

Form can be recognized as form by touching it, either with the hand or with an instrument. Form is that which offers resistance, that which cannot be penetrated; it takes up space and is an obstacle to another form occupying that space. It is also said by some Abhidharma masters that form is characterized by being breakable, by deteriorating, or by being transformable. (AKB I:13d)

SKANDHA OF FORM
Eleven Dharmas

Five Sense Organs	*Five Sense Objects*	*One Imperceptible*
Eye	Visible form	Form arising from a vow
Ear	Sounds	
Nose	Smells	
Tongue	Tastes	
Body	Tangibles	

According to the Sarvāstivādin Abhidharma

The skandha of form includes causal form and resultant form. The four great elements are known as causal form because they are the basis for the arising of all other forms. Eleven kinds of form that result from the combinations of the four great elements are known as resultant form. (KJ 2b.1–5a.2).

Causal Form

The four great elements are earth, water, fire, and wind. The earth element is solid, and its function is to form a basis. The water element is fluid, and its function is cohesion. The fire element is heat, and its function is maturation. The wind element is motion, and its function is expansion.

"The elements are called great because they are the point of support for resultant forms; because they assemble on a large scale as the mass of the earth, water, fire, and wind, where their modes of activity manifest together. What activity establishes the existence of these elements and what is their nature? Their activity proves that the elements exist. The activities are support, cohesion, maturation, and expansion." (AKB I:12a-d)

The smallest unit of form is the atom, called the limit of form, or that which cannot be divided further, being conceived of as partless and indivisible. Atoms assemble in a regular fashion to form larger aggregates, which have been given names indicating some aspect of their properties. Seven atoms make a "fine" particle. Seven "fine" particles make an "iron" particle. Seven "iron" particles make a "water" particle, seven again make a "rabbit" particle, and so forth through "sheep" particle, "ox" particle, "dust mote," "louse-egg," "louse," "barley grain," and "finger-width." The next measurements are based on proportions: Twenty-four "finger-widths" are called an "arm-span;" four arm-spans make one "bow;" five hundred "bows" are called the "reach of hearing," and eight "reaches of hearing" are called a measure. (AS I,II, AKB II:22, III:85–88)

Resultant Form

The resultant forms include the five sense organs and the five sense objects. The five sense organs are the eye, ear, nose, tongue, and body as organ of touch. Each sense organ is a condition for the arising of its respective consciousness, such as eye-consciousness, ear-consciousness and so forth.

The subtle form of each organ has a distinctive arrangement of atoms. The inner subtle form of the eye is said to be round and blue like a sesame flower. The inner subtle form of the ear is like the twisted curl of birch bark. The inner subtle form of the nose is like two parallel copper needles. The inner subtle form of the tongue is like the crescent moon. The inner subtle form of the body as the organ of touch (the skin) conforms to the shape of the body. The inner subtle form of the organ is the causal force, the sensory capacity. (AKB I:44a-b)

The five sense objects are visible forms, sounds, smells, tastes, and tangibles. (AS I, KJ 3a.1) Visible forms can be classified according to variations of color and shape. Color variations include the four primary colors of blue, yellow, white, and red and their many distinct combinations. Secondary aspects that affect the coloration of form are: degrees of cloudiness and smokiness, dustiness and mistiness, sun and shade, light and darkness. Shape variations include long, short, square, round, high, low, fine and gross, even and uneven, with more subdivisions such as triangular, oblong, and so forth. Visible forms can also be classified as good, bad, or neutral depending on their associations in context. (AKB I:29c-30a)

Also included under visible forms are forms such as reflections, the perceptible form of actions and gestures such as making a prostration, and the uniform blue color of the sky. (KJ 3a.2)

Sounds, the objects of the ear, are classified by their cause and their function. The primary causes of sounds are the four great elements, but these elements may or may not be associated with a sentient being. Sounds made by sentient beings include voices, hand clapping, finger snapping, and so forth. Sounds made by elements not associated with sentient beings include the sound of the wind or trees or water flowing. There are also combinations of both when a sentient being makes a sound by means of an inanimate object like a drum. Sounds are either articulate, expressing a meaning, or inarticulate and meaningless. Meaningful sounds are made either by noble individuals such as Dharma masters or by ordinary worldly persons. Sounds can be pleasant, discordant, or neutral, depending on their associations.

Smells are the objects of the nose and are classified as fragrant, unfragrant, or neutral; naturally arising or manufactured.

Tastes, the objects of the tongue, are classified as sweet, sour, salty, bitter, pungent, or astringent. Many combinations arise from mixing these six together. Tastes can also be classified as pleasant, unpleasant, or neutral, and as natural or manufactured.

Tangibles are the objects of the bodily sense of touch. Tangibles include the solidness of the element earth, the wetness of the element water, the warmth of the element fire, and the movement of the element wind. Arising from combinations of the four elements are an additional set of tangibles: smoothness, roughness, heaviness, lightness, hunger, thirst, and cold. There are also inner experiences of the body: being flexible, slack, tight, sated, ill, aged, dying, refreshed, or possessed of physical courage.

Imperceptible Form

Taken together, the five sense organs and five sense objects make ten categories of form. According to the Abhidharmakoṣabhāṣya, an eleventh category consists of imperceptible forms that arise from taking a vow. These forms are not perceptible to others. Yet the vow holds whether or not one is awake and aware; once the vow is taken, an imperceptible form arises depending on the four great elements and remains intact until the vow is abandoned. (AKB I:11)

Objects of Mind

According to the Mahāyāna Abhidharma as presented in the Khenjug, the eleventh category of form includes not only imperceptible form as mentioned in the Abhidharmakoṣabhāṣya, but also four other categories given in the Abhidharmasamuccaya. Together these five are objects of mind belonging to the skandha of form.

The first of the five objects of mind is the most subtle form of all, the atom. The atom is not perceptible by the five senses but is known through mental analysis.

The second are forms that belong to space, such as reflections and empty space. These are not tangible and do not impede the presence of another form. These can be objects of the eye as well as objects of the mind.

The third are forms that arise from making a vow; these are the forms counted by the Abhidharmakoṣabhāṣya as non-manifesting, imperceptible form.

The fourth are forms that are produced by the imagination, such as hallucinations and dreams.

The fifth are forms that arise from meditative power. These do not depend on an aggregation of atoms but are brought about by different causes.

These five are objects of mind; the majority of the objects of mind are not in the skandha of form but in the skandha of motivational factors. (AS I, KJ 3b.5) The five types of objects of mind are perceptible by the mental organ, the mind, but not by the sense organs (with the exception of mirages and reflections). These forms do not offer resistance, which is the hallmark of most form, but are nonetheless classified as form. (KJ 2b.4)

CHAPTER NINETEEN

Skandha of Feeling

The skandha of feeling refers to the pleasant, unpleasant, or neutral feeling tone that arises in conjunction with all experience. The Abhidharmakoṣabhāṣya says: "The skandha of feeling is the threefold mode of experiencing pleasure, pain, and what is neither painful nor pleasant [neutral]." (AKB I:14c, KJ 5a.3–5a.5)

Sixfold Feeling

The basis for feeling is contact. As organ, consciousness, and object make contact, feeling arises. With each sense organ, a particular type of feeling arises, creating a sixfold division of feeling:

1. feeling arising from the contact of eye, visible form, and eye-consciousness

2. feeling arising from the contact of ear, sound, and ear-consciousness

3. feeling arising from the contact of nose, smells, and nose-consciousness

EIGHTEEN TYPES OF FEELING

Feeling based on	*Tone*	
Eye	pleasant unpleasant neutral	sensory
Ear	pleasant unpleasant neutral	sensory
Nose	pleasant unpleasant neutral	sensory
Tongue	pleasant unpleasant neutral	sensory
Body	pleasant unpleasant neutral	sensory
Mind	pleasant unpleasant neutral	mental

4. feeling arising from the contact of tongue, tastes, and tongue-consciousness

5. feeling arising from the contact of body, tangibles, and body-consciousness

6. feeling arising from the contact of mind, mental objects, and mental-consciousness

Each of these six can be pleasant, unpleasant, or neutral, making a total of eighteen types of feelings. Feelings can also be classified according to whether they arise in conjunction with the five sensory consciousnesses or whether they arise in conjunction with the mental consciousness. Again, each of these can be pleasant, unpleasant, or neutral. (AKB II:7–8, AS:I, KJ 5a.4)

Other Classifications

Feeling can also be understood by classifying it into five types: physical pleasure, mental pleasure, physical pain, mental pain, and indifference. Physical feeling is feeling that accompanies any of the five sense consciousnesses; mental feeling is feeling that accompanies mental consciousness.

The Mahāyāna Abhidharma states that feeling can also be classified as: disturbed, undisturbed, clinging, and nonclinging.

Disturbed feeling arises in conjunction with all self-oriented experience, based on appropriating the five skandhas as a self: Feeling is "my" feeling. Undisturbed feeling is not associated with self-oriented experience; it includes feeling arising with experience associated with seeing the absence of a self.

Clinging feeling is associated with the five sensory objects and the qualities of the desire realm, and it fosters addiction to the desire realm. Nonclinging feeling is free of clinging; it supports renunciation and meditative states. (AS I, KJ 5a.3, MBP 21–22)

CHAPTER TWENTY

Skandha of Perception

The skandha of perception refers to the process of recognition of an object. Perception means taking hold of the characteristic of the object. Perception consists of grasping specific characteristics such as blue, yellow, long, short, male, female, friend, enemy. (AKB I:14c–d)

Six Kinds of Perception

Each particular perception is linked to one of the sense organs, giving six kinds of perception.

1. Perception arising from the contact of eye, visible forms, and eye-consciousness

2. Perception arising from the contact of ear, sounds, and ear-consciousness

3. Perception arising from the contact of nose, smells, and nose-consciousness

4. Perception arising from the contact of tongue, tastes, and tongue-consciousness

SIX KINDS OF PERCEPTION

1. Arising from contact of eye, visible form, eye-consciousness
2. Arising from contact of ear, sound, ear-consciousness
3. Arising from contact of nose, odor, nose-consciousness
4. Arising from contact of tongue, taste, tongue-consciousness
5. Arising from contact of body, tangibles, body-consciousness
6. Arising from contact of mind, mental objects, mental-consciousness

5. Perception arising from the contact of body, tangibles, and body-consciousness

6. Perception arising from the contact of mind, mental objects, and mental-consciousness (KJ 5a.5)

Six Classes of Perception

Perception is sixfold when classified according to having or not having characteristics and according to what realm of existence it belongs to:

1. Perception with characteristics, which is of two kinds: perception that grasps an object as being blue or yellow, etc., and perception that grasps the proposition, "This is a man," etc. There are as many subdivisions here as there are knowable things. (KJ 5a.6)

2. Perception without characteristics, which is of three types: perception of an unfamiliar object, for which the name is not known; perception of markless space; perception during meditative absorption in the highest meditation realms at the summit of existence.

3. Lesser perception that operates in the desire realm

4. Vast perception that operates in the form realm

SIX CLASSES OF PERCEPTION

1. Perception with characteristics
   - characteristics of an object
   - characteristics of expressions
2. Perception without characteristics
   - not knowing the name
   - space
   - summit of existence
3. Lesser perception
4. Vast perception
5. Immeasurable perception
6. Perception of nothing whatsoever

5. Immeasurable perception that operates in the formless realm in the spheres of infinite space and infinite consciousness

6. Perception in the sphere of nothing whatsoever in the formless realm. (AS I, KJ 5b.1 MBP 23-25)

CHAPTER TWENTY-ONE

Skandha of Motivational Forces

Motivational forces are those formative forces that bring about activity. The characteristic of this skandha is to build, create, and direct into action. This skandha includes most conditioned dharmas.

Any conditioned thing is included in four of the five categories of the knowable: form, mind, events associated with mind, and events not associated with mind or form. (The fifth category is the nonconditioned and does not include conditioned things).

These four categories are characterized in the following way: Form is that which consists of atoms and is equivalent to the skandha of form. Mind is characterized by knowingness and cognizance and is equivalent to the skandha of consciousness. Most events associated with mind are included in the skandha of motivational forces. Events associated with neither form nor mind are included in the skandha of motivational forces because they resemble mind more than form.

FIVE CATEGORIES OF THE KNOWABLE

1. Form	skandha of form
2. Mind	skandha of consciousness
3. Events associated with mind	skandha of motivational forces skandha of feeling skandha of perception
4. Events not associated with mind or form	skandha of motivational forces
5. Nonconditioned	no skandhas

Events Associated with Mind

The mental events associated with mind are presented in the Abhidharmakoṣabhāṣya using the dharma analysis of the Sarvāstivādin and Vaibhāṣika schools. Mental events are of five major kinds:

1. omnipresent events that accompany all states of mind
2. virtuous events that accompany virtuous states of mind
3. nonvirtuous events that accompany nonvirtuous states of mind
4. events that accompany emotionally afflicted states of mind
5. events that are lesser emotions (AKB II:23c–d)

Omnipresent Events

Ten omnipresent mental events are present in every moment of mental activity: feeling, intention, perception, interest, contact, discernment, mindfulness, attention, determination, and concentration. The Mahāyāna Abhidharma texts divide these into two groups of five, the omnipresent and the object-determining. The ten omnipresent events are described as follows:

MOTIVATIONAL FORCES	
Associated with Mind	*Nonassociated with Mind*
10 omnipresent	14 events
10 virtuous	
2 nonvirtuous	
6 emotionally afflicted	
10 lesser emotions	
8 variables	

Feeling is the experience of pleasure, pain, or neutrality arising from the contact of the five senses and their consciousness with the appropriate sense object. This is also categorized as the skandha of feeling.

Intention is the mental activity that urges the mind forward. It directs the mind toward what is virtuous, nonvirtuous, or neutral.

Perception refers to the process of apprehending experience, either conceptually or nonconceptually, through the six senses. Perception grasps the characteristics of the object and thereby recognizes it. This is also categorized as the skandha of perception.

Interest is the force of intention, the willingness to act to attain the object of desire, and it is the basis for action.

Contact is the conjunction of sense organ, object, and mind. It forms the basis for feeling.

Discernment is prajñā, which is certain and exact knowledge of the object of perception. Its function is to remove doubt about the nature of the object. The Mahāyāna Abhidharma enumerates four procedures by which prajñā distinguishes the nature of the object: knowing what must be done, knowing relationship, knowing how validity is obtained, and knowing the absolutely real. This complete investigation dispels all doubt about the object. (MBP 37)

Mindfulness is not forgetting the object once one is familiar with it. The function of mindfulness is to prevent being distracted.

Attention is the mental engagement that keeps the mind focused on a specific object of observation. While intention leads the mind toward an object, attention makes the mind stay fixed upon the object.

Determination is the act of staying with the object that has been selected for investigation, or with what the mind has established as valid. Its function is to remain firm.

Concentration is samādhi, the tendency toward the union of mind and object. It culminates in one-pointedness of mind that focuses completely on the object. It functions as a support for knowing.

The ten omnipresent events are present in every moment of mind. According to one school of thought discussed in the Abhidharmakoṣabhāṣya, when these ten are distorted by emotional forces, they then proceed wrongly or poorly. Concentration when afflicted is distractedness; mindfulness when afflicted is known as forgetting; determination when afflicted is a wrong resolve; discernment when afflicted is incorrect or inexact understanding. (AKB II:25, 26a–c)

The Abhidharmakoṣabhāṣya explains that it is difficult to note all the events even in a sequential way; it is even more difficult to note them within a single moment, although they are all present. Like a soup made of various ingredients, a moment of mind seems to have one simple flavor, but it is, in fact, a complex blend of many flavors. These can be discerned if one is attentive. (MP III)

Ten Virtuous Events

Ten virtuous mental events are found only in virtuous states of mind and are found in all virtuous states of mind: faith, conscientiousness, alert ease, equanimity, self-respect, propriety, nonattachment, nonaversion, effort, and nonviolence.

Faith clears up the mind like a "water-clearing gem" that clarifies cloudy water. Faith also means to have insight, conviction, or confidence in what has value, what is real, and what is possible.

Faith provides a basis for determination, out of which arises effort, which in turn is the basis for developing all good qualities. There are three types of faith: admiring faith, longing faith, and trusting faith. Admiring faith comes from seeing the value of the Buddha, Dharma, and Sangha. Longing faith arises from the desire for freedom from suffering and the desire to obtain the benefits of Dharma practice. Trusting faith is based on conviction and leads to complete reliance on the Dharma. (AKB II:25, KZLZ II:I)

Conscientiousness means taking responsibility for protecting virtuous actions and attitudes and preventing nonvirtuous ones. It forms the basis for all the worldly and transworldly excellent qualities. Conscientiousness fosters virtue by assuring the absence of the three poisons—attachment, aversion, and confusion. It is accompanied by effort.

Alert ease refers to fitness for action that freely applies the full energy of body and mind toward good purposes. This ease comes from relaxing rigidity, and it removes all obstacles.

Equanimity is the mind resting naturally, abiding free of attachment, aversion, and confusion. Its function is to prevent the possibility of emotionality. The mind governed by equanimity is disinterested, stable, and energetic.

Self-respect is to avoid what is objectionable from one's own perspective or from the perspective of the Dharma. Its function is to support disciplined action that avoids misdeeds.

Propriety is to avoid what is objectionable from the perspective of others or from the perspective of society.

Nonattachment is an attitude free from desire for worldly goods and for worldly existence; it prevents engagement in negative actions. It is a mental state in which there is no discontent.

Nonaversion is an attitude free from the tendency to hurt others or respond with malice or rage. Nonaversion supports nonhatred, never blaming others, even in frustrating situations, and never inflicting suffering on those who cause frustration.

Effort means being actively devoted to what is positive and to what prevents the unwholesome. Effort channels and directs the tendency toward well-being first activated by faith.

Nonviolence is an attitude of loving-kindness based on nonaversion. It is patient acceptance and complete freedom from the wish to harm oneself or others. In the Vinaya, nonviolence is spoken of as the heart of the Buddha's teachings.

Among the ten virtuous mental events are two of the three roots of good: nonattachment, which is absence of attachment, and nonaversion, which is absence of aversion. The third root is absence of confusion. These three roots are the absence of the three poisons. (AKB II:25)

Two Nonvirtuous Events

Two events are present in all nonvirtuous mental states: disrespect and absence of propriety. Disrespect is a lack of veneration of good qualities in others and a lack of regard for one's own good qualities. Absence of propriety means that in regard to other people one feels no shame for one's transgressions.

Six Emotionally Afflicted Events

Six events exist exclusively and always in emotionally afflicted (kliṣṭa) mental states: confusion, nonconscientiousness, laziness, faithlessness, torpor, and restlessness.

Confusion includes ignorance, lack of knowledge, and lack of clarity. Nonconscientiousness is the opposite of conscientiousness; it prevents the cultivation of virtuous mental events. Laziness is the opposite of energy; it is heavy, inert, and clumsy. Faithlessness is the absence of faith. Torpor is inactivity of body and mind, the opposite of alert ease. This physical and mental heaviness obstructs action and supports emotionality. Restlessness is an unsettledness of mind that is attracted to pleasure; it obstructs mental stability.

All of these events are present when the mind is involved in emotional turmoil. For example, restlessness and torpor may seem contradictory, but are always found together, the restlessness being oriented toward an object of desire, while the torpor persists in relation to performing virtuous activity. If any of these six are present, the others are present as well.

FORTY-SIX DHARMAS
Skandha of Motivational Forces

Ten Omnipresent

Feeling
Intention
Perception
Interest
Contact
Discernment
Mindfulness
Attention
Determination
Concentration

Ten Virtuous

Faith
Conscientiousness
Alert ease
Equanimity
Self-respect
Propriety
Nonattachment
Nonaversion
Effort
Nonviolence

Six Emotionally Afflicted

Confusion
Nonconscientiousness
Laziness
Faithlessness
Torpor
Restlessness

Two Nonvirtuous

Lack of self-respect
Lack of propriety

Eight Variable

Worry
Sleepiness
Investigation
Analysis
Desire
Anger
Pride
Doubt

Ten Lesser Emotions

Vindictiveness
Resentment
Spite
Malice
Jealousy
Dishonesty
Deceit
Hypocrisy
Avarice
Haughtiness

According to the Abhidharmakoṣa

FIFTY-ONE MENTAL EVENTS

Five Omnipresent

Feeling
Perception
Intention
Contact
Attention

Five Object-determining

Interest
Determination
Mindfulness
Concentration
Discernment

Eleven Virtuous

Faith
Conscientiousness
Alert ease
Equanimity
Self-respect
Propriety
Nonattachment
Nonaversion
Effort
Nonviolence
Nonconfusion

Six Basic Emotions

Desire
Anger
Pride
Ignorance
Doubt
Opinionatedness

Twenty Proximate Emotions

Vindictiveness
Resentment
Spite
Malice
Jealousy
Dishonesty
Deceit
Hypocrisy
Avarice
Haughtiness
Lack of self-respect
Lack of propriety
Torpor
Restlessness
Faithlessness
Laziness
Nonconscientiousness
Forgetfulness
Inattentiveness
Distractedness

Four Variables

Worry
Sleepiness
Investigation
Analysis

According to the Mahāyāna Abhidharma

Ten Lesser Emotions

A class of ten factors known as the lesser emotions includes vindictiveness, resentment, spite, malice, jealousy, dishonesty, deceit, hypocrisy, avarice, and haughtiness. (AKB II:27)

Eight Variable Factors

A class of eight variable factors are worry, sleepiness, investigation, analysis, and four of the emotions: desire, anger, pride, and doubt. The first four are variable in that they may be found in either virtuous or nonvirtuous mental moments.

The last four—desire, anger, pride, and doubt—are variable in a different sense. These four cannot coexist in the same mental state. In an afflicted state of mind, only one of these four can be present at a time, together with the six emotionally afflicted events. (AKB II:27–29b)

The emotions classified by the Vaibhāṣikas with the variable factors are classified by the Mahāyāna Abhidharma—together with ignorance and opinionatedness—as the six root emotions. The Vaibhāṣikas single out these six as the six latent emotions (anuśayas).

This classification system yields forty-six mental events or factors: ten events that accompany all mental states; ten that are found in virtuous states; six that accompany emotionally afflicted states; two that accompany nonvirtuous states; ten that are considered lesser emotions; and eight that are variable.

Afflicted Mind and Virtuous Mind

"The emotionally afflicted mind is called small because it is loved by the small-minded. A virtuous mind is called large because it is loved by great persons . . . An afflicted mind is worth little for it is easily obtained, while a virtuous mind is worth much for it requires great effort to develop." (AKB VII:11d)

Disturbed by emotions, the mind functions far below its peak capacity. Its ability to recognize and sustain what is virtuous is limited, and its power over destructive emotionality is weak. An afflicted mind is distracted, untrained, and unfree, whereas a virtuous mind is manageable, unified, well-trained, and can be liberated. (AKB VII:11d)

The virtuous mind is always associated with twenty-two mental events: the ten omnipresent, the ten virtuous, and two variable events—investigation and analysis. When worry occurs, it makes a total of twenty-three. A nonvirtuous mind manifests twenty mental events: the ten omnipresent, six emotionally afflicted events, two nonvirtuous events, and two of the variables, investigation and analysis. It may also be associated with one of the four variable emotions, in which case it manifests twenty-one mental events. There are other divisions that arise when mental states are analyzed in relation to particular realms of existence and stages of meditation. (AKB II:28a–30b)

Events Not Associated with Mind

According to the Abhidharmakoṣabhāṣya, there are fourteen nonassociated motivational factors. These nonassociated motivational factors belong neither to form nor to mind; they are included in the skandha of motivational forces together with the mental events. (AKB II:35a-47d, KJ 9b.2)

Acquisition is a force that binds other dharmas to an individual so that pride or anger or faith "belong" to that person. It is through acquisition that a mental event or a perception, for example, stays within the person's stream of experience and does not "drift" into another's stream of experience.

Nonacquisition is the force that allows those dharmas that have been bound to an individual to disengage. Thus both positive and negative qualities can be lost. Not all the Śrāvaka schools accepted acquisition and nonacquisition. The Abhidharmakoṣabhāṣya contains a long debate on this subject (AKB II:36–41).

Similarity of state is a force that causes resemblance between living beings. The Abhidharmakoṣabhāṣya says: "By virtue of the force known as similarity, resemblances exist among living beings, as well as among dharmas that belong within the stream of living beings." Similarity is both general and particular. Because of the general type of similarity, all living beings resemble one another to some degree. Because of the particular type of similarity, beings are differentiated according to the realm they inhabit, their type of birth (from egg, womb, heat-moisture, magical), their sex, their species, as well as what state of understanding they possess (layperson, monk, Noble One, or Arhat). (AKB II:41a)

Absorption of cessation is the first of three special states that exert a particular arresting force on the mind. All three stop the mind and mental events just as a dam blocks a river. The absorption of cessation is a meditative state marked by a temporary tranquility; it is the highest state of worldly samādhi. (AKB II:41b–43g)

Absorption of nonperception, which is a meditative state of nonperception, is the second of these states.

Nonperception, which is a state within the god realms, is the third of these states.

Life force is the power that causes the continuation of the individual, supporting warmth and consciousness. The strength of the life force results from the actions of a previous existence, which determine how long from the moment of conception the skandhas of the individual will renew themselves. (AK II:45a-b)

Birth is the first of four characteristics of conditioned things that are considered distinct forces. Birth causes something to pass from the future into the present.

Duration causes something to last.

Aging causes it to pass from the present into the past.

Impermanence finishes it. There is a lengthy discussion of this subject in the Abhidharmakoṣabhāṣya. (AKB II:45c–46d).

Names are a force that cause ideas to arise.

Phrases contain the essentials of an idea in short statements such as, "He reads," or "Motivational forces are impermanent." Phrases give rise to understanding activity, quality, and time.

Letters refer to the consonants and vowels that make up words. (AKB II:47a-b)

Twenty-four Factors

The Mahāyāna Abhidharma adds ten more motivational factors, which are listed in the Abhidharmasamuccaya.

The state of an ordinary being is the force that refers to the absence of the noble qualities of one on the path.

Continuity is the force of connection between causes and effects.

Diversity maintains the separation between cause and effect so that they are distinct, while supporting one another.

Rapidity indicates the rapid succession of causes and effects.

Relatedness assures that the result will follow from the cause.

Order controls the sequence of events.

Temporality controls the timing of events, spacing them out over time so they are not simultaneous.

Spatiality places the events in relation to the ten directions of space.

Countability allows events to be enumerated.

Collection allows events to coexist in time and in space

CHAPTER TWENTY-TWO

Skandha of Consciousness

The characteristic of the skandha of consciousness is recognition. It functions to apprehend the presence of a sensory or mental object. The Abhidharmakoṣabhāṣya says: "The skandha of consciousness is the bare grasping of each object by mind, the impression of the object." (AKB I:16a)

The Madhyāntavibhaṅga says: "Seeing the object is consciousness. Distinguishing special qualities are mental events." Vasubandhu's commentary on this text explains that consciousness sees the simple object while mental events such as feeling, etc. distinguish the special qualities in relation to that object. (MAV I:8b, MBP 9–10)

Just how consciousness connects to the object is a subject of discussion and debate among Buddhist schools. The Vaibhāṣikas claim that consciousness grasps the object "nakedly," meaning directly, with nothing intervening between mind and object. The Sautrāntikas say consciousness grasps an "aspect" or mental form of the object.

Six Kinds of Consciousness

Consciousness functions with each of the six sense organs and is classified into: eye-consciousness, ear-consciousness, nose-consciousness, tongue-consciousness, body-consciousness, and mind-consciousness. The objects of each type of consciousness are distinct so that, for example, the eye-consciousness grasps visible form and not sound.

The six consciousnesses have their own function distinct from the functions of the other skandhas. Eye-consciousness, for example, grasps the presence of color and shape but does not know that the color is "blue," which is the function of the skandha of perception; it does not know that the color is "pleasant," which is the function of the skandha of feeling.

Mind, Consciousness, and Intelligence

The Abhidharmakoṣabhāṣya defines mind as the equivalent of consciousness and intelligence: "The names mind (citta), intelligence or mental organ (manas), and consciousness (vijñāna) refer to the same thing." Further, it explains that mind is called citta because it accumulates; it is called intelligence (manas) because it knows; and it is called consciousness (vijñāna) because it distinguishes its object. (AKB II:34a–b)

The Abhidharmasamuccaya agrees that all three are included within the skandha of consciousness: "What is the definition of the skandha of consciousness? It is mind (citta), intelligence (manas), and consciousness (vijñāna)." The Abhidharmasamuccaya makes distinctions, however, among these three, relating each to different levels of consciousness. (AS I) Other Mahāyāna works contain extensive explorations of types and levels of consciousness. For example, Yogācāra texts distinguish mind-consciousness (mano-vijñāna) from an afflicted mind-consciousness and from an all-ground consciousness.

A Mistake of Consciousness

The belief in a self is based on a mistake made by the skandha of consciousness, which confusedly and naively grasps "something" that is not present. The texts often give the illustration of misidentifying a rope as a snake. If the light is dim, if conditions are hazy or foggy, it is possible to take a coil of rope for a snake. So convincing is this perception that the perceiver may be startled with fear.

Candrakīrti quotes the Pratītyasamutpāda Sūtra as saying: "O monks, even ignorance has its basis, its conditions, and its cause. O monks, what is the cause of ignorance? It is an erroneous act of consciousness, a confused act of consciousness arising from illusion." (PSP XXIII)

The confused act of consciousness bifurcates experience into opposites of self and not-self, subject and object, is and is-not. The divisive tendency of consciousness creates the underlying illusion of "selfhood" in all its aspects.

Four Afflictions

The Abhidharmasamuccaya explains the fundamental confusion in terms of four afflictions (kleśa) that are always present except when one is deeply engaged in the path or has reached the path of no more learning. (AS I) Vasubandhu also lists these four in the Triṁśikā:

1. mistakenness about a self (bdag-tu-rmongs-pa)
2. seeing in terms of a self (bdag-tu-lta-ba)
3. pride of self (nga-rgyal)
4. cherishing a self (bdag-tu-chags-pa) (TSK 6)

Lama Mipham explains in his commentary on the Triṁśikā that mistakenness about a self is ignorance, the loss of intrinsic awareness; seeing in terms of a self is taking the five skandhas as "I" or "mine;" pride of self is egotism and arrogance; and cherishing a self is attachment to self.

Mistakenness is recognizing as "I" what is not in fact self. Then this self is appreciated as "me" and also "mine." There is a position and territory that belongs to "I." "I" is now connected with objects: my head, my body, my thought, my desire, my idea, my property, my view. That territory must then be possessed or else "I" suffers. The territory expands to include objects, ideas, people, mental and physical events—everything imaginable could become part of "my" territory. Moreover, "I" enjoy and relish all of this: It is my business, my pleasure, and my life.

Twenty Possibilities

Ordinarily, the identification of the self with the five skandhas is firmly entrenched. However, we can penetrate this illusion by questioning the relationship between self and each of the five skandhas. Nāgārjuna explains in the Suhṛllekha that there are four special relationships to explore:

1. that skandha is the self
2. that skandha is possessed by the self
3. that skandha exists in the self
4. that skandha is where the self resides (SL 49)

We could also imagine that the self is completely unrelated to the five skandhas. But then what possible significance could this kind of self—a nonagent beyond all attributes—have for human life? How could it be connected to the five skandhas of our experience if it is completely "other"?

Nāgārjuna points out: "If the self were the same as the five skandhas, it would arise and perish. If it were other than them, it could not be characterized in terms of personal existence." (MMK XVIII:1)

Exploring the four special relations in regard to each of the five skandhas brings up twenty possible ways that we might imagine a self to exist. We may ask, for example, "Is consciousness the self, or are mental events possessed by the self?" "Is feeling where the self resides, or does feeling exist within the self?" Even posing these questions intellectually can liberate us from some forms of suffering. Investigating them thoroughly through meditative analysis leads to incisive knowledge.

Lama Mipham encourages us in this way: "Once you fully understand the five skandhas, you will become disillusioned with samsara. The mistaken opinion that takes the self to be unitary will change, and the self will be understood as a composite thing."

The shadow of identity, the "self-evidence," appears as not-knowing. Not-knowing has no real basis, but itself becomes the basis for false identity. As long as there is no realization, the fundamental not-knowing and suffering continue. If one awakens and not-knowingness is eliminated, then suffering comes to an end. Realizing the self does not exist, one no longer accumulates suffering, and a way of life free of the shadow of "self"—almost unimaginable to us now—becomes possible.

Further Readings

Mahāpuṇṇam Sutta. Majjhima Nikāya, CIX. On views of self.

Dhātuvibhaṅga Sutta. Majjhima Nikāya, CXL. On analyzing experience.

Brahmajāla Sutta. Digha Nikāya, I. A discourse on wrong views.

Milindapañha. Chapter I. On the self.

Abhidharmakoṣabhāṣya, by Vasubandhu. Chapters I,II. Extensive skandha, dhātu, and āyatana analysis with discussions.

Abhidharmasamuccaya, by Asaṅga. Chapter I. Extensive skandha, dhātu, and āyatana analysis.

Pañcaskandhaka Prakaraṇa, by Vasubandhu. A condensed analysis.

Visuddhimagga, by Buddhaghosa. Chapter XIV. On the skandhas.

Blo-gsal-mgul-rgyan, by Ye-shes-rgyal-mtshan. "Necklace of Clear Understanding," in *Mind in Buddhist Psychology.* Mahāyāna Abhidharma text giving the fifty-one mental events with discussion.

Sems-dpyod-rnam-sbyong, by Lama Mi-pham. "Wheel of Analytic Meditation," in *Calm and Clear.* On analytic meditation.

SECTION NINE

Patterned Potentials

CHAPTER TWENTY-THREE

Eighteen Dhātus

The experience of seeing, hearing, smelling, tasting, touching, and thinking arises within an established patterning. Each sense organ, sense object, and sense consciousness possesses a particular potential, a "program" that is ready to operate under the proper conditions. This patterned potential is created by emotionality (kleśa) and actions driven by emotion (karma) that leave imprints on the body and the mind. The potentials are activated according to the way they are programmed and once set in motion, are self-stimulating.

Under the influence of karma and kleśa, the miraculous ability of our "body of knowledge" to retain and transmit patterning and to be immediately responsive becomes a force of delusion. We become locked in to the sensory realm, which becomes a realm of desire filled with unsatisfied imaginations revolving around an illusory self. By carefully analyzing the patterning process within direct experience, we can see how sense perceptions join with thoughts, memories, and imaginations to create the world of fictions that the self inhabits.

EIGHTEEN DHĀTUS

Organ	*Object*	*Consciousess*
Eye	Forms	Eye-consciousness
Ear	Sounds	Ear-consciousness
Nose	Smells	Nose-consciousness
Tongue	Tastes	Tongue-consciousness
Body	Tangibles	Body-consciousness
Mind	Mental objects	Mind-consciousness

Organs, Objects, and Consciousnesses

Experience can be classified into eighteen patterned potentials, the eighteen dhātus: six sense organs, six sense objects, and six sense consciousnesses. All that we know or can know, the conditioned and nonconditioned dharmas, are contained within these eighteen dhātus.

Each organ functions together with its particular object and consciousness. For example, the eye operates in conjunction with visible form and eye-consciousness. The three are intimately related. Form is that which becomes visible when seen by the eye; the eye is that by which one sees the form; and consciousness is a response to a form that has the eye as its basis and form as its object. (AŚ I)

The six organ dhātus are the eyes, the ears, the nose, the tongue, the body as an organ of touch, and the mind. The six object dhātus are visible forms, sounds, smells, tastes, touchables, and all things that are objects of the mind (dharmas). The six consciousness dhātus are eye-consciousness, ear-consciousness, nose-consciousness, tongue-consciousness, body-consciousness, and mind-consciousness.

Beginning to observe experience in terms of the eighteen dhātus, we see shifting surface patterns as we first distinguish the operations of the six senses from one another: seeing, hearing, smelling, tasting, sensing, thinking.

The Visuddhimagga explains that the teaching on the dhātus reveals that consciousness is not a unity, nor is it permanent or stable. (VM XV:32) Further, these six distinct consciousnesses can be discerned and observed in relationship to their respective organs and objects. Each of the three aspects of each sensory operation can be isolated: Here is the organ, here is the object, and here is the consciousness.

Definitions

The term dhātu, meaning potentiality, can also signify realm, such as a realm of existence, or element, such as earth, water, fire, and wind.

The Abhidharmakoṣabhāṣya explains that dhātu means source or mine. Just as a mountain rich in minerals and metals has distinct and different iron mines, copper mines, silver mines, and gold mines, the human embodiment has eighteen mines, each giving rise to its own precious "ores." The eye, for example, is a mine or source for the later moments of the existence of the eye. (AKB I:20a-b)

"The six organ dhātus from eye to mind are the cause, lineage, or seed that brings about grasping the object. Similarly, the dhātus of forms, sounds, smells, tastes, tangibles, and mental objects (dharmas) are that which is grasped. The six consciousness dhātus from eye-consciousness up to mind-consciousness are the cause, lineage, or seed of actually taking hold of the object. Thus dhātu signifies cause, lineage, or seed." (KJ 12b.2)

Dhātu is seed because it contains the potential for further experience; it is the lineage that transmits the past forward toward the future; and it is the cause as generating source. Working with this analysis, we can begin to see that no self is required to be the cause of experience.

Dhātus of Mind

In distinguishing the mental organ, mental objects, and mind-consciousness as a threefold functioning, the mental organ is called mind, while the mental objects are called dharmas.

The Abhidharmakoṣabhāṣya explains what is meant by mind as an organ: "Could a mind or the dhātu of mind be distinct from the six classes of consciousness, distinct from the sense consciousness and from the mind-consciousness? There is no mind-organ distinct from the consciousness. Of these six consciousnesses, the one that is continually passing away is called mind." (AKB I:16d–17a–b)

In this analysis, the last previous moment of consciousness is considered the basis or support for the next moment of consciousness, and so it functions like an "organ." Just as each of the five sensory consciousnesses has an organ as a support, the support of mental consciousness is called "mind" as if it were an organ.

The objects of mind or mental objects (dharmas) make up the dhātu of dharmas. All dharmas can be objects of mind. Visual consciousness has visible things as objects, while mental consciousness has all the dharmas as objects. So for example, a chair can be an object of sight and also an object of thought. (AKB II:62c, AKB I:48a)

There are seven divisions within the dhātu of dharmas: the three skandhas of feeling, perception, and motivation; imperceptible form; and the three nonconditioned dharmas. (AKB I:15b–d)

The three nonconditioned dharmas are: two types of cessation (one based on comprehension and one not based on comprehension) and space. The Abhidharmakoṣabhāṣya explains that space is not conditioned: "Space is that which does not obstruct. Its nature is not to hinder form, while form resides freely in space; moreover, space is not obstructed by form nor is it displaced by form." (AKB I:5c)

Cessation based on comprehension gives rise to nirvana, the ceasing of the afflictions brought about by the comprehension of the four noble truths. Because wisdom has been applied as an antidote to ignorance and grasping, the conditions do not exist for afflictions to arise. (AKB I:6a)

Cessation not based on comprehension is like a state of potentiality: When a particular consciousness does not arise because all the conditions are not present for its arising, then there is a cessation of the hindered consciousness. For example, when the eye-consciousness is occupied with certain visible things, other eye-consciousnesses are not actualized. If one is engaged in looking at the trees on the left, one is not seeing the lake to the right. That possible eye-consciousness is hindered. (AKB I:6c–d).

Mahāyāna Analysis of the Dhātu of Dharmas

A Mahāyāna analysis distinguishes sixteen mental objects in the dhātu of dharmas rather than seven: five kinds of form that the Śrāvaka schools do not discuss, three skandhas, and eight nonconditioned things (dharmas). (AS I)

The five forms are: atoms, form belonging to space, form arising from a vow, imaginary form, and form arising from meditative power. (See the eleventh category of form in the discussion on the skandhas.)

The three skandhas are feeling, perception, and motivation.

The eight nonconditioned things (dharmas) are: space and the two cessations, three kinds of suchness—the suchness of virtuous things, the suchness of nonvirtuous things, and the suchness of neutral things; and two kinds of absorptions, the absorption of cessation and the absorption of nonperception.

Eighteen Classifications

The eighteen dhātus can be further classified according to eighteen different types of inquiry relating the dhātus to the path.

Which dhātus are associated with form?

Which dhātus are demonstrable?

Which dhātus are mutually obstructive?

Which dhātus are corrupt, promoting emotional instability?

Which dhātus belong to specific realms?

Which dhātus are associated with virtue, which with nonvirtue, and which with neutrality?

Which dhātus are external and which internal?

Which dhātus have an object?

Which dhātus are associated with conceptual thought?

Which dhātus are appropriated as "mine"?

Which dhātus are permanent and which impermanent?

Which dhātus are subjective and which are objective?

Which dhātus are associated with investigation and analysis?

Which dhātus are accumulations of atoms?

Which dhātus interrupt or are interrupted?

Which dhātus are removed on the path of seeing and which on the path of meditation?

Which dhātus arise as a result of previous actions? Which arise from accumulation of matter? Which arise from similar causes?

Which dhātus are associated with properly functioning organs or faculties? (AKB I:29–37, KJ 12b.4)

The Abhidharmakoṣabhāṣya contains discussions of these distinctions. For example, which dhātus are corrupt and which uncorrupt? The three dhātus of mental organ, mental consciousness, and mental objects can be corrupt or uncorrupt. They are uncorrupt if they are associated with the truth of the path or the nonconditioned. The remaining fifteen dhātus are always corrupt. (AKB I:31c–d)

Which dhātus exist in the beings of each of the three realms? All dhātus exist in the beings residing in the desire realm. Only fourteen dhātus exist in beings dwelling in the realm of form, who have no dhātu of smell or dhātu of taste, no dhātu of nose-consciousness or dhātu of tongue-consciousness. Only three dhātus exist in beings dwelling in the formless realm: mental organ, mental consciousness, and mental objects. (AKB I:30a–b)

Which dhātus are associated with virtue, nonvirtue, or are neutral? Eight dhātus are neutral: the five sense organs together with three objects (smells, tastes, and tangibles). Other dhātus are associated with virtue or nonvirtue or are neutral depending on conditions. For example, sounds can be good or bad depending on whether they issue from a virtuous or nonvirtuous mind. Virtuous mental events and nonvirtuous ones and neutral mental events are included in the dhātu of dharmas. The seven dhātus associated with the mind, the six consciousnesses and mind as organ, are virtuous, nonvirtuous, or neutral depending on whether or not they are associated with the roots of good—the absence of attachment, the absence of aversion, and the absence of confusion. (AKB I:29c)

Which dhātus take an object? The six consciousnesses and the mental organ are all able to be "subject" for an object. In addition, feeling, perception, and motivational factors associated with mind are able to have objects. The nonassociated motivational factors are not able to have objects. (AKB I:34a–b)

Which dhātus are associated with investigation (vitarka) and analysis (vicāra)? The five sensory consciousnesses always include analysis and investigation for they are always turned toward externals. The three dhātus of mental organ, mental objects, and mental consciousness sometimes are associated and sometimes are not associated with analysis and investigation depending on whether one is in the desire realm, the form realm, or the formless realm. (AKB I:32a–b)

These few examples show how the dhātu analysis can be used to penetrate the fabric of ordinary experience. Understanding experience as a series of interdependent interactions of the eighteen dhātus unravels the fabrication of the self as the source or cause of experience. (KJD 4b.2)

Further Readings

Abhidharmakoṣabhāṣya, by Vasubandhu. Chapter I. On the dhātus.

Abhidharmasamuccaya, by Asaṅga. Chapter I. On the dhātus.

Visuddhimagga, by Buddhaghosa. Chapter XV. On the dhātus.

Pañcaskandhaka Prakaraṇa, by Vasubandhu.

SECTION TEN

Instant Sense Fields

CHAPTER TWENTY-FOUR

Twelve Āyatanas

Āyatana analysis classifies experience into two groups: one group of six organs and one group of six objects. The six organs are eye, ear, nose, tongue, body, and mind. The six objects are forms, sounds, smells, tastes, tangibles, and mental objects (dharmas). Together these organs and their objects comprise the twelve āyatanas.

Āyatana Analysis

The Khenjug explains the term āyatana (skye-mched) as arising and spreading: from the gateway of the subject and object, consciousness arises (skye) in relation to the object and spreads (mched). (KJ 14b.2)

The six object āyatanas from form to mental objects are called "what is grasped." The six organ āyatanas from eye to mind are called the subject, "the grasper."

Categorizing experience into the twelve āyatanas highlights the connecting "point" between subject and object as sense

TWELVE ĀYATANAS

Organ	*Object*
Eye	Forms
Ear	Sounds
Nose	Smells
Tongue	Tastes
Body	Sensations
Mind	Mental objects

organs and sense objects make contact. Sense organs and their corresponding objects are charged with potential, like positive and negative poles; when the circuit or gateway between them opens, the current flows. Instantaneously, sense fields arise between the two responding poles.

Observing experience in this way counteracts the view that a subtle self within the senses is required as the enjoyer or experiencer. Once subject and object have been established, experience flows "between" subject and object spontaneously.

The self does not receive experience—"self" is a fabrication falsely transposed onto the dynamic interaction of organ and object. Even the concept we now have of self is simply the result of an interaction between the mind and a mental object (dharma), one of a progression of subtle sensory interactions that can be traced with great precision upon careful analysis.

The Khenjug explains the purpose of āyatana analysis in this way: "By understanding the six outer gateways (sense objects) as what is to be enjoyed and the six inner gateways (sense organs) as that which does the enjoying, one counteracts holding to the self as the enjoyer of experience." (KJD 5a.5)

Āyatana of Mind

The āyatana of mind includes the five sensory consciousnesses and the mental consciousness. In general, mind makes known the significance of things (dharmas). Its function is to choose what to be involved with and what to turn away from. If the mind is virtuous, all other consciousnesses are virtuous; by the power of mind, consciousness engages or disengages with objects.

"Mind precedes the object. Mind is swift, it is the chief."(KJ 15a.3)

The mind can operate both conceptually and nonconceptually. The five sensory consciousnesses are nonconceptual, while mind consciousness can operate either way. The conceptual mind remembers objects such as a vase and creates a generalized idea of a vase. The generalized idea is associated with the sound of the name, "vase."

In order to recognize a particular vase at a specific time and place, first a nonconceptual consciousness arises through the operation of the senses of sight, hearing, touch, taste, or smell. This consciousness deals with the particular vase, not the generalized idea of a vase. Only when the particular object of appearance is linked to the generalized object of remembrance does one recognize a "vase." The mind forms a concept of a vase as a particular type of thing with inherent integrity (self-ness) and identifies the general concept with the unique impermanent actual vase composed of clay, water, and paint. Impermanent unique things are thus established as existing through time.

Once an object is identified and named, the self can engage it in various ways. Now the object can be liked or disliked, possessed, discarded, or used. The subject's involvement with objects reinforces the identities of both subject and object: The self becomes the enjoyer, and the unique and impermanent object becomes a "thing" to be enjoyed. (KJ 14b.6–16a.4)

Equivalencies

Five organ āyatanas are equivalent to the organs in the dhātu analysis, and five object āyatanas are equivalent to the objects in

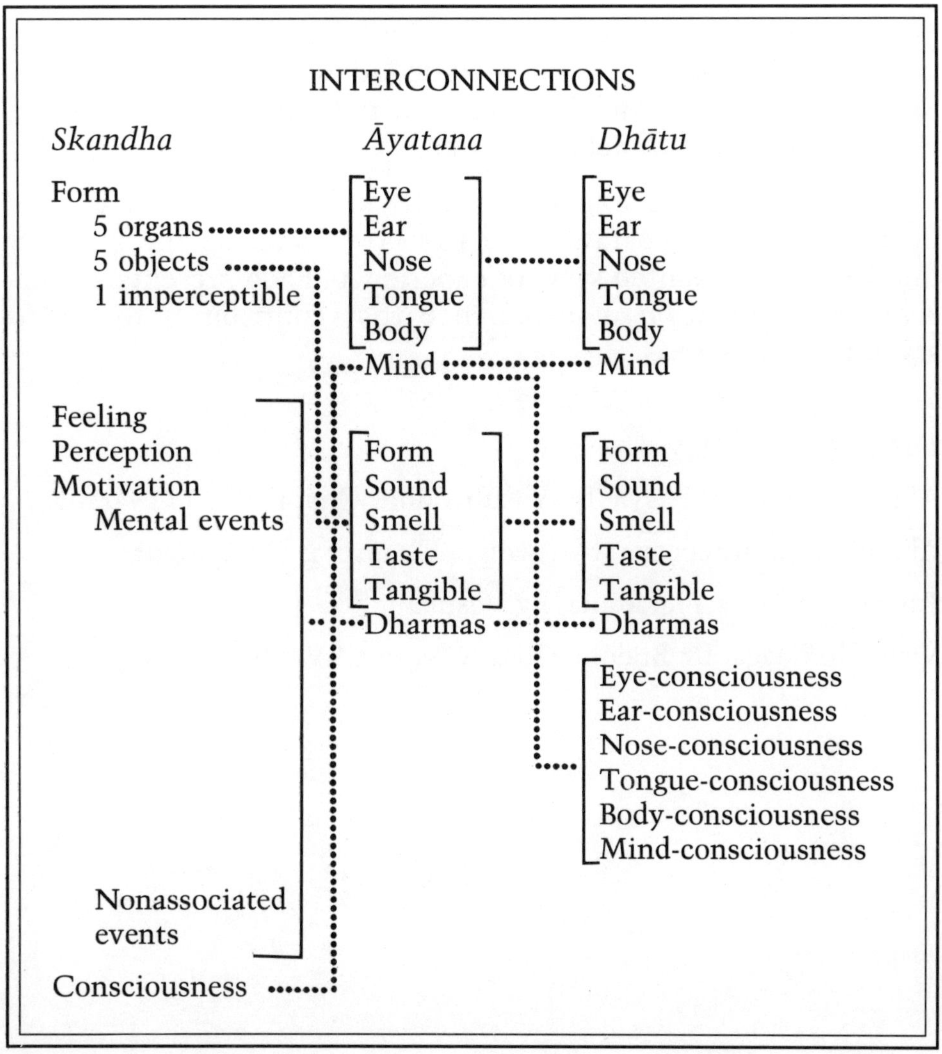

the dhātu analysis. Likewise, the dharma-āyatana is equivalent to the dhātu of dharmas. But the seven dhātus that are classified as consciousness (the five sense consciousnesses, one mind consciousness, and mind as mental organ) are grouped together in the mind āyatana.

In both the dhātu and āyatana analyses, the nonconditioned dharmas are included in the category of dharmas. However, the three nonconditioned dharmas are not included in the skandha analysis. The nonconditioned dharmas are not discussed in terms of the skandhas because the skandhas are not appropriate for that purpose. (AKB I:22a–b) Since āyatanas and dhātus include the non-conditioned dharmas, they include all seventy-five dharmas. Skandhas, āyatanas, and dhātus can be mapped onto one another, but they do not completely overlap.

The analyses of experience into skandhas, āyatanas, and dhātus are three separate means of counteracting the ordinary uncritical self-oriented view of experience. Each presents a cohesive systematization of experience that contributes to understanding selflessness.

Further Readings

Abhidharmakoṣabhāṣya, by Vasubandhu. Chapter I. On āyatanas.

Abhidharmasamuccaya, by Asaṅga. Chapter I. On āyatanas.

Pañcaskandhaka Prakaraṇa, by Vasubandhu.

Visuddhimagga, by Buddhaghosa. Chapter XV. On āyatanas.

SECTION ELEVEN

Interdependent Co-operation

CHAPTER TWENTY-FIVE

The Twelve Links

What is this remarkable obscurity that makes the world not see the play of interdependent co-operation, which exists, but see the self, which does not exist? (MSA VI:4)

On the night of the enlightenment the Buddha completely penetrated this obscurity, breaking the bonds of samsara by comprehending the inner workings of consciousness within all realms of existence. Transmitted to his disciples on numerous occasions, this realization became known as the teaching of pratītyasamutpāda, interdependent co-operation.

The Buddha has said: "Whoever sees interdependent co-operation sees the Dharma. Whoever sees the Dharma sees interdependent co-operation." (MN XXVIII)

Buddhism is the only tradition that teaches interdependent co-operation. Proper study of this teaching removes extreme views such as eternalism, nihilism, fatalism, and materialism. Thus, the Buddha's teaching is known as the middle way, for it avoids extremes and transcends partial views. Only this perfected understanding can lead sentient beings to enlightenment.

THE TWELVE LINKS
OF INTERDEPENDENT CO-OPERATION

1. Ignorance	7. Feeling
2. Karmic Propensities	8. Craving
3. Consciousness	9. Grasping
4. Name and Form	10. Existence
5. Six Organ Āyatanas	11. Birth
6. Contact	12. Old Age and Death

Fundamental Questions

In a general way, interdependent co-operation indicates the interconnectedness of life, the balance of nature, and the interactions between environment and living beings. In particular, interdependent co-operation points out twelve "links" that the Buddha determined were of crucial importance for the operation of samsara: ignorance, karmic propensities, consciousness, name and form, six organ āyatanas, contact, feeling, craving, grasping, existence, birth, and old age and death.

Karma depends on ignorance; body and mind depend on karma; birth and death depend on body and mind. Scientists seeking a unified theory of existence may eventually discover the importance of this teaching for arriving at a satisfactory understanding of fundamental questions such as the connection between mind and matter and the relationship of cause and effect.

The depth of the teaching of interdependent co-operation has been brought out in treatises by masters of all Buddhist traditions. The Abhidharma of the Śrāvaka schools focuses on the cause and effect relationships among the twelve links to explain the operation of samsara, especially karma and kleśa, rebirth, and the process of purification. The Mahāyāna understanding, which ultimately transcends all forms of duality including cause and effect, sees in interdependent co-operation the demonstration of the emptiness of all elements of reality.

"Since all things are empty of own-being, the incomparable Tathāgata teaches interdependent co-operation regarding all things . . . Since what is dependent lacks own-being, how can it exist?" (SST 68, 71)

The Purpose of Studying Interdependent Co-operation

Analysis of experience in the light of interdependent co-operation reveals how appearance arises. The Buddha explains in the Lalitavistara:

"The eye is impermanent and nonenduring,
likewise, the ear and nose;
also the tongue, the body, and the mind.
They are by nature suffering, without self,
empty, and hollow; they are like
grass or a wall, not independent.
They do not even have a self, a name, or life.

All these dharmas come forth
in dependence on causes;
they are free from the two extremes
of existence and nonexistence.
They are like the sky.
There is neither creator nor enjoyer.
Only the karma of virtuous and nonvirtuous actions
carries on." (LAL XXVI)

In particular, the purpose of the study of interdependent co-operation is to counteract the idea of self as agent: "Since nothing is without cause, and does not arise from anything other than a cause, by understanding how things appear due to interdependent co-operation, one counteracts holding to self as the agent or doer." (KJD 5b.6)

The Khenjug further explains that things do not originate from an uncaused independent permanent cause such as a self, time, or a creator. What is called interdependent co-operation is arising that depends on the coming together of respective causes and conditions. (KJ 20b.2)

All experience can be understood to result from the conjunction of causes and conditions. When the required causes and conditions for a particular result are present, then the result will definitely occur; if the required causes and conditions are not present, then the result will not occur.

Causes and Conditions of Outer Phenomena

Both outer and inner phenomena arise as a result of causes and conditions. Outer phenomena, the things of the physical world, arise in a series of seven steps. The texts use the example of a seed giving rise to a plant that gives rise to a fruit. The seven steps are: seed, sprout, leaflets, stemmed plant, bud, flower, fruit. Each stage succeeds the previous one in time and in order, each giving rise to the next.

Contributing to the development of any outer phenomena are six conditions: earth, water, fire, wind, space, and time. These six perform the following functions: Earth stabilizes, water causes cohesion, fire causes maturation or ripening, wind expands, space accommodates, and time gradually transforms.

Causes and Conditions of Inner Phenomena

Inner phenomena refer to the functioning of sentient beings and the operation of the five skandhas. Inner phenomena arise as the result of causes and conditions; the necessary causes are the twelve links of interdependent co-operation, while thirteen additional conditions support the operation of these twelve. (AKB III:20–36, KJ 18a.6)

In the Lalitavistara the Buddha expresses his insight into interdependent co-operation at the time of his enlightenment: "Then this came to the mind of the Bodhisattva: What by its very existence gives rise to old age and death? What is the cause of death? Then there came to his mind: Since birth exists, old age and death come forth; the cause of old age and death is birth . . . What by its very existence gives rise to birth? What is the cause of birth? And there came to his mind: When existence exists, birth comes forth. The cause of birth is existence. What by its very existence gives rise to existence? And there came to his mind: When grasping exists, existence comes forth . . ." (LAL XXII)

In this way the Buddha perceived how samsara appears through interdependent co-operation. Because ignorance exists, karmic propensities arise. Because karmic propensities exist, consciousness arises. Because consciousness exists, name and form arise. And so forth through birth, old age, and death. In the same way, karmic propensities will cease if ignorance ceases, and so forth down to old age and death.

Ignorance The first of the twelve links of interdependent co-operation is ignorance. Ignorance is a state of not knowing the truth that all conditioned things are impermanent, sources of suffering, and without self. Imagining a self that is single, whole, and continuous, ignorance stubbornly holds to a fiction that is not in accord with reality. (KJ 18b.4)

Karmic Propensities Through the power of ignorance, there arise virtuous, nonvirtuous, and nonagitated actions that are produced by the emotions of attachment, aversion, and confusion. These actions plant the seeds of the next existence. Thus, virtue supports rebirths in the happier, higher realms, while nonvirtue supports rebirths in the more painful lower realms. Nonagitated actions support rebirth in the form and formless realms.

Consciousness Karmic propensities give rise to a particular kind of consciousness. Once the seed of karmic propensities is placed in the consciousness, consciousness projects the next birth. At this stage consciousness is called the projecting consciousness. When the conditions for rebirth have all come together, the consciousness that results goes to the place of rebirth, and at this stage it is called the projected consciousness.

Name and Form Through the power of this projected consciousness, there is transition to the womb. Name here refers to four skandhas—consciousness, feeling, perception, and motivation—while form refers to the skandha of form. By mutually supporting one another, name and form give rise to the physical body of the next existence, which is then appropriated by consciousness.

The Six Organ Āyatanas From the full development of name and form, there arise the inner organs of the eye, ear, nose, tongue, body, and mind.

Contact Once the sense organs are operating, then sense organ, object, and sense consciousness unite, and attention becomes restricted to the object appropriate to each sense.

Feeling From contact arise three feelings: pleasant, unpleasant, and indifferent. The Lalitavistara points out that even the smallest feeling, whatever it may be, proceeds to craving.

Craving From feeling arises craving towards the objects of the senses. There is the craving of desire that wishes not to be separated from what is pleasant, the craving of fear that wishes to be rid of what is unpleasant, and an abiding in indifference. Craving means to relish the taste of the object (which is caused by feeling) and to hold the object by clinging and enjoyment. Craving can be divided into three kinds: craving in the desire realm, in the form realm, and in the formless realm.

Grasping From craving arises grasping, the development of craving to the point of complete, eager involvement with the objects of desire. There are four types of grasping: grasping at desirable objects, holding to wrong views, holding certain types of discipline and ritual to be supreme, and holding to belief in a self.

Existence Craving makes manifest the karma that establishes the next existence in terms of body, speech, and mind. Existence can be divided into three kinds: existence in the desire realm, existence in the form realm, and existence in the formless realm.

Birth Through the power of existence, there arises birth. Birth means being born in the new birthplace, in the appropriate family, with a complete embodiment. Birth creates the basis for all the various kinds of sufferings.

Old Age and Death From birth there arise the changes in the stream of the skandhas called old age and the complete stopping of this stream, which is called death. The mental and physical pain we experience as death approaches is the prime example of samsaric suffering.

The Conditions of Inner Phenomena

The Khenjug summarizes the additional conditions that support the operation of the twelve links as a set of two conditions, a set of six conditions, and a set of five conditions. The links of ignorance and karmic propensities function in cooperation with two conditions: mental objects and the inner organs. The seven links from name and form to existence function in cooperation with six conditions: the elements of earth, water, fire, wind, space, and consciousness. These relate to bodily existence in various ways, establishing the firmness of the body, the liquidity of fluids, the warmth of digestion, the inhalation and exhalation of breath, the internal cavities and spaces, and consciousness. The link of consciousness functions in cooperation with five conditions: the organ or faculty, the object focused on, the actual appearance, the presence of unobscured space, and the operation of the mind. (KJ 20a.5, JO XVI)

CHAPTER TWENTY-FIVE

Operation of Samsara

The relationship between cause and effect in interdependent co-operation is described in the Khenjug as distinctive in five ways: It is impermanent, uninterrupted, not transferred, nonproportional, and possesses similarity of continuity.

Neither cause nor effect is permanent, just as a sprout arises after the seed has ceased and not while the seed is uninterruptedly present. The relationship between cause and effect is not, however, interrupted, just as the sprout does not arise from the stopping of the seed. The stopping of the seed and the arising of the sprout occur in the manner of the rising and falling of the sides of a balance. Cause is not transferred into the effect because seed and sprout are not the same, each having its own function and nature. Nonproportional means that a small cause can produce a big effect, just as a small seed can produce a large fruit. Similarity of continuity means that a wheat seed will produce a wheat plant and not a rose. In the same way, a virtuous cause will result in happiness. See the Abhidharmasamuccaya for a similar discussion. (AS I, KJ 20b.4)

Four Methods of Understanding

The Visuddhimagga explains that there are four methods of understanding interdependent co-operation: the method of identity, the method of diversity, the method of disinterest, and the method of regularity.

The method of identity understands interdependent co-operation to mean that there is no interruption between the links, just as a seed becomes a tree by going through all the intermediate stages. Seeing such continuity removes nihilistic views that assume there is no connection between cause and effect. It also removes clinging to eternalist views that assume continuity of cause and effect means continuing identity.

The method of diversity focuses on the arising of each new state. This erodes the eternalist view, for one sees that continuity does not mean persistence of the same state. Diversity can be misunderstood as a form of nihilism, however, if one takes the newly arising state to mean a break in continuity.

The method of disinterest points out that the links of interdependent co-operation arise without any actor or maker causing them to arise. The cause is the previous link, not an outside agent. Each link possesses the power to be a cause, for it is in the very nature of each link to give rise to the next link. One who sees this properly abandons the view of a creator self. Misunderstanding this method, one focuses on the fact that ignorance "is not interested" in giving rise to the next link. The lack of intentionality is mistaken for a lack of inherent connection between cause and effect.

The method of regularity shows that a result accords with its specific causal condition. Only some results, and not others, occur in conjunction with certain causes. One who understands this abandons the view that events are uncaused and the view that there is no moral retribution. Misunderstanding this method, one mistakes it for fatalism, imagining that a particular result must inevitably follow from a cause without seeing that many other conditions may modify the result. (VM XVII:310–313)

Continous Rounds

The Khenjug focuses on two ways to understand interdependent co-operation in relation to time: as continuous and as momentary. Interdependent co-operation functions continuously as an ongoing flow from link to link throughout samsaric existence. One full cycle can be understood as extending over three lifetimes: Ignorance and karma existed in the previous life; the present life is consciousness up through existence; birth, old age and death will occur in the future life. One full cycle can also be understood to require two lives to complete. (AKB III:20a–21, KJ 21a.5, VM XVII:287)

Momentary Rounds

It is also possible to understand interdependent co-operation as occurring in the one moment of completing an action. The example given in the Abhidharmakoṣabhāṣya is the act of killing:

"Ignorance is getting involved in the action; karmic propensities is the action; consciousness is the awareness at that time; name and form, the six senses, and contact are the experience of using the weapon; feeling is one's own pleasure and the other's pain; craving and grasping are the enthusiastic involvement; existence is the state of the five skandhas at the moment of the deed; this leads to birth of the present and what follows; old age and death are the change and cessation of that experience." (AKB III:24d)

Condensing the Twelve Links

The Abhidharmakoṣabhāṣya also describes the twelve links in an abbreviated form: "This twelvefold chain is also threefold: kleśa, karma, and foundation." (AKB III:26a–b)

The Khenjug further explains these three aspects. Ignorance, craving, and grasping are called kleśa; karmic propensities and existence are called karma; and the other seven are known as the foundation for suffering. (KJ 22a.4)

A helpful image from the Sūtras is repeated in the Khenjug: The seed of suffering is planted in the field of karma by ignorance

CONDENSING THE TWELVE LINKS

Ignorance	kleśa	projecting
Karmic propensities	karma	projecting
Consciousness	foundation	projecting
Name and form	foundation	resulting projected
Six organ āyatanas	foundation	resulting projected
Contact	foundation	resulting projected
Feeling	foundation	resulting projected
Craving	kleśa	establishing
Grasping	kleśa	establishing
Existence	karma	establishing
Birth	foundation	established
Old age and death	foundation	established

Kleśa arises from kleśa, just as grasping arises from craving.

Karma arises from kleśa, just as karmic propensities arise from ignorance.

Foundation arises from karma, just as consciousness arises from karmic propensities.

Foundation arises from foundation, just as name and form arise from consciousness.

Kleśa arises from foundation, just as craving arises from feeling.

Continuous Rounds:
Ignorance and karmic propensities exist in the past existence; birth, old age and death will exist in a future existence; and the eight other links exist in the present.

and the other kleśas. Karma is like a field; consciousness is like a seed; ignorance sows the seed. Once moistened by craving, the sprout emerges as name and form.

Kleśa, karma, and foundation are also known as the pervasive affliction of kleśa, the pervasive affliction of karma, and the pervasive affliction of life because all sentient beings are subject to them. These three are also known as the dependency of kleśa, the dependency of karma, and the dependency of suffering.

From the three links called kleśa come two links called karma, and from the two links called karma come seven links called sufferings, and so forth around again.

"In this way from kleśa arises karma and from karma arises suffering; since suffering gives rise to karma and kleśa, the wheel will revolve until ignorance is reversed." (GTD 19b.6)

When the twelve links are condensed into just four, then ignorance, karmic formations, and consciousness are the projecting links; the four of name and form, the six organ āyatanas, contact, and feeling are the resulting projected links; the three of craving, grasping, and existence are the establishing links; and the two of birth and old age and death are the established links.

Twelve Links in Two Orders

The "forward" or progressive order of the twelve links leads into samsara. It begins with the first five links, which are the truth of the origin of suffering. The remaining seven are the truth of suffering. This order shows how suffering is created.

Understanding the "reverse" order leads to nirvana. Old age and death will cease when birth ceases; birth will cease when existence ceases, and so forth back to ignorance. When ignorance disappears, then karmic propensities disappear, and so forth. Reversing the first five is the truth of the path. The cessation of the following seven bases for suffering is the truth of cessation. This shows how suffering is brought to an end. Meditation on the reverse order is a special focus of the Pratyekabuddha. (JO XVI, GTD 19b.3ff)

Action of Cause and Effect

The study of causes and conditions is complex, "very hard to see and likewise difficult to teach." Lack of understanding of cause and effect is part of the ignorance that gives rise to suffering. (VM XVII:25).

The study of interdependent co-operation demonstrates in general that action always produces a result and that the result is not random; it accords with its causes. Our own actions of body, speech, and mind are creating our future, moment by moment. At the same time, understanding causality is the key to transformation. Positive results will be obtained once we know their causes, and emotional disturbances can be removed when we know their causes.

No unified single cause can be isolated as creator of any given event, for many causes and conditions work together. It follows that consciousness is not a unified permanent agent, for it too arises from an assembly of factors.

Blind Operation

Within the twelvefold chain, consciousness is a key link because it mistakenly sees a self within the skandhas where there is no self. Ignorance allows the karmic patterns to operate blindly, giving rise to obscured consciousness. Based on consciousness, names come forth as forms, and these forms reinforce consciousness as the seer of the forms. Each link supports and reinforces the one "before" and the one "after" it.

Nāgārjuna says in the Suhṛllekha: "The skandhas are not created accidentally nor by means of time, nor from themselves; nor are they preexisting. They do not come from a creator nor are they without a cause. You should know that they are produced from craving and ignorance." (SL 50)

Lama Mipham's commentary on the Suhṛllekha further explains that the skandhas are produced when the cause (ignorance) and the conditions (karma and kleśa) are combined.

The threefold chain—karma, kleśa, and suffering (foundation)—is a short description of the way samsara works. Like an engine driving a machine, or like a factory putting out a product, the chain of causation puts out karma, kleśa, and suffering. This reality is described in the first and second noble truths. Karma, kleśa, and suffering recreate each other endlessly through ignorance, giving rise to conditioned existence characterized by impermanence, suffering, and no-self. Name and form arise and perish, but there is no self within. Feeling arises and perishes, craving arises and perishes, but there is no self within. Nonetheless, karma and kleśa continue to create their product: existence, birth, and death, the ground of suffering.

"In this way suffering arises
in dependence on the skandhas
and watered by desire, it increases greatly . . .

"When delusive mental activity is understood,
this complex of production is no more.
The ignorance that brings it forth
does not arise—
there is nothing for it to come from.

"When the cause of karmic motivations is removed,
there is no driving influence
drawing one thing after another.
It is in dependence on this driving influence
that consciousness comes forth."

And so forth, until:

"Knowing the way things are,
there is no more ignorance.
When there is no more ignorance,
all the links of existence do not arise . . .

"This succession of connected circumstances
the Tathāgata has understood.
Therefore, self-arising, he taught himself.
The skandhas and heaps of senses are not 'the Buddha'.
Buddha is the understanding of causes—
only that." (LAL XXVI)

Further Readings

Lalitavistara. *The Voice of the Buddha: The Beauty of Compassion,* chapters XXII, XXVI.

Mahānidāna Sutta, Digha Nikāya XV. Discourse on the links of interdependent co-operation.

Abhidharmakoṣabhāṣya, by Vasubandhu. Chapter III. On the twelve links.

Abhidharmasamuccaya, by Asaṅga. Chapter I. On the twelve links.

Visuddhimagga, by Buddhaghosa. Chapter XVII. Extensive discussion of interdependent co-operation.

Dam-chos-yul-bzhin-nor-bu-thar-pa-rin-po-che'i-rgyan, by sGam-po-pa. *The Jewel Ornament of Liberation,* chapter XVI. On outer and inner phenomena and the two orders.

SECTION TWELVE

Powerful Properties

CHAPTER TWENTY-SEVEN

Twenty-two Indriyas

Sentient beings possess twenty-two powerful properties known as indriyas. The Sanskrit root of the word indriya means supreme authority or ruler, and each of the twenty-two exercises a special influence over embodiment. (AKB II:1) Indriya has been variously translated as faculty, organ, capacity, or power. There is no single English term that fits all the uses of the Sanksrit.

Description of Indriyas

The first five indriyas are the sense organs: eyes, ears, nose, tongue, and body. These "rule" the physical appearance of the individual; they determine how well one relates to the physical environment, such as being able to feed and protect oneself. These five indriyas contribute to the production of sensory consciousnesses and various mental states, while each one has its own special mode of functioning, such as seeing, hearing, smelling, and so forth. (AKB II:1a–c)

The mental organ or mind predominates in regard to rebirth as well as being the ruler over all the mental events.

THE TWENTY-TWO INDRIYAS

1–5. Five sense organs of eye, ear, nose, tongue, and body	14. Faith
6. Mind	15. Effort
7. Male gender	16. Mindfulness
8. Female gender	17. Concentration
9. Misery	18. Wisdom
10. Pleasure	19. Will to know the unknown
11. Joyful mind	20. What is unknown
12. Unhappy mind	21. Possessing all-knowingness
13. Indifference	22. Life

The Dhammapada says:

"All things have the nature of mind. Mind is the chief and takes the lead. If the mind is clear, whatever you do or say will bring happiness that will follow you like your shadow.

"All things have the nature of mind. Mind is the chief and takes the lead. If mind is polluted, whatever you do or say leads to suffering, which will follow you as a cart trails after a horse." (DP I:1–2)

The sexual indriyas are the predominating influence over the differentiation of living beings into male and female. They govern all the specific characteristics of physical build, size, voice, and so forth, associated with this differentiation.

There are five indriyas associated with feeling: the power of pain, the power of pleasure, the power of happiness, the power of unhappiness, and the power of indifference (the intermediate feeling of neither pleasure nor pain). With these faculties we experience physical pain and pleasure, mental happiness and unhappiness, and indifference.

These five predominate with regard to becoming involved with the emotions. Attachment is supported and sheltered by the feeling of pleasure; aversion is supported and sheltered by the feeling of displeasure; confusion is supported and sheltered by the feeling of indifference. For this reason, these indriyas are said to predominate with regard to defilement.

With regard to purification, five other indriyas are the guiding influence: faith, effort, mindfulness, meditative concentration, and wisdom. It is through the operation of these five that the path toward purity is traveled. (AKB II:3)

There are three pure indriyas that control the approach to nirvana: the power that is the will to know the unknown, the power of actually having the superior knowledge that belongs to the Arhat, and the power of knowing that this has been accomplished. Nirvana appears through the first pure indriya; it endures through the second; and its blessedness is fully experienced and enjoyed through the third. (AKB II:4)

There is also a "life organ" that has influence over the arising of a sentient being and the length of its life.

These twenty-two faculties can be discussed and classified in a variety of ways, for example whether they are contaminated or uncontaminated by the emotions; whether they arise as a result of karma maturing; whether they are virtuous, nonvirtuous, or neutral; which faculties are possessed by beings in different realms; whether they are abandoned along the path and how this comes about; how they are lost or gained. (KJ 28b.4) The Abhidharmakoṣabhāṣya contains detailed discussions of these classifications. (AKB II:9–21)

Determining the Direction

The purpose of studying the indriyas is to better understand the processes of defilement and purification. The endless rounds of samsara are supported through the five sense organs, mind, the indriya of life and the sexual indriyas that allow these organs to arise and endure, and the five feelings. Nirvana is supported by the five indriyas beginning with faith together with the three pure indriyas.

These powerful properties determine the direction of our lives: If we rely on feelings of pleasure, displeasure, and indifference to make decisions, we remain circling within the bounds of samsara. All sensory and mental contact gives rise to feeling, and feeling gives rise to craving and grasping, which pitch us into the world of emotions. Based on ignorance, the three feelings of pleasure, displeasure, and indifference readily become the causes of the three poisons of attachment, aversion, and confusion.

Operating within samsaric cycles, human embodiment is highly vulnerable to emotional affliction. The indriyas of the senses and feelings are extremely sensitive, readily engaging objects with a strong grasping potential. This possessive engagement stimulates the readiness to respond and creates reflections or echoes that confirm the process of engagement. The consequences invisibly reinforce the patterns of engagement, firmly binding us to samsara.

The deceptive and unstable patterns of pleasure and displeasure increase our vulnerability. Nāgārjuna explains in the Suhṛllekha that one cannot trust any of samsara's pleasures. Pleasant situations are unstable; pleasant companions are not reliable; and pleasant surroundings are transient. But once a pleasant feeling arises, it stimulates more grasping and involvement. With our intelligence and energy engaged in this way, it is difficult to see clearly where our actions will lead. (SL 69–76)

Following the Lead of the Self

Following feeling, relying on liking or wanting, we are not free. The freedom to "do as we like" is not freedom of choice because we are ruled by the powerful property of feeling; we cannot choose apart from liking and disliking. Likes and dislikes may be articulated in the form of sophisticated-sounding opinions, but the decision is made for us by feeling.

The Western world places a high value on personal feelings and opinions: Each individual "has a right" to an opinion. But rarely do we question how we have arrived at our opinion. Upon examination, we may discover that opinions tend to stem from convenience, familiarity, and selfishness—what feels good or what is pleasing or comfortable to us. Upon this basis, we act, and receive the consequences of our action.

Even if we compile a large number of such opinions, there is no guarantee that we will develop a wise perspective as a ground for action. Often this process only creates a mass of confusion, for opinions of one individual tend to conflict with the opinions of another. If there appears to be agreement, we tend to assume this agreement will remain stable. But agreement only means that the needs of the individuals involved are temporarily similar, and when those needs shift, agreement will evaporate.

To make certain decisions, we rely on logic or scientific findings, which are supposedly free from personal opinion but are still weighted with the opinions of a particular culture. This style of knowing is founded on particular distinctions and ignores other possibilities. The evidence is clear that the scope of modern scientific knowledge is limited, for this knowledge is not yet able to predict and control the side-effects resulting from its own use. Its solutions in turn create more problems, reinforcing the circular patterns of samsara. Only understanding that penetrates to the root causes of problems can break this circularity. Until we explore the depths of consciousness, we cannot resolve the fundamental questions that face human beings.

New Directions

If we learn to rely on faith, effort, mindfulness, concentration, and wisdom, we can explore these questions in depth and move toward resolution. Educating ourselves by means of these five spiritual faculties, we become capable of distinguishing what is truly creative and positive from what is ultimately limiting and negative. Shedding light in the darkness, these five faculties can guide us toward meditative calm and insight and eventually toward the higher stages of the path. All five play a crucial role on the path of linking that connects the path of preparation with the path of seeing. Nāgārjuna explains:

"Faith, effort, mindfulness,
meditative concentration, and wisdom—

only these five refer to the highest possible realization.
Strive after these unshakable faculties and powers,
which become the culminating point of the path." (SL 45)

The Śikṣāsamuccaya explains that through these spiritual faculties one is able to avoid being captured by samsaric influences. If these five are developed, one cannot be overcome by emotionality or diverted from the path to enlightenment.

"First, one develops faith in all the qualities of the Buddha, and then: The qualities one has confidence in by faith one attains by effort. The qualities one attains by effort, one preserves by mindfulness. The qualities one preserves by mindfulness, one focuses intently on by concentration. The qualities one focuses on by concentration, one learns to understand by wisdom. This wisdom not dependent on another is called the power of wisdom. These five faculties, joined together and developed, complete the Buddha's qualities." (SS XVIII)

Process without Selfhood

The operation of the twenty-two powers explains the process of defilement and purification without reference to a self controlling the processes. "Understanding the way the indriyas function, one clears up confusion about the self as the site [where the process of defilement and purification take place]." (KJD 6b.5)

The Mahāyānasūtrālaṁkāra explains that this imaginary controller or "king" does not really exist. One illusory king rules over defilement, and another illusory king rules over purification. The defeat of one by the other does not establish the existence of either. They are just two different images of the fictitious self.

"It is like an illusory king being conquered
by another illusory king—
thus the sons of the Buddhas look upon all dharmas
as free from pride in a person that holds to a self." (MSA XI:29)

Further Readings

Milindapañha. Chapter I. On the five spiritual faculties.

Abhidharmakoṣabhāṣya, by Vasubandhu. Chapter II. On the twenty-two indriyas.

Abhidharmasamuccaya, by Asaṅga. Chapter I. On the indriyas.

Visuddhimagga, by Buddhaghosa. Chapters IV (verses 45–49) and XVI. On balancing the five spiritual faculties and descriptions of the indriyas.

Śikṣāsamuccaya, by Śāntideva. Chapter XVIII. On how to practice with the five faculties.

SECTION THIRTEEN

Expressions of Time

CHAPTER TWENTY-EIGHT

Many Times

Ordinary experience seems bound within a flow of time that we call past, present, and future. In the Abhidharma texts, these three are known as the three times.

"What is the entity (dharma) we call time? It is not an eternal substance as some would have it; the term 'time' is an expression through which conditioned things are designated as being past, present, or future." (AKB IV:27a–b)

The Abhidharmakoṣa calls conditioned things "pathways" or the time periods of past, present, and future because their nature is "having gone," "going on," and "will be going." (AKB I:7c–d)

Past, present, and future can be defined in terms of the completion of the process of cause and effect. When the activity of both the cause and effect are finished so that what arose earlier and came to completion has now ceased—this is called the past. When the cause exists, but the action is not complete, so that the result is still missing—this is called the future. When the cause is active, but the result has not yet come to completion—this is called the present.

Ways of Measuring

Time can also be classified in terms of a duration ranging from short to long. We can imagine time as a series of instants, where an instant is a period of time that cannot be further divided. Some texts say that there are one hundred and twenty instants in a moment, sixty moments in the next division, and so forth, up to days, weeks, years, and collections of years.

Divisions of time differ depending on the culture and even on the field of knowledge within a single culture. Measures may be based on planetary motion, on the cycle of the breath, on the motion of atomic particles, or on the procession of religious commemorations. Stages of life such as birth, childhood, youth, and so forth, can be used to divide time, as can stages of growth in the natural world (seed, sprout, plant, and fruit) so that, for example, there is planting time and harvest time.

Another way of measuring time is from the beginning of an undertaking up to its completion. One "moment" might be as short as a snap of the fingers, or as long as the period from the first rising of the thought of enlightenment in an individual up until the achievement of complete awakening, a process said to require many kalpas. Here we can see clearly that the divisions depend on our perspective. For example, the path of a Bodhisattva and that of a Śrāvaka differ considerably in relation to time, the one requiring three kalpas and the other requiring as little as three lifetimes, according to some sources.

Kalpas of Time

In the vastness of cosmic time, our world-system is only a brief spectacle. All forms arise, endure for a time, and decay to arise in new forms. Our universe is only one of a long succession; like those before it, it has arisen and will endure for a great kalpa or aeon, a nearly incomprehensible span of time; then, as all forms, it too will decline and pass out of existence.

How long is a kalpa? The Samyutta Nikāya explains: "It is as if there were a mountain of rock a league in height without a break, a cleft, or a hollow. If every hundred years a man were to rub it with a silk cloth, that mountain of rock would wear down and vanish more quickly than a kalpa would come to an end."

Another image is based on the sands of the Ganges River. If one grain of sand were removed every hundred years, the total time for the removal of all the sand is said to be one "sara." Three hundred thousand saras constitute one kalpa.

Within this great kalpa that defines the lifespan of the universe are eighty lesser aeons: twenty aeons of creation, twenty aeons of stability, twenty of decay, and twenty of emptiness before the formation of the next universe.

The Abhidharmakoṣabhāṣya explains that our world-system is now in the midst of the twenty aeons of stability; when these twenty aeons have passed, our world will enter into the twenty aeons of decay. The first signs of this decay appear in the hells; beings continue to die in the hell realms, but are no longer reborn there. When the hells are emptied of beings, the hells cease to exist, and the period of destruction begins. While beings continue to die in the realm of the hungry ghosts (pretas) and among the animals of the ocean, beings are not reborn there; when these realms are emptied, they too cease to exist. Human beings and the animals who live with them are the next to pass out of existence in the same manner, and the realm of human beings ceases to exist. So also the demigods and the gods of the heaven realms disappear, and the realms they inhabited cease to exist.

With the world-system emptied of beings, the collective action which maintained the world is exhausted. When this happens, seven suns appear in succession; the world-system is first consumed in fire, then deluged in water, and then devastated through wind. This ends the aeons of decay, and twenty aeons of emptiness ensue. The place where the world-system once existed is but empty space, and the beings who dwelt in the world abide in the Ābhāsvara heaven, one of the formless realms.

After twenty aeons of emptiness, the collective action of beings initiates the world's re-formation. Winds arise in space, auguring the beginning of twenty aeons of creation. Gradually increasing in intensity, the winds form a circle; upon this circle, a circle of water takes shape, and upon the water forms a sphere of gold. From the sphere of gold rises Mt. Meru, the axis mundi; around Mt. Meru, arranged in concentric circles, rise seven great mountain ranges separated from each other by oceans. Beyond the seven mountain ranges lies a vast salt ocean, bounded by the Cakra, or Wheel Mountains that form the world-system's outermost rim.

One after another the heaven realms take form and beings are again born there. In time four great continents appear in the great salt ocean and the realms of humans, animals, pretas, and hells take form. Beings are reborn in each of these realms according to their karma. With the birth of the first being in the hells, the period of creation is ended, and the period of duration begins anew. (AKB III:89–93)

Investigating Time

The division of time into moments is governed by conventions based on the idea of a stream of time composed of a series of instants that arise and perish. (KJ:33b.4–6) If one investigates closely how such instants could create the flow of experience, a different perspective begins to unfold. If moments join together, then they must either join gradually or all at once. If they join gradually, then moments are not indivisible; if they join all at once, a kalpa elapses as a moment. If they do not join, then what could be in between two moments? If another moment could enter this "space," it would destroy the indivisibility of moments. If there cannot be anything in between, but there is no joining, then how could moments be added together to create the experience of duration? Though the idea of moments appears valid, when closely examined, it gives rise to inconsistent and contradictory positions. If time is not what it appears to be, there is room for a vastly different way of understanding.

One might also consider how the divisions of time are influenced by the intentions of individuals. For example, time is regarded from different perspectives depending on whether one is very young, in one's youth, middle-aged, or old. The sense of time shifts as life passes, yet one's own life is always the dividing line for past-future distinctions. Thus, we might consider that our ordinary time conventions are very dreamlike, depending on the distinction-maker.

Timeless Time

The Śrāvaka schools considered time closely. The Vibhāṣa records different explanations of how things "move through time." The Abhidharmakoṣabhāṣya contains discussions on time in terms of momentariness and causality. (AKB II:45–46)

The Mahāyāna reveals a completely unlimited vision of time that transcends even these sophisticated philosophical perspectives. Longchenpa speaks of "Samantabhadra time:"

"Samantabhadra time,
in which the three aspects of time are timeless,
in which ultimately everything is equal and perfect,
is pure from the very beginning." (KB I:XIII)

While it appears that some things are in the past, some in the present, and some in the future, these distinctions arise through the power of discrimination. In reality, in the past there is no ceasing; in the present there is no being born; and in the future there will be no arising. If one realizes the equality of the three times, this is the genuine understanding of time.

The study of the topic of time counteracts the notion of the self as eternal. "By developing knowledge of time, one knows all things to be impermanent, and this understanding counteracts holding to the self as permanent. This study also brings forth comprehensive knowledge of what is a conventional expression and what is the real meaning." (KJD 7a.4)

Further Readings

Aggañña Sutta, Digha Nikāya XXVII. On the origin of world-systems and beings.

Abhidharmakoṣabhāṣya, by Vasubandhu. Chapter III, verses 85–100. On instants and kalpas.

Chos-'byung, by Bu-ston Rinpoche. *History of Buddhism,* part I, pp. 90–100. On kalpas.

SECTION FOURTEEN

World of Suffering

CHAPTER TWENTY-NINE

System of Suffering

Seven weeks after the enlightenment, the Buddha proceeded to Vārāṇasī to the Deer Park of Sārnāth where he first turned the wheel of the Dharma. During the last watch he gave the first five disciples the twelvefold teaching on the four truths. The Buddha taught the four noble truths on many occasions and in many different ways.

The four truths are the truth of suffering, the truth of the origin of suffering, the truth of the cessation of suffering, and the truth of the path that leads to the cessation of suffering. The Enlightened One explains in the Lalitavistara Sūtra and in the Dharmacakrapravartana Sūtra that these four truths had never been heard before, for they had not been handed down by tradition, but were independently discovered by the Buddha.

Twelvefold Teaching

In the Lalitavistara the Buddha explains the twelve stages of understanding through which he progressed during the night of the enlightenment. He first set his mind on discovering the nature of suffering, the nature of the origin of suffering, the nature of the cessation of suffering, and the nature of the path to cessation of suffering. He persisted until, he says:

"I produced knowledge, vision, and realization, abundant knowledge, deep humility, and wisdom—and light came forth."

The next step was to comprehend and penetrate suffering, to forsake the source of suffering, to manifest the cessation of suffering, and to cultivate the path. Again, he persisted until:

"I produced knowledge, vision, and realization, abundant knowledge, deep humility, and wisdom—and light came forth."

The final step was to complete and accomplish each of those endeavors: to completely understand suffering; to completely abandon the source of suffering; to make manifest the cessation of suffering; and to follow the path to its end. And once again:

"I produced knowledge, vision, and realization, abundant knowledge, deep humility, and wisdom—and light came forth."

Only after completing this twelvefold cycle did the Buddha declare that he had attained complete and perfect enlightenment. (LAL XXVI)

In following the way of the Buddha, we begin with understanding the inner nature of each of the four truths. To understand the world of suffering and how this world is structured, we study the three realms, the six destinies, and the characteristics of samsara. To understand the causes of suffering and how they operate, we study karma and kleśa, actions and emotional patterns. To understand the cessation of suffering, we study the achievement of the Arhats, Bodhisattvas, and the Buddha. To understand the path, we begin with a study of the five stages of the path.

Studying the First Noble Truth

The Abhidharma texts describe the relationship of sentient beings and the environment with the image of a vessel (the external environment) with a content (sentient beings). (AKB III:45) Although the environment seems independently given, the apparent vessel has arisen from the collective actions of the sentient beings. Abhidharma texts explain that the qualities of the land, the nature of the society, and other aspects of the external world are reflections of the past and present actions of sentient beings. Thus the world we live in is our responsibility in an intimate way.

World and Beings

There are six different classifications of beings, known as the six destinies: hell-beings, hungry ghosts, animals, humans, demigods, and gods. Each destiny is characterized by distinctive emotional patterning. Hell-beings are dominated by hatred and aggression, ghosts by greed and yearning, animals by dullness and ignorance, humans by passion and desire, demigods by paranoia and envy, and gods by self-absorbed pride.

These six basic emotions provide the fundamental causal momentum to experience, giving rise to subsidiary emotions whose interweaving patterns establish the nature of the whole of samsara with its six destinies.

These six destinies form a coherent system within which every sentient being circulates. The potential for each destiny resides within the mind; thus human beings experience all the emotions and can relate to the distinctive patterns that characterize the other destinies. Likewise, the potentials of human nature persist in the minds of beings in other destinies.

This patterning also manifests physically. The more intense and continuous the emotional energy, the more solidly embodied it becomes. Certain minds manifest the potential of virtue and naturally surround themselves with beauty; others manifest suffering and neurosis, attracting and accumulating harmful, unpleasant experiences.

Each pattern of emotional energy creates a particular kind of mental and physical environment; when a pattern of mind becomes dominant, it leads to a particular destiny. For example, if hatred and anger predominate, they evolve into a self-destructive energy that burns or freezes life. Although human experience is not thoroughly dominated by the energy of anger, we can touch the quality of that destiny. We can imagine anger growing uncontrollable, creating suffering and mental anguish so immense that all possibilities of peace, joy, self-respect, or confidence are lost, and body and mind are damaged beyond repair.

Though we are in the human realm now, these other realms are not far from us; there is no guarantee that under some extraordinary circumstance we will not find ourselves in one of them. The timing of such an event is unpredictable. Just as the sudden shaking of an earthquake may open a crack in familiar ground, the mind may suffer a shock that propels it into an unfamiliar realm. Under the appropriate conditions, the emotional patterns of any of the six destinies can be activated, since these "programs" are latent in human consciousness.

World of Endurance

Inside the world of the apparent vessel, the beings of the six destinies undergo all kinds of experiences. These experiences are dominated by ignorance that separates self and other, and this results in selfish discrimination and harm. Harmful thoughts and actions in turn increase the darkness of ignorance. Caught in this cycle, beings cause endless miseries for themselves and one another. Thus, this world is also known as the world of endurance (sahalokadhātu).

The root causes of the six destinies, the six emotional afflictions, can be transcended by profound and all-embracing meditative concentration and by a penetrating understanding. Together concentration and understanding can become powerful enough to erase the patterning and restructure the "programming."

The ordinary untrained mind does not possess the means to work skillfully with the suffering of samsara. The mind untrained in concentration endures cycles of misery without knowing how to transcend them: Its powers are diffused and its intelligence confused. Unguarded by the developed power of concentration, the doors of the mind and the senses stand wide open to whatever influences arise. We do not choose what to engage; rather, engagements choose us.

This lack of control permits the mind to scatter and move toward disorder and even chaos. With its energy diffused, the mind is inherently dissatisfied, unwhole, unprotected, and insecure. Lacking the "holding power" or strength to consistently pursue and protect what is meaningful, it is unable to negotiate its way through the complexities and uncertainties of life.

Three Realms

Abhidharma cosmologies describe a complete world-system as including three realms of existence: the realm of desire, the realm of form, and the formless realm. These can be visualized as lying vertically above one another. The desire realm includes Mount Meru and the lower levels of the aerial heavenly realms; the four continents, including the continent Jambudvīpa, where humans and animals live; and the hell-realms beneath Jambudvīpa. (AKB III:45–57)

The three-realm system extends throughout all worlds. One world-system includes a set of continents, heavens, hells, and a Mount Meru world axis. One thousand of these worlds makes up a small chiliocosm; one thousand small chiliocosms make up a dichiliocosm; and one thousand dichiliocosms make up a trichiliocosm. (AKB III:73–74)

Beings of all six destinies living in the desire realm are dominated by attachment to the senses. The three lowest destinies—hell-beings, hungry ghosts, and animals—are considered unfortunate, while the three higher destinies—humans, demigods, and gods—are known as fortunate. Beings of all six realms are nonetheless subject to suffering. (AKB III:4a–d)

Beings in the two lowest destinies (pretas and hell-beings) reside beneath Jambudvīpa, while animals and humans inhabit Jambudvīpa and three other continents. The demigod and the god realms belonging to the desire realm are located on Mount Meru or above it in aerial abodes.

The two higher realms of form and formlessness include states of existence termed godlike, characterized by temporary bliss and peace. Beings born into the form and formless realms belong only to the destiny of gods. They live a refined existence with subtle emotions and attachments. The residences of the gods in the form realm are considered aerial, but those of the formless realm cannot be located in a particular "place." These higher realms can be temporarily experienced by human beings through meditation.

All-Pervasive Suffering

A study of our world reveals that samsara cannot fulfill its promise of happiness. Nowhere within the three realms can freedom from suffering be found. From the highest levels of the formless realm to the bottom of the hells, there is no enduring happiness in any samsaric realm or destiny.

This understanding becomes all the more significant if one appreciates the scope of the Buddhist view: There may be many kinds of experience and ways of being, but they are all included within the desire realm, the form realm, or the formless realm.

"What is called samsara is like a potter's wheel, a water pulley, or bees circulating inside a jar. When the bee is inside the jar, it remains within the bounds of the jar no matter where it flies, for there is nowhere else it can go. Likewise, wherever you are born, in the lower or higher destinies, you have not passed beyond the dimensions of this samsara. The top of the jar is like the higher destinies of gods and men, and the lower part of the jar is like the lower destinies. According to virtuous or nonvirtuous karma, one travels from one destiny to another in birth after birth, and so it is called samsara, going round and round." (KZLZ I:III)

Six Destinies: Three Lower Realms

The three lower destinies are those of hell-beings, hungry ghosts, and animals. The hell realms comprise eight hot and eight cold hells, together with surrounding hells, each with its own fearsome characteristics. In the hot hells, beings are tortured with overwhelming heat; in the cold hells, suffering is so intense that the body splits and shatters. The hell realms arise in connection with aversion and hatred.

Hungry ghosts have huge bodies with swollen bellies, narrow necks, and tiny mouths. Unable to satisfy their hunger, they are consumed by needing and craving. No matter what nourishment appears, they cannot make use of it. Tantalized by the possibility of satisfying their endless hunger, the ghosts will rush toward fruit trees and refreshing lakes, only to have the trees turn barren and the lakes turn to sand; any food or drink they put in their mouths turns to chaff or molten metal.

The animal realm is filled with immeasurable misery on all sides. Dominated by the need to eat and reproduce, wild animals live in constant fear of predators and hunters; their lives may last no longer than a year, a week, or even a day. Domestic animals are either slaves, subject to the whims of their owners, or raised simply to be slaughtered for food and clothing. This realm is characterized by overwhelming ignorance. Animals cannot assume responsibility for their own lives or comprehend how to reach a better state of existence.

These three lower realms are characterized especially by the suffering of suffering, which is so powerful that the more subtle types of suffering are hardly noticed. Enslaved by ignorance and having no idea of the Dharma, these beings are bound to repeat the patterns that brought them to the lower realms. Thus the beings born into these destinies tend to remain there for many lifetimes. (KZLZ I:III)

Six Destinies: Three Higher Realms

The three higher destinies are those of demigods, gods, and human beings. The demigods possess strong bodies, radiant health, and great wealth, but their existence is dominated by their envy of the gods' greater splendor and power. Their obsession with gaining what the gods enjoy causes them to engage in ceaseless battle and to suffer continuously from the agitation of obsessive striving. The demigods are driven by jealousy and desire for power. They live by intrigue and manipulation; being ill-disposed toward the success and accomplishment of others, even their own kind, they cannot forge any unity among themselves. Though this destiny appears powerful and desirable, it is fraught with anguish.

Classifications that give only five destinies omit the demigods as a separate group. The higher levels of demigods are placed together with the gods and the lower levels of demigods are grouped with the animals.

The gods live long lives that appear to be filled with pleasure and happiness and freedom from suffering. Their desires are fulfilled as they arise; their health never diminishes; their bodies exhibit no signs of aging. There is little in their reality to rouse them to question their way of life. Perceiving no problems, they have little motivation to practice the Dharma. Since the gods' lives are so long, they are oblivious to mortality until they approach death. But as death draws near, they experience the suffering of change in an extreme degree. Knowing they will lose the godly state of being, they are deeply shocked by the realization that it is too late to do anything about it. Not having cultivated worthy actions, wisdom, or compassion, they have laid no positive basis for the future. After indulging in bliss for aeons, they have exhausted the merit that earned them birth in the heavenly realms. As death approaches, they see clearly their future state as a hell-being, hungry ghost, or animal, and their suffering is immense.

The human realm is characterized by desire. Striving to reach an ideal, constantly wishing, searching, and grasping, the human mind fills with thoughts and judgments based on comparing and selecting. The intellect is most active in this destiny. Three kinds of misery dominate human experience: the suffering of suffering, the suffering of change, and the suffering of the conditioned. Although suffering torments everyone without exception in the human realm, the degree of suffering varies with circumstances. This mixture of more and less suffering allows humans to contemplate samsara in ways impossible in other destinies.

Only in the human realm is enlightenment possible. This is the only realm where the necessary conditions, the opportunity, and the desire for liberation arise. The gods are temporarily impervious to suffering, the demigods too busy fighting to care, the animals, ghosts, and hell-beings too immersed in their own ignorance and suffering to form the resolve required for transformation. (KZLZ I:III)

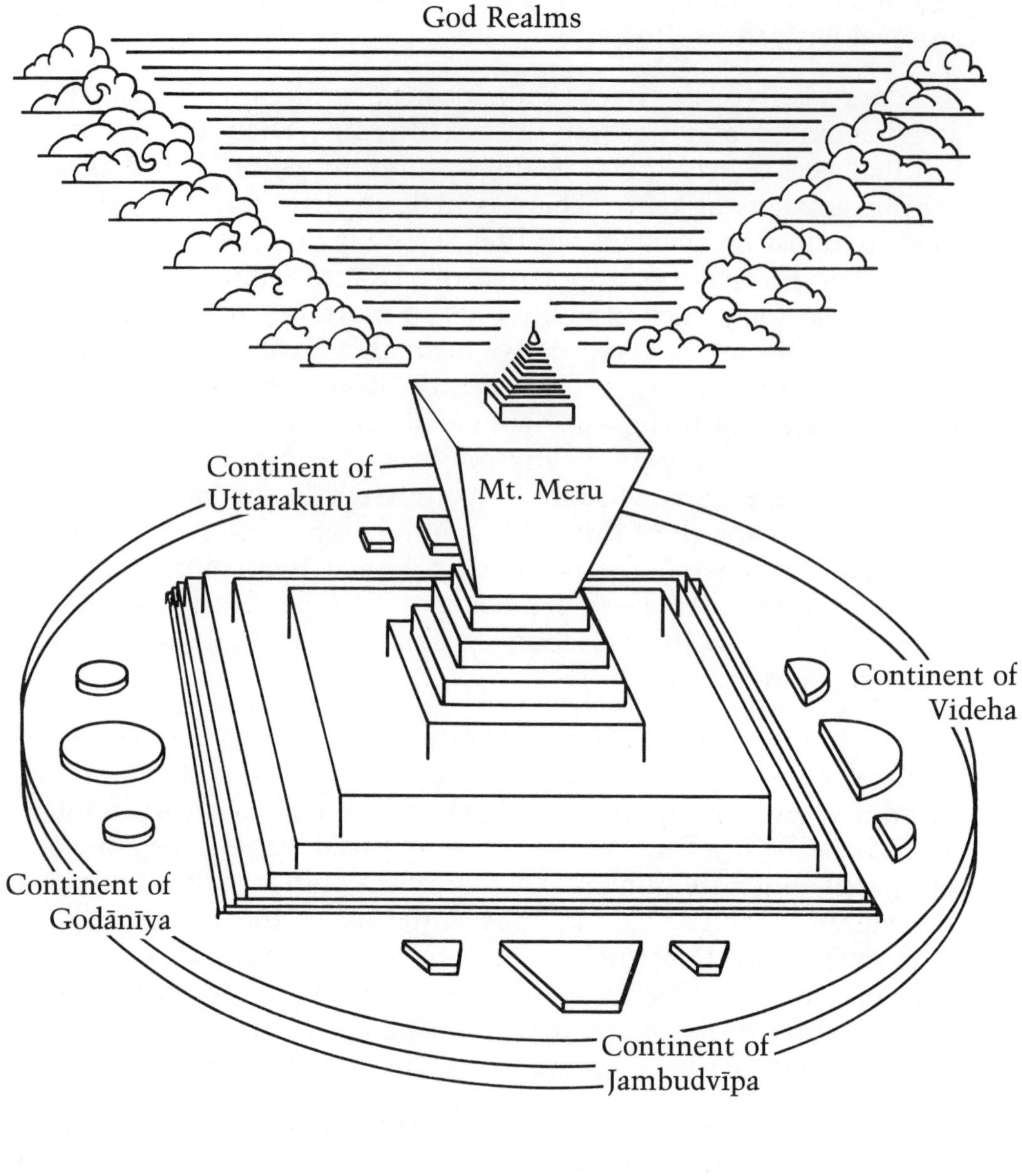

Cosmic Mandala

Formless Realm	Gods of Formless Realm	Sphere of Neither Perception Nor Nonperception Sphere of Nothingness Sphere of Boundless Consciousness Sphere of Boundless Space
Form Realm	Gods of Form Realm	The Pure Reaches Great Maturity Increasing Merit Cloudless Extensive Virtue Virtue Immeasurable Virtue Limited Clear Light Boundless Light Limited Light Great Brahmā Acolytes of Brahmā Brahmā's Realm
Desire Realm	Gods of Desire Realm	Constant Pleasure Delighting in Creation Blissful Ones Free from Strife The Thirty-three Four Great Kings
	Humans Animals Hungry Ghosts Hell-beings	

CHAPTER THIRTY

Living in Suffering

The nature of samsara can be glimpsed by examining the world we know today, imagining its centuries of past history, and projecting its possible futures. Can we see the inordinate amount of suffering that has taken place in the course of time—the wars, famines, plagues, the personal suffering, the heartaches, confusion, and disappointments? Can we possibly imagine that the sufferings we see in our world today have occurred in endless cycles, in every part of the world, in every era? Can we add to this mass of suffering the agonies of hell-beings, hungry ghosts, and animals?

"If the tears shed in the past in suffering from hunger, thirst, and cold had never dried up, they would surpass the waters of the great oceans." (KZLZ I:III)

Innumerable beings have wandered endlessly round the six destinies without ever finding a resting place. There is no release, only circling within the three realms. Beings have taken birth in many different forms from beginningless time: "From beginningless samsara up until the present, there is scarcely any kind of being in whose form you have not been born." (KZLZ I:III)

Types of Birth

Beings are born through four different processes. Some beings are born from eggs, such as geese, parrots, cranes, and other birds and reptiles. Some, such as many types of animals and humans, are born directly from wombs. Others, such as insects and worms, are born from within droplets of water. Magical birth includes beings that arise spontaneously in their fully developed form, such as gods, hell-beings, or beings in the intermediate state between birth and death. (AKB III:9, KJ 36b.2)

Types of Nourishment

Once beings have been born, there are four types of nourishment that support them. The first is what is usually understood by "food:" nourishment eaten by mouth and physically digested. This nourishment supports the growth of the body. The second nourishment supports the senses: the contact between the individual's consciousness, sensory organ, and sense object. Contact leads to the arising of experience in all of its associated feeling tones, and this nourishes the mind.

The third nourishment is volition or mental intention. The power of intention gives rise to hope that helps beings endure. For example, sailors at sea tormented by hunger and thirst may survive for many weeks if they have sighted land in the distance. If this hope were somehow crushed, the sailors would quickly die. The fourth nourishment is consciousness, which is the sustainer of life. When a being is reborn, the new existence is produced from the seed of consciousness upon which the actions of the past are imprinted and which sustains the momentum of future existences. (AKB III:38d, KJ 37a.5)

Just as the physical body is supported by food, the other three nourishments support senses, mind, and life as they function within the cycles of samsara. Contact leads to feeling, which leads to craving and the rest of the links of interdependent co-operation. Intention is the driving force of karma that maintains the twelve links. Consciousness deluded about a self is reborn moment to moment. These three factors—contact, intention, and consciousness—fuel the engines of samsara. The Abhidharmakoṣabhāṣya adds: "Contact, intention, and consciousness are considered nourishment only when they are impure." (AKB III:40a–b)

If contact, intention, and consciousness are pure, they do not increase the momentum of samsara; thus purification of these factors is an essential part of the Buddhist path. The Śrāvaka purifies contact by guarding the senses. The Bodhisattva purifies intention through mindfulness focused on benefiting others. The Bodhisattva purifies consciousness by liberating it from judgmental tendencies and conceptual limitations.

Types of Endings

The Enlightened One saw clearly that samsara by nature has limitations and is incapable of sustaining and maintaining what we most value. Everything we care about comes to an end; every story ends in tragedy or decay. Human purposes are eventually cut short, and our investment of time and energy is lost. Our short-sightedness does not easily recognize endings and so sees permanence in what is by nature impermanent.

The Bodhicaryāvatāra says: "This day of health and its nourishment, this present lack of danger, this momentary life in a borrowed body—all this is deception." (BCA IV:16)

Life begins with birth, is sustained by the four kinds of nourishment, and ends with death. Not only is physical life brought to an end, but all things that make up lived experience likewise come to an end. The Tibetan term "'jig-rten," which translates the Sanskrit "loka" (world), literally means support for what is destroyed. There are four endings in particular:

All life ends in death.

All associating ends in separation; we must depart from friends, lovers, and families.

All wealth ends in decline; all goods accumulated over a lifetime will be dispersed here and there after our death. We must give up everything we have accumulated.

All that is raised up ends in falling low; one who is prominent and famous today is forgotten or defamed tomorrow. (KJ 37b.3)

"All things are changing, unstable, like clouds, like flashes of lightning, like drops of dew." (LAL XV)

It is in the nature of samsara that everything is eventually interrupted. In the short range, there is success: We experience security, love, happiness. We may even be able to transmit something of value from generation to generation, but if the samsaric way of life is our only alternative, we cannot establish any genuine basis for meaning. In the longer range, our accomplishments fall short: No matter what is gained, something else is still hoped for. A price must always be paid for success, but if success does not bring what we wished, our efforts are ultimately wasted.

These limitations apply to more than the material level of our lives. Everything "slips through our fingers:" Good intentions vanish; deep insights dissipate. We glimpse alternatives but are powerless to enact them. We do not understand the importance of integrating the energies of body and mind. Lacking this knowledge, we cannot accumulate enough strength or momentum to achieve much of lasting value.

Waiting, hoping, wishing, and wondering, the ordinary mind cannot penetrate the dreamlike deception of samsara. Something is always wrong, but the problems cannot be isolated, penetrated, and completely resolved. A subtle confusion leads us to believe that all solutions are to be found somewhere in the future.

Crisis after crisis erupts, fueled by hatreds and desires; conflicts and disputes attract energy and attention away from positive pursuits, and rob us of valuable time for accomplishment. Indecision, restlessness, and worry weaken clarity and resolve. As energy is diverted into confusion, there is less energy available to penetrate and resolve problems and get solid results.

These patterns of limitation operate in our personal lives and in our societies. When we observe closely, we can see that the knowledge presently at our command is incapable of transcending these samsaric patterns. If we were to explore the nature of these patterns directly, we could begin to free ourselves from their limitations.

The Time of Trouble

While the option of questioning these limitations remains available to us, it is becoming more and more difficult to study the Dharma deeply enough to effect a change in our views and actions. Just as the individual experiences distinct stages of growth, stability, and decline, so do world-systems arise, flourish, and come to an end. Although our world is now in a period of twenty aeons of stability, we are currently passing through the era called "The Time of Trouble" (kāliyuga), in which our world-system moves from stability toward decay. This degeneration is evident in five areas: lifespan, time, emotionality, views, and basis of being. (AKB III:94a–b, KJ 39.a.4)

The degeneration of life means that despite advances that promote longer lifespans, the life force itself is growing weaker. The degeneration of the time means that enjoyment and vitality are decreasing, life is losing its savor, and endeavors of all kinds are more difficult to bring to fruition. The degeneration of emotionality refers to the increasing emotional instability in the lives of ordinary people, while the degeneration of views refers to the increasingly lax practices of monks and nuns. The degeneration of the basis means that the bodies and minds of sentient beings are increasingly subject to illnesses and pains. The Abhidharmakoṣabhāṣya explains that the degeneration process affects both physical and mental realms, diminishing bodily health, beauty, intelligence, memory, energy, and stability.

Our situation is thus doubly difficult: We are locked within the limitations of samsara during a period of degeneration. Mind is weakened, easily confused, readily agitated, and unable to make clear distinctions between wholesome and unwholesome pursuits. Self-confidence is hard to develop, and commitments are extremely difficult to maintain. The decline of the Dharma makes our situation even more serious.

The Longevity of the Buddha's Teachings

Although the brilliance of the Dharma shines like the sun, untouched by time, emotionality and confusion gradually thicken like clouds, obscuring the Dharma's beauty and power.

As the kalpa begins to degenerate, the light and warmth of the teachings are filtered through ever denser layers of negativity.

Thus like everything in the conditioned world, the teachings of a Buddha do not endure forever. Various texts describe the longevity of the Dharma in the human realm as 1,000 years, 2,000 years, 2,500, and 3,000 years. In the highest god realms, the teachings will endure until the end of the great kalpa.

A commentary on the Prajñāpāramitā explains that the Buddha's teaching endures 5,000 years, passing through ten stages of 500 years each. The first three stages are the period of the Arhats or the period of living knowledge. The next three stages are the period when the three trainings remain well practiced. The next three stages are the period when only the theory of the Abhidharma, the Sūtras, and the Vinaya remains. The tenth and final stage is the period when only the outward signs of the teaching remain.

As the power of samsara grows and confusion and emotionality increase, the understanding, practice, and transmission of the Dharma diminishes. When the power of the kleśas grows strong and the power of contemplation weakens, the more subtle teachings are not accurately practiced or well implemented. The meaning behind the words is not properly understood, making the Dharma seem remote from life experience. Lacking a sense of the inner meaning, individuals do not readily engage the teachings or make a commitment to study and practice. Without preparation and commitment, little can be accomplished.

Even when instructions are clear and direct, it is difficult now for people to become involved with serious study and practice. Efforts are sidetracked again and again because the goal is not clear and commitment is not strong. Individuals remain largely confined to the theoretical plane of experience. Much time is spent discussing, criticizing, and wondering about the teachings and the teacher, rather than proceeding in a direct and orderly way to identify, penetrate, and remove obstacles to progress. Following this approach, efforts to resolve problems only intensify them, generating thickening layers of obscurations, like billowing clouds of smoke.

A spiritual orientation of any kind is now hard to develop, while to most people the advanced path of the Bodhisattva is almost unimaginable. And yet, if we sincerely wish to connect with the Dharma, we can regard these obstacles as inspiration for transformation. The transformation process is based on our fundamental and enduring human heritage: the potential for enlightenment that all beings possess, the teachings of the Enlightened One, which have been preserved by the masters of the past, and spiritual friends to guide us along the way.

When we know that the purpose of life is transformation and can make a commitment to the process of education, each obstacle only sharpens the sword of wisdom. This sword, forged by an intelligence that is not deceived about priorities and values, can cut cleanly through confusion and delusion.

Unique Opportunity

In a world where everything eventually deteriorates, in the midst of these troubled times, the conjunction of our lives with the Buddha, Dharma, and Sangha is most fortunate. In the lifespan of a world-system, enlightened beings arise only at certain times. Buddhas appear only in periods of stability before the lifespan grows too short and sentient beings become hopelessly confused. (AKB III:94a–b) To live in the world as a human being at the same time that the Buddha's teachings are present offers a unique opportunity to travel the path to enlightenment. The two main components of this opportunity are known as leisure and endowment.

Leisure and Endowment

Leisure means freedom from eight unfavorable conditions while endowment is the possession of ten qualities: five that depend on oneself and five that depend on others. Leisure and endowment are described in Mahāyāna texts such as the Karuṇāpuṇḍarīka and the Gaṇḍhavyūha Sūtra. In the Tibetan tradition the Ngal-gso-skor-gsum (*Kindly Bent to Ease Us*) by Longchenpa, the Thar-pa-rin-po-che'i rgyan (*Jewel Ornament of Liberation*) by Gampopa, and the Kun-bzang-bla-ma'i-zhal-lung transcribed by

Patrul Rinpoche give extensive discussions of the significance of leisure and endowment.

The leisure to study and practice the Dharma depends on freedom from eight unfavorable states in which there is no inclination or time to practice the Dharma. These eight states are: the three lower realms of existence (hell-beings, hungry ghosts, and animals), cultures whose customs are opposed to the most basic principles of the Dharma, the long-lived gods, heretics holding doctrines contrary to the Dharma, those born in periods when no Buddha arises, and those born with deficient faculties.

Ten special conditions make up the endowment. The five conditions found within oneself are: to be a human being, to be born in a civilized country, to have faculties intact, to be engaged in a wholesome vocation, and to have faith in the Dharma. Five conditions are dependent upon others who have created the opportune time and place: That the Buddha has appeared, that he has preached the Dharma, that the Dharma continues to exist, that the Dharma is being practiced, and that teachers are available.

When these conditions are present and our determination is strong, even the overwhelming suffering of our world can be overcome. As Śāntideva says: "Enlightenment is obtained by a fraction of the effort required to survive millions of years of suffering in samsara." (BCA VIII:83)

Awakening to the reality of our situation—pervasive impermanence and suffering, increasing confusion, and decreasing spiritual light—we recognize the responsibility that we have in this place and time. The teachings of the Buddha are universal. They are the birthright of all individuals who wish to awaken. If we wish to participate in this golden lineage of light, our task is to nourish the growth of understanding in the heart and mind of a committed human being. The commitment to embody compassion and wisdom gives life a threefold meaning that holds up under all adversity: to benefit ourselves, to benefit others, and to benefit the Dharma.

"Like a flash of lightning in the darkness of night, may the gesture of the Buddha turn the thoughts of the world toward goodness for a moment." (BCA I:5)

Further Readings

Mahāvastu. *The Mahāvastu,* in 3 volumes. On the genesis of the world.

Dam-chos-yid-bzhin-nor-bu-thar-pa-rin-po-che'i-rgyan, by sGam-po-pa. *The Jewel Ornament of Liberation,* chapters II, IV, V. On leisure and endowment, the nature of suffering, and the six destinies.

Ngal-gso-skor-gsum, by Klong-chen-pa. *Kindly Bent to Ease Us,* volume I, chapters I, II, III. On leisure and endowment and the nature of samsara.

Chos-'byung, by Bu-ston Rinpoche. *History of Buddhism,* part II, pp. 171–180. On the longevity of the Dharma.

Klong-chen-snying-thig-sngon-'gro, by 'Jigs-med-gling-pa. *The Dzogchen Preliminary Practice of the Innermost Essence,* part II, pp. 28–43. On leisure and endowment, the nature of samsara, and the benefit of liberation.

Kun-bzang-bla-ma'i-zhal-lung, by Patrul Rinpoche. *Kun-zang Lamay Zhal-lung,* chapters I, II, III. On leisure and endowment and the nature of samsara.

bsTan-pa'i-rnam-gzhag and Chos-'byung, by Dudjom Rinpoche. *The Nyingma School of Tibetan Buddhism,* book II, p. 944. On the longevity of the Dharma.

SECTION FIFTEEN

Causes and Conditions

CHAPTER THIRTY-ONE

Circular Momentum

The Dharma teachings explain that all-pervasive suffering arises because of ignorance. Depending on ignorance, karma (actions) and kleśa (emotionality) create the vicious cycle of suffering called samsara.

"The Buddha has declared that pleasures and sorrows,
the heights and depths of samsara,
have come from previously accumulated karma." (KB I:IV)

Studying the Second Noble Truth

Out of ignorance, the self misleads itself. Although we may have good intentions, unknowingly and innocently we choose the wrong directions. These choices further deepen ignorance and confusion so that good decisions become more and more unlikely. Decisions grounded in confusion result in intense pain that the texts delineate as the eight forms of suffering. Each of the eight is fraught with anxiety, uncertainty, and frustration on subtle emotional and mental levels.

"The root of karmic activity is the loss of pure awareness. It is made up of attachment, aversion, and confusion. What is engendered by them are the black and white deeds that initiate samsara." (KB I:IV)

Not recognizing that our own actions and emotional reactions have created the confusion, we do not see the cause or know how to end our own suffering. We imagine the cause of suffering to be "elsewhere"—a creator god, society, or the actions of others. We believe that if these externals would change, we would no longer suffer.

The Buddha's teachings emphasize the importance of clearly examining the cause of suffering and learning to look for its root in our own thoughts and actions. Then we can perceive how we ourselves create suffering: Through active or passive actions, we continually strengthen the bonds of karma and kleśa.

Active Control

Actively, we are motivated by the never-ending desires of the self. We are compelled to pursue whatever the self imagines will satisfy its desires. We are convinced that satisfaction of desire is the source of true happiness.

Yet the very nature of desire does not permit happiness. Like trying to quench one's thirst by drinking salt water, satisfying desire only stimulates the flow of desire. In the wake of fulfillment, desire once more stirs and reaches out. There is never lasting satisfaction, not even completion.

"Even a rain of gold could not satisfy your desires, for the smallest taste of enjoyment leads to the suffering of more desire. A truly wise person understands this." (DP XIV:8)

Desire is like a flame, brightly beautiful, fascinating, and yet dangerous. Caught up in desire, the mind has little understanding of past, present, or future. As for the past, we do not remember how little satisfaction and how much frustration we have actually experienced. Any small amount of satisfaction is magnified out of proportion, and the distorted memory obligates us to pursue desire further. In the present moment, we lose mindfulness as we surrender to the momentum of fascination. So strong is the burning need of the present that we can scarcely imagine the future consequences of our actions.

The Abhidharma texts refer to this blind emotion-driven activity as nonvirtuous conduct. It has no positive benefits and leads only to more suffering, more compulsive action, and more emotional instability. Yet, habituated to the drama of desire, we enjoy the feeling of yearning and wanting. We keep desire alive with memories and images, elaborating upon them, creating myths of satisfaction that we elevate to a goal. If we do not reach that goal, we are deeply disappointed; if we do reach it, we find it does not last or was not worth the price. Still we cannot stop. We have become addicted to desire and are caught in a pattern of yearning and wanting.

Eventually, the mind tires of yearning and wanting, either from surfeit or from frustration; it loses its stability, gives up hope, or becomes completely uninterested. These three symptoms mark the end of the cycle of desire and reveal its true nature: Desire burns on and on; feeding the flame only makes it burn brighter, until at last the fuel is spent, and the fire goes out. Though desire rigorously controls the mind and body, we accept its rule and even learn to enjoy it.

Passive Control

Passively, we create suffering by promoting cycles of karma and kleśa that revolve around laziness. Gloominess, feelings of inadequacy, unwillingness to make commitments, and indifference are all related to laziness. We do not care to set goals and work to achieve them. Logic and reason support laziness, creating the explanations and excuses for lack of accomplishment.

With the passing of time, so little is accomplished that problems and difficulties begin to manifest. But the lazy mind cannot risk its superficial comfort by engaging the problems. Easily overwhelmed, the lazy mind retreats into a deeper gloom of laziness and inactivity.

At a certain point, deeply poisoned by laziness, we give up all discipline and allow events to take their own course. Problems now increase dramatically, undermining any remaining positive intentions. Experiences of failure and confusion reinforce feelings of inadequacy, which promote further withdrawal. Refusing responsibility, we become incapable of making good decisions or getting results, which confirms our sense of inadequacy and incompetence. Disconnected from struggling, the lazy mind tells us that nothing can be done about our situation. Eventually this cycle leads to deep boredom and lack of interest in life that mature into cynicism and pervasive bitterness.

Investigating Karma and Kleśa

These two forms of self-inflicted suffering are extremely effective means of perpetuating patterns of ignorance and confusion. The more intense the suffering, the more confusion is generated. Once the momentum of emotional reaction → compulsive action → emotional reaction develops a certain directional strength, it is very easy to be pulled into these cycles and very difficult to get out of them. The circular momentum seals the pattern, leaving no apparent escape.

Endless repetition of this pattern traces deep grooves in our consciousness. Activated by the proper conditions, our energy readily flows along these grooves. Abhidharma texts liken the latent patterns to seeds. When seeds are activated by conditions such as rain and sunshine, they are able to bring forth a complete plant. The seeds from this plant, once sown, faithfully transmit the pattern.

Karmic patterns, accumulated over long periods of time, even many lifetimes, run through the depths of consciousness, like strata laid down in rock. The power of an action does not disappear; whatever has been done in the past will have an effect at some point in time.

In addition to individual karmic patterns, which accumulate lifetime after lifetime, there is vast collective karma that we share, for example, as citizens of a country or members of a race. Myriad individual actions of body, speech, and mind have joined to create the collective motivations of a culture and the resultant rise and fall of its fortunes.

The workings of karma are very difficult for the untrained mind to trace because it does not understand the inner connections between events. It does not know what kinds of events result from what kinds of actions. Moreover, memory is limited to such a small percentage of actual experience that the mind cannot make the proper connections between events.

We can, however, understand the basic principles of karma and kleśa, which allow us to comprehend the cause of suffering and to develop the three trainings. By identifying actions and emotions clearly, we can recognize the direction in which we are moving. We begin to cultivate virtuous actions and discontinue nonvirtuous actions of body, speech, and mind. This disciplined conduct brings stability and confidence to our lives and allows the development of further training.

With continued study and observation, and with practice in meditative concentration, we gradually free ourselves from the manipulation of emotionality and direct our actions more wisely. Conscious direction of our actions requires strength of mind and clarity of purpose that arise from training in both meditative concentration and wisdom.

As wisdom deepens, the actual nature of the operation of karma and kleśa becomes clearer. We can see how the dramatic arousal of the emotions hypnotizes the mind, like the spell of a magician. The emotions support the illusion of the self, and the illusion of the self generates and justifies the emotions. Entranced by the displays circulating around the illusion of a self-existent "I", the audience does not notice the absence of a self at the center.

CHAPTER THIRTY-TWO

Cause and Effect

The diversity of the world arises from karma. The diversity of the world arises from the actions of living beings . . . What is action? It is intention and that which is produced through intention." (AKB IV:1a–b)

The law of cause and effect takes into account the intention behind action. Intention is the mental willing; what arises from intention is the action that has been willed, which is made up of the various acts of speech and body. Thus there are said to be three kinds of karma: karma of mind, speech, and body.

Virtuous and Nonvirtuous Action

Actions can be classified as good (virtuous), bad (nonvirtuous), or neutral. The law of karma says that good gives rise to happiness (resulting in less suffering) and bad gives rise to unhappiness (resulting in more suffering).

The Abhidharmakoṣabhāṣya explains that the essential component of the result of action is feeling (vedanā). Virtuous actions are beneficial and result in pleasant feelings. Nonvirtuous actions are harmful and result in unpleasant feelings, which increase suffering. Neutral action has neither harmful nor beneficial effects and is ethically neutral. It results in a feeling that is neither pleasant nor unpleasant. (AKB IV:45–47, 57)

Actions classed as good or bad may be absolutely good or bad, good or bad in and of themselves, or good or bad through association. For example, nirvana is absolutely good. The absence of attachment, the absence of aversion, and the absence of confusion, known as the three roots of virtue, are good in themselves. The attitudes that are associated with these roots of virtue, such as the other virtuous mental events, are good by association. Actions are also good by reason of their original cause, the intention of the mind. (AKB IV:8)

Bad action works the same way. Actions can be bad absolutely, like samsara as a whole. The roots of nonvirtue (attachment, aversion, and confusion) are bad in themselves. Actions associated with these roots are also bad, as are any actions whose original cause is bad. (AKB V:20a–b)

Ten virtuous and ten nonvirtuous actions are listed in the Abhidharma texts as the ten good courses of action and the ten bad courses of action. Actions are further divided into those associated with body, speech, and mind. Nonvirtuous actions of the body are killing, stealing, and sexual misconduct; nonvirtuous actions of speech are lying, slander, harsh words, and idle talk; three nonvirtuous actions of the mind are covetousness, ill-will, and wrong views. The ten good courses of action are the opposites of these ten bad courses.

An action can also be classified according to whether it is meritorious, demeritorious, or nonagitated. Meritorious action is virtuous action in the realm of desire. Virtuous actions in the realms of form and formlessness do not result in agreeable feelings but foster nonagitation and the feeling of indifference. (AKB IV:45–46a–b)

Results of Action

Action can be classified as projecting results or as completing results. Action that projects results determines a future existence in whatever realm of rebirth is suitable. Action that completes results develops the specifics of experience: how much happiness or suffering arises within that future existence. The Abhidharma-koṣabhāṣya gives the example of sketching an outline (projecting) and filling in the details (completing). (AKB IV:95a–b).

Depending on previous actions, one takes birth as a hell-being, a hungry ghost, an animal, a human, a demigod, or a god. The quality of life in that realm and the quality of the sense faculties are determined by previous actions; so is the environment one inhabits, the patterns that shape one's behavior, the length of one's life, one's health, and one's wealth. The effects of previous actions mature correspondingly. Thus killing results in a short lifespan; stealing results in poverty; lying results in being criticized and deceived; slander results in being surrounded with disunity and dissension; sexual misconduct results in having quarrelsome partners; idle talk results in a lack of courage and in others not believing you; and ill-will results in fear. (AKB IV:85, KZLZ I:IV)

The effects of the ten virtuous and ten nonvirtuous actions are of three kinds: matured results, outflowing results, and predominating results. When a bad course of action results in birth in a hell realm, this is called the matured result. Outflowing refers to the resemblance between cause and effect. For example, when a bad course of action results in shortening the lifespan or in poverty though one is born into the human realm, this is called an outflowing result. When a bad course of action results in changes in one's environment, such as land becoming infertile, this is called a predominating result. (AKB IV:85)

Likewise, good courses of action result in three kinds of effects: the matured result is being born in the higher realms; the outflowing result is having a long life or living under good conditions; and the predominating result is having a healthy and fruitful environment.

The five mortal transgressions are deeds so negative that their results cannot be mitigated by any combination of virtuous actions or antidotes. If one commits matricide, patricide, or kills an Arhat, causes a schism in the Sangha, or intentionally wounds the Buddha, one is reborn in one's next life in a hell-realm without any intermediate existence. (AKB IV:96).

Classifications

The study of karma also involves classifying causes and effects in terms of six causes, four conditions, and five resultant forces. (AKB II:49–65) Abhidharma texts also review karma from various perspectives such as how complete is the process of cause and effect, how determined or undetermined is this process, and how strong are the effects.

Some actions are set in motion and completed; others are set in motion but remain incomplete. The cause that sets action in motion is called the causal promoter, which projects or produces the action. The condition operating at the very moment of the action that allows the action to proceed is called the contemporary promoter. If the contemporary promoter is not active, the action will not take place even if it has been projected. For example, even though an action has been begun, it depends on the actor remaining alive in order to be completed. If the actor dies, the action is not completed. (AKB IV:10)

Determined action will have a result in the present life or later—the fruit will definitely ripen. Indeterminate action is uncertain either in regard to its time for retribution or whether it will have a result at all. The results of most actions can be counteracted or altered by means of the results of other actions. (AKB IV:55c–d)

Action can also be considered in terms of how weak or strong are its effects. The strength of an action's effect depends on the depth of motivation, the intensity of the effort, the "field" that received the action (whether one harmed a monk or a layperson, for example), and other factors. (AKB IV:55a–b, KJ 43b)

Protecting Virtuous Action

An understanding of karma inspires the Śrāvakas to take vows to protect virtuous behavior, and keeping these vows constitutes the training in moral discipline. The Abhidharma describes three types of discipline: prātimokṣa, the ethics for beings in the desire realm; the discipline produced through meditation, which is the ethical behavior of the realm of form; and unafflicted, pure discipline, which is the ethical behavior arising from the path itself. Pure discipline is the ethical behavior of very advanced practitioners. (AKB IV:13c–d)

The Abhidharmakoṣabhāṣya says:"The prātimokṣa discipline is morality, good conduct, karma, and discipline." It is morality (śīla) because it cools the passions. It is good conduct because it is praised by the wise. It is karma or action by its very nature. And it is discipline (saṁvara) because it restrains body and speech. (AKB IV:16a–b)

There are eight types of vows within the prātimokṣa discipline: the vows of ordained monks and ordained nuns, the vows of men and women novices, the vows of lay men and women, temporary vows, and beginners' vows. The lay person takes five vows; the lay person taking vows for a short time takes eight vows. The novice takes ten vows, while the fully ordained individual follows the ten vows as well as the rules stated in the Prātimokṣa Sūtra, which contains about 250 rules for monks and 350 rules for nuns. (AKB IV:14–15)

Manifest and Nonmanifest Action

To explain how vows operate in terms of cause and effect, the Vaibhāṣikas considered that not all actions were manifest or visible. If nonmanifest karma did not exist, the action of taking a vow would make no sense. The intention gives rise to an action of speech or body that is concrete and can be noted. That concrete act then has effects. Though the form of the vow itself cannot be seen, it too has an effect.

The Abhidharmakoṣabhāṣya says: "Intention is action of mind; it gives rise to action of speech and action of body." (AKB IV:1c–d)

Actions of body and speech are either manifest or nonmanifest. Action that manifests physically is the actual shape that is visible to another (some masters said it was movement). A nonmanifest action of the body may follow a manifest action of the body; it resembles a mental action (intention), but it has a kind of "shape" just as do actions of the body. Although this form cannot be seen, its presence can be known. (AKB IV:2b–3b)

Taking a vow is first a mental action of intention, from which follow specific acts of body and speech associated with formally taking a vow. At the same time as these actions of body and speech manifest, there arises an invisible, nonmanifest action which the Vaibhāṣikas said was form, not mind or mental. Once a vow is taken, this form persists. Thus one remains a monk or nun even when acting in sinful ways.

Another example of nonmanifest action is renunciation. Renunciation has an effect that everyone can experience: It is like a dike or a dam holding back a flood of unwholesome actions. Although this renouncing has no visible form, its inner effect is clear and certain. The concept of nonmanifest karma also explained how one who commanded another to commit a deed would receive the karmic results of the action. (AKB IV:4a–b)

Mastering Karma

The Mahāyāna understanding that sees all experience in the light of śūnyatā ultimately transcends causality and duality. Longchenpa expresses the nature of karma as artistry: "From the very beginning, karma, though nothing in itself, is there manifesting itself and is like an artist creating everything."

And yet, Longchenpa cautions us: "Karma accompanies you like a shadow following your body. It does not change place but is there as the body's pleasure and pain. It is difficult to divert, like a waterfall. Like a ruler over all that live, it makes beings rise and fall. It is vast and wide like the expanse of the sky. It is distinctly black and white, just like a blue or white lotus. . . .

"He who denies the karmic effect of actions is holding to the extreme view of nihilism and only goes from bad to worse. Having started a bad journey, such a one will never find freedom from evil situations and will drive happy existences farther and farther away." (KB I:IV)

Taking to heart the laws of cause and effect is essential for understanding the operation of samsara and for developing the knowledge that eventually transcends karma. "It is important that you always believe in the system of cause and effect, and consider what to do and what to avoid. Dharma discussions about high doctrinal views should not undermine your following the law of cause and effect." (KZLZ I:IV)

Padmasambhava urges his disciples to be very careful in this regard: "The more you realize the real nature of ultimate truth, the more cautious you should be in dealing with the law of cause and effect." (KZLZ I:IV) Fully seeing how the illusion of self is perpetuated by karma and kleśa, one accepts responsibility for manufacturing suffering and recreating confusion and ignorance. The effects of our actions, both positive and negative, are very powerful. They create worlds and realms of existence, like echoes or reflections of mind that we actualize out of ignorance. Though the vicious cycles of samsara may be like a dream, the nightmare continues until each of us awakens completely, and the suffering is real enough. With a deep understanding of the operation of karma, one can master its force and turn it toward the benefit of oneself and others.

CHAPTER THIRTY-THREE

Emotional Afflictions

The world arises from karma, but what is the root of karma? The Abhidharmakoṣabhāṣya says: "The roots of existence, of rebirth, or of karma, are the anuśayas." (AKB V:1a)

The Sautrāntikas regard the anuśaya as the latent trace of a kleśa. While an emotional affliction (kleśa) is in a state of quiescence, it is called an anuśaya. The emotion is not manifesting, but the potential to manifest is present, as in a seed. Just as a rice seed is capable of producing a rice plant, the anuśaya can produce an activated emotion. (AKB V:2a)

The Vaibhāṣikas considered that the kleśa and the anuśaya were essentially the same. The anuśaya of a kleśa is just that kleśa itself. (AKB V:2a)

These emotional afflictions, whether latent or activated, are the root of existence, which means they are the root cause of rebirth and of karma. If the kleśas are completely cleared away, karma has nowhere to take hold. When the basis for action has been transformed, the liberated one acts solely from compassion and wisdom.

The Abhidharmakoṣabhāṣya explains the meaning of anuśaya this way: "They fix and they flow, they carry away, they attach, they seize: Such is the meaning of the word anuśaya . . . By means of the anuśayas, the mental stream of the individual flows into the objects." (AKB V:34,39–40, AS II)

Activation of Emotion

When an emotional affliction (kleśa) is activated, ten operations take place. Each of these operations can be carefully studied in experience:

1. The kleśa solidifies its connection to the person.

2. The kleśa continues to reproduce itself.

3. The kleśa prepares the individual to be the basis where the emotion can arise.

4. The kleśa gives birth to its offspring, the associated emotions.

5. The kleśa leads to action (karma).

6. The kleśa reinforces its causes, which are incorrect judgments.

7. The kleśa gives rise to mistakenness about the objects of perception.

8. The kleśa deflects the mental stream of the individual toward the object or toward rebirth.

9. The kleśa promotes falling away from what is good.

10. The kleśa becomes a fetter that keeps the individual bound to the three realms. (AKB V:1a)

An emotional affliction becomes active under three conditions. According to the Khenjug, these are:

1. When the latent trace of emotion (anuśaya) is not perfectly known and not completely abandoned

2. When the objects that provoke its manifestation are present

3. When the mind is not functioning in accord with truth (KJ 49a.4)

The Abhidharmakoṣabhāṣya gives three causes for the arising of emotion:

1. The latent traces (anuśayas)
2. The presence of the object that provokes the emotion
3. An erroneous judgment

While the presence of an object of the emotions and the erroneous judgments prepare the way, the actual cause of the arising of an emotion is the latent trace. (AKB V:34) This runs counter to ordinary understanding, which claims that circumstances "make" us emotional. In fact, the emotion is already potentially present, waiting for the object to appear to complete the conditions for its arising.

Having arisen, emotion increases in two ways: by becoming involved with the object or by association with other emotions, feelings, and kinds of consciousnesses that favor its growth. (AKB V:32a–b,39, KJ 49b.5)

Certain emotions mutually support and "feed" each other, while others do not. For example, desire is not nourished by anger or doubt, but it is fed by envy and other emotions. Desire is further supported by pleasant feelings, mental happiness, and indifference. Interconnections for each major emotion can be analyzed in detail. The Khenjug describes these analyses. (KJ 50a.5)

The Abhidharmakoṣabhāṣya lists six anuśayas: desire, anger, pride, ignorance, false views, and doubt. When desire is further divided into desire for sensual pleasure and desire for existence, then seven are counted. If the five false views (see p. 241) are all separately enumerated, and only one desire is counted, then there are ten anuśayas.

Ignorance

The Arthaviniścaya Sūtra explains that ignorance means the ignorance of thirteen things:

1. The past, present, and future
2. The internal states and the external world

3. Action and the results of action

4. Good and bad action

5. Cause and effect

6. Interdependent co-operation

7. Buddha, Dharma, and Sangha

8. Suffering, the cause of suffering, the cessation of suffering, and the path to the cessation of suffering

9. Meritorious and demeritorious action

10. What supports enlightenment and what does not support enlightenment

11. What is to be practiced and what is not to be practiced

12. What is inferior, debasing the mind and body, and what is superior, ennobling mind and body

13. What is negative, opposing enlightenment, and what is positive and pure, an immaculate aid to enlightenment

Ignorance is absence of knowledge, lack of insight, lack of realization, lack of light, and infatuation. (AVS V)

Similarly, the Pañcaskandhaka Prakaraṇa says that ignorance is lack of knowledge about the four truths, the Three Jewels, and karma. The Abhidharmasamuccaya describes ignorance as absence of understanding of the three realms. It functions as a basis for the appearance of emotions, errors, and doubts.

The Abhidharmakoṣabhāṣya describes ignorance as confusion about the four truths and explains the relation between ignorance and wrong views: "From confusion, there arises doubt. From doubt come forth false views, and from false views arises the belief in a self." (AKB V:32c–e)

Five False Views

The five false views are: belief in a self, holding extremist views, holding perverted views, holding a limited view in esteem, and holding ascetic practices and discipline to be paramount.

Belief in a self as a permanent or unitary entity is false; there is nothing fixed in this "accumulation of things that perish" that could be called a self. All the other false views develop based on the belief in a self. (AS I, MBP 73)

To believe that there is a self that continues eternally or that there is complete dissolution at death (eternalism or nihilism) are both extremist views. To hold a perverted view is not just to assert a false idea, but it is to deny what is actually true, as in denying the operation of cause and effect. Holding a limited view in esteem means that one considers excellent what is actually an impure perspective that should be abandoned.

Holding ascetic practices and discipline to be paramount is to consider effective what is not in fact effective for liberation. For example, one regards morality and ascetic practices to be sufficient for release from all suffering. (AKB V:8)

These erroneous views are associated with the four fundamental errors: taking what is impermanent to be permanent; taking what is suffering to be happiness; taking what is impure to be pure; and taking what is not-self to be self. (AKB V:9)

Enumerating Emotions

The five views are added to the other five latent emotions—desire, anger, pride, ignorance, and doubt—to make altogether ten latent emotions. These ten become ninety-eight when counted in all their variety in the three realms. In the desire realm there are thirty-six latent emotions: twelve views, four doubts, five desires, five angers, five ignorances, and five prides. In the form realm there are thirty-one because the five angers do not exist there; in the formless realm there are also thirty-one. (AKB V:3–5) There are other ways of enumerating the latent emotions. The Mahāyāna Abhidharma lists 128 of them.

Ninety-Eight Emotions

The ninety-eight latent emotions are removed either on the path of seeing or on the path of meditation. For example, in the desire realm, thirty-two latent emotions are removed through insight into the four truths. This insight occurs as one enters the path of seeing. Insight into the first noble truth counteracts certain emotions; insight into the second noble truth counteracts certain other emotions; insight into the third noble truth counteracts a third set of emotions; and insight into the fourth noble truth counteracts yet another set of emotions. Other forms of latent emotions in the desire realm are removed only by the path of meditation. Similarly, the latent emotions in the form realm and the formless realm are removed partly on the path of seeing and partly on the path of meditation. (AKB V:3–5)

Non-Buddhist meditation practices bring about the removal of some emotional afflictions, but do not remove what must be removed by seeing the four truths. By definition, a non-Buddhist path does not include insight into the four truths. For example, though one may develop detachment through various meditation and concentration practices, one might still hold erroneous views, such as a belief in a self.

Contaminations, Floods, Yokes, and Clingings

In addition to the ninety-eight latent emotions, there are ten emotional events called wrappings of attachment: lack of self-respect, lack of propriety, jealousy, avarice, restlessness, regret, torpor, languor, vindictiveness, and hypocrisy. (AKB V:47, KJ 53a.4) Together these make 108 emotions that are categorized in four different ways: as the three contaminating influences, the four floods, the four yokes, and the four clingings.

Three Contaminating Influences Contaminating influences (āsrava) are the influence of pleasure, which includes forty-one emotions in the desire realm; the influence of existence, which includes emotions in the form and formless realms; and the influence of ignorance. (AKB V:35a–36d)

The Four Floods The four floods are the flood of desire for sense objects, which includes desires, prides, doubts, and the ten wrappings in the desire realm; the flood of existence, which includes emotions of the form and formless realms, such as desires, types of pride, and doubts; the flood of views; and the flood of ignorance, which pertains to all three realms and is made up of five types of ignorance. The four floods carry us away.

The Four Yokes The four yokes cause one to be attached. They are: the yoke of desire for sense objects, the yoke of existence, the yoke of views, and the yoke of ignorance.

The Four Clingings The four clingings seize their objects. They are: clinging to objects of pleasure, clinging to views, clinging to morality and ascetic practices, and clinging to a belief in a self. (AKB V:34,37,38, AS II, KJ 53a.5)

Fetters, Bonds, Residues, Hindrances, and Poisons

Nine Fetters Nine of the emotions are called fetters: desire, anger, pride, ignorance, wrong views, overestimation (parāmarśa), doubt, jealousy, and avarice. These attach the individual to cyclic existence within the three realms by encouraging bad courses of action and not encouraging good courses of action. As a result one is fettered with suffering. (AKB V:41–45, AS II, KJ 51b.6)

Three Bonds Three emotions—attachment, aversion, and confusion—are called bonds because they are bonded to pleasant, unpleasant, and indifferent feelings. Attachment lodges in agreeable feeling and takes it as its object. Aversion lodges in disagreeable feelings; and all three lodge in the feeling of indifference. (AKB V:45d, AS II, KJ 54a.1)

Seven Residues Seven emotions are called residues (latent emotions): sensual desire, desire for existence and becoming, anger, pride, ignorance, false views, and doubt. (AS II, KJ 52b.6)

Five Hindrances Five hindrances or obstacles are sensual desire, anger, torpor-languor, restlessness-worry, and doubt. The five hindrances obstruct the three trainings: Desire and anger destroy moral discipline; torpor-languor destroys wisdom; and restlessness-worry destroys meditative concentration. (AKB V:59, KJ 53b.5)

Three Poisons The three poisons of attachment, aversion, and confusion are known as the three bonds, three stains, three sins, three thorns, three accessories, three bad ways of conduct, three ruinations, three burnings, three battles, three plagues, three dense forests, three obstructions, and three impurities. (AS II, KJ 54a.2)

Eight Worldly Dharmas

"Taking essenceless samsara as an essence,
devoted to food and clothes,
we forget the ultimate truth.
Although we have everything necessary,
again and again we want more.
Our mind is cheated by untrue illusion."

—*Bla-ma-rgyang-'bod*

Involvement with the eight worldly dharmas keeps beings imprisoned in the realms of samsara and renders them susceptible to the hosts of emotions. The eight worldly dharmas are: praise and blame, gain and loss, fame and disgrace, happiness and suffering.

The eight worldly dharmas constitute our attachment to hopes and fears: We hope for praise, gain, fame, and happiness while fearing blame, loss, disgrace, and suffering. Entangled in these eight concerns, we give our energy and intelligence to the pursuit of these hopes and the avoidance of these fears. Our way of thinking is completely dominated by these eight concerns, which the world proclaims to be of utmost importance. But Śāntideva reminds us that to achieve true peace of mind, one must ". . . turn this thinking upside down," becoming indifferent to hope and unmoved by fear.

"By means of calm one achieves insight. The calm person destroys emotionality when he has become calm. The chief goal worthy of one's desire is tranquility, and this comes through indifference to the ways of the world." (BCA VIII:4)

CHAPTER THIRTY-FOUR

Deadly Influences

The human mind does not easily discern who are its friends and who are its enemies. A delusive, seductive drama presents situations in a certain light, centered on the forceful concerns of the self and its stories.

The drama of the self is controlled by forms of emotionality that are metaphorically referred to as demons or mārayas (deadly influences). Mārayas are obstacles to enlightened awareness created by fear and the false view of a self that sees emotions, thoughts, etc. as belonging to "I." When we abandon false views of a self, we see clearly that the mārayas have no reality.

Four major deadly influences are the māraya of the skandhas, the māraya of death, the māraya of emotionality, and the māraya of divine delights.

The Lalitavistara explains why the Buddha is called Jina, the Conqueror: "He has conquered the māraya of the skandhas, the māraya of death, the māraya of emotionality, and the māraya of divine delights." (LAL XXII)

Sentient beings are deceived by these four "lords of illusion" that tempt us away from awareness. These deadly influences control samsaric existence; we do not control our own lives until we are free from obsession with the skandhas, the kleśas, death, and delights.

Operation of the Deadly Influences

Lacking knowledge and training, the human mind is easily exploited and tricked. Its powers of concentration are easily fragmented; its freely operating intelligence can be confused and dimmed; its energies can be diverted into emotionality. The deadly influences are pervasive, like subtle waves or vibrations that work their way into the mind. Gradually, they take over, and there is no longer room for more authentic ways of being.

The mārayas operate by showing two different faces. At first there is the friendly face, offering something pleasing or interesting. Because we do not know how to find satisfaction without depending on the alluring offerings of the mārayas, we are enticed. Once we become involved, the face gradually grows malevolent. What seemed to be a source of happiness now creates misery, and some simple pleasure ends in a prolonged and difficult drama.

"These unknowing ones are harmed by sweetness, like someone licking honey off the blade of a razor." (LAL XV)

Until we learn to protect ourselves, our lives are not fully ours. The simple truth is that we know that we are suffering, but we cannot understand it; we cannot isolate the cause. Not knowing how to separate ourselves from the deadly influences, we cannot protect the heart and mind from suffering.

We have many reasons why we do not develop this knowledge: It seems we have no choice, no alternatives, and no power; there is no time, or we do not know how. And so the mind wanders in superficial reasoning, wondering what to do, finding one excuse after another why nothing can be done. Such "wondering" may appear to be inquiry into the human situation, but it is just another instance of the mārayas at work.

Four Deadly Influences

The deadly influence of the skandhas constantly involves us with the world of things. Objects become all-important, dominating our time and energy to care for them and enjoy them. Machig Ladronma, the great twelfth-century Tibetan yoginī, explains: "This loving and hating objects as though they were real, this whole obsessive attitude toward sense perceptions—these are the very conditions that cause such suffering and misery to sentient beings. They bind all beings to the frustrating flow of constant becoming. For that reason they are called demons."

The deadly influence of the emotions seduces us and then diminshes our strength. Tantalizing us with a small taste of pleasure, the emotions deceive us into spending our time, energy, and intelligence chasing memories, false images, and imaginations. Filled with longing, we vacillate between hope and fear. We lose the object, or it turns sour, or we cannot get enough of it; our lives are dominated by either desire or despair. Can we even imagine being free from the imprint of these emotions?

Machig Ladronma explains: "Experiences that frighten or upset us we call demonic, while pure experiences of gaiety and ebullience we call divine. If you embroil your mind in either of these, it is bound to become emotionally unstable. Although the emotions do not exist tangibly and do not manifest any substance as real, concrete objects, they still have a definite ability to harm you as you run here and there trying to adjust to them."

The deadly influence of delights tempts us with great heights of joy, such as romantic love, thrilling music and art, and any other sources of ecstasy. This group of experiences includes the sweetness of leisure and the peacefulness of meditative states. Deeply satisfying but transient, these experiences seduce the mind and orient it toward searching and wishing for more.

The deadly influence of death is the illusion of a self that lives and dies, the māraya of birth and death. Free of the belief in a self, one is free of the deadly influence of death. Who is born and who dies, if the self does not exist?

These four mārayas arise based on the belief in a self. Machig Ladronma explains: "If the self exists as real, then demons also exist. If such a self does not exist, then demons are also nonexistent. And there can be no obstacles or hindrances for a self that does not exist."

Deadly Poisons

The demonic energy of emotions is toxic to the human mind and body, creating confusion and delusion. Under the influence of emotional energy, the natural "immune system" of the mind is deactivated so that poisons of all kinds can be released without alerting the mind that something has gone wrong. Similar to the way a virus invades a cell and takes over its operating systems, the individual's faculties and abilities are taken over and used to manufacture more karma and kleśa. Thus emotions create more emotions until the mind is completely deluded. In this way a human life becomes mechanical, and we become enslaved to emotion while imagining that we are free.

In the undisciplined mind, imagination becomes the great weapon of the mārayas. Fueled by the erratic energy of the emotions, the mind spins forth a bewildering array of images. In our confusion we do not know how to distinguish the imaginary from the real, and stories about ourselves and our lives replace insight.

The Mahāyāna master Śāntideva describes the grip of the emotional influences in this way: "Like one hypnotized, I have no understanding, not realizing by whom I am driven crazy or who dwells within. My enemies, desire, hatred, and the rest, are destitute of hands and feet; they have no courage or wisdom. How can they enslave me? They dwell within my own mind and strike me at their leisure. And still, how slow am I to anger—how pathetic my unwarranted patience!"

And again: "I must be a warrior in this! Intent on waging warfare . . . I am stupid only because I make no effort. Through the operation of wisdom, the deadly emotions can be subdued." (BCA IV:27–29,43–46)

To awaken from the deadly dramas of samsara requires great courage. Breaking with the conspiracy created by emotion takes strength and knowledge: First, to recognize that samsara is a deceiver and does not deliver what it promises; and second, to refuse to be drawn into the dramas created by the emotions.

Upon awakening, one is free from involvement with this nightmare. No longer controlled or manipulated, one is no longer subject to suffering. The feeling of freedom is clear and clean; smooth, light, and open; courageous, fearless, and independent. These are the qualities the Arhat admires and emulates. Likewise, the Bodhisattva will gladly trade the seeming joys of samsara for the beauty of this path so that he can awaken others from the nightmare.

The human heart and mind have the power to recover integrity and depth. A glimpse of life free from the control of the emotional demons brings great joy. Other joys and happinesses are based in not-knowing, but this is the joy of knowing. The joy of freedom does not belong to the demons and cannot be appropriated by them, only imitated. With knowledge, we can protect life so that it cannot be suppressed or controlled. Even if full enlightenment is not reached, what lies ahead is beautiful, and unfolding the potential of knowing makes every moment of life worthwhile.

CHAPTER THIRTY-FIVE

Reversing the Direction

Whatever one plants will grow if the conditions are right. From nonvirtuous seeds will come the voracious weeds of suffering; from virtuous seeds will come happiness and the beautiful flowers of wisdom and compassion. Though it is not material, virtue has substance and weight; it has a powerful impact on the momentum and direction of karma and kleśa. The power of virtuous action is called merit.

Power of Virtue

Compassion and wisdom are stronger than karma and kleśa—if they were not, the vicious cycle of samsara could never be transcended. History has shown that even those who committed terrible crimes were able to confess their actions, purify their hearts, and attain the state of Arhat or Bodhisattva. Though the momentum of nonvirtuous karma is continuously recreating itself, it is not fixed or eternal. It can be transformed by accumulating virtue and transcended by deepening wisdom.

The power of virtue is dependent on the intention and motivation that underlie action. Outwardly virtuous action performed with a lazy or neurotic mind has much less merit than virtuous action undertaken with concentration and mindfulness. Positive qualities reinforce one another: Discipline, patience, effort, confidence, concentration, joy, appreciation and a host of other qualities mutually support one another. Just as the negative effects of karma and kleśa create a cycle of increasing darkness and suffering, virtue's power creates a cycle of increasing light and joy.

Accumulating Merit

Performing virtuous actions consciously for the benefit of others creates tremendous merit. The more selfless and pure the intention, the more powerful the merit. The gift of even a single flower has tremendous positive effects if it is offered for the purpose of benefiting others. The most meritorious actions are those performed with the most selfless aim in mind, the enlightenment of all sentient beings. Nāgārjuna explains: "By generating the thought of enlightenment for the benefit of all beings, a mass of merit is collected. If this merit took form, it would more than fill the expanse of space." (BCV 107)

The Bodhisattva accumulates merit by dedicating all merit accruing from his actions to the liberation of others. By "turning over" merit to others, the Bodhisattva recreates endless resources, a treasury of unending positive goodness. This is the alchemy of the Mahāyāna, the transforming power of selfless love and compassion.

"May all living beings everywhere who are suffering any affliction of body or mind obtain by my merit oceans of happiness and joy." (BCA X:2)

Training in Virtue

A king who admired the way of the Buddha but found the practices too difficult once asked for a simple path to enlightenment. He was given a single practice: to wish all beings well. The king was to wish that everyone be happy and to derive his happiness from theirs; if anyone was happy, the king would then be happy too. This simple but extremely difficult practice expresses the essence of virtuous intention.

Practicing virtuous action and dedicating its merit to others are common Buddhist practices. But developing the truly selfless orientation that generates great merit requires intensive training. The six perfections and other Mahāyāna practices strengthen and transform the attitude of wishing others well into the actual power to bring about beneficial results for others.

The prayers and Dharma activities the Sangha performs with pure-minded devotion produce immeasurable merit. The Sangha continually turns over this merit for the benefit of all beings. Like golden honey poured into a dark and bitter drink, the flow of merit into the world makes it possible for living beings to survive the sufferings of samsara and to awaken to the possibility of enlightenment.

Three Sources of Merit

Three kinds of action are special sources of virtue and merit: giving, self-discipline, and meditation. These three areas offer the occasion for meritorious works. (AKB IV:121–123)

Nāgārjuna refers to giving, self-discipline, and meditation as the three lamps and encourages us to live by their light: "Take hold of happiness, which is the light produced by the three lamps." These three dispel the darkness of samsara, "which even the sun and moon cannot illuminate." (SL 76)

Giving is a special source of merit if it is not accompanied by fear and hope; if one joyfully gives something of one's own with no thought of personal gain, giving generates great merit. Giving is excellent when it accords with three excellences: that of the giver, that of the object given, and that of the "field" receiving the gift. The giver is excellent if he or she is endowed with faith, discipline, learning, generosity, wisdom, and few desires. When the giver is excellent, the gift is automatically excellent.

The field is excellent depending on the destiny of the recipient. Although a positive seed will produce some small positive result even sown in a bad field, it will be much more fruitful when sown in a good field. Giving to human beings, for example, creates more positive results than giving to beings in the lower destinies, who have diminished capacities for practicing virtue and developing wisdom. If one gives to a person who is suffering intensely, this also has very powerful results. Giving to one's benefactors, such as parents or teachers, is very positive, as are gifts to the Sangha and to those with excellent spiritual qualities.

Gifts are meritorious for two reasons: because of the merit from the giver abandoning a possession, and because of the merit produced by the enjoyment and benefit created for the recipient. Gifts made in honor of stupas and the like are positive because of the willingness of the giver to abandon a possession and because of the devotion that motivates honoring the Buddha.

The self-discipline of keeping the precepts produces powerful merit especially when it is free from any taint of self-centered interest. Such pure action possesses effectiveness in five ways. The deed itself is pure; the attendant mental events are pure; the deed generates no disturbing emotions; it is associated with mindfulness of the Buddha, Dharma, and Sangha; and it leads toward nirvana.

There is also a scale of effectiveness in terms of motivation, with fear being the lowest motivation for discipline and attachment to pleasure or honor being the next lowest. Discipline undertaken in conjunction with the seven branches of enlightenment is genuinely effective; and the highest discipline is completely free from emotionality (attachment, aversion, confusion, and the subsidiary emotions).

Meditation gives rise to powerful merit because it allows the mind to be "impregnated" or "perfumed" with the positive and the good. The deeper the meditation, the more perfumed the mind becomes. In the Milindapañha, the monk Nāgāsena gives twenty-eight advantages of practicing meditation, including lengthening life, developing strength, removing faults, increasing a good reputation, banishing discontent, removing fear and instilling confidence, removing laziness and generating energy, and removing attachment, aversion, and confusion. Meditation makes the mind alert, pliant, one-pointed, and joyful. Filling the practitioner with delight and peace, meditation reveals the true nature of reality. (MP VIII)

The Importance of Meditative Concentration and Analysis

Like a lake that appears quiet on the surface, but whose depths ripple with fish swimming in many directions, the mind may appear still, while at deeper levels its rhythms are constantly shifting. The patterning of karma and kleśa occurs at these deeper levels where ordinary attention does not reach. An emotional pattern is activated, takes shape, and comes into play before it registers on ordinary consciousness. The dynamic is faster than conscious intention, and the momentum is more forceful than our untrained concentration can control. Consciousness is easily deceived by the continuous display of reflections and reverberating echoes produced through the patterning of karma and kleśa.

Mental activity develops in three stages: in the beginning, thought arises; in the middle, thought takes form, manifesting its emotional character, imagery, words, and direction; and in the end thought disappears into a mysterious "gap" or space from where a jump is made to the next thought. Moment by moment, thought after thought arises, like half-remembered dreams or music playing softly but constantly in the background.

This close examination of the arising and cessation of thought is so new to us in the West that we do not even have names for its various aspects. Learning to observe and then disengage from this incessant and elaborate activity requires mental stability developed through concentration and meditation practice, together with mental clarity developed through study and analysis.

Turning the Mind toward the Dharma

Studying the first two noble truths is the foundation for turning toward the Dharma. Within these two truths are four crucial topics that when contemplated seriously over time orient the heart and mind toward the teachings of the Buddha. The first four chapters of the Kun-bzang-bla-ma'i-zhal-lung give detailed discussions of each of these four topics.

1. Rarity of obtaining a human birth

2. Impermanence and death

3. Defects of samsara

4. Law of cause and effect

Rarity of Human Birth

Terdag Lingpa explains in the *Jewel Ladder* that contemplating the rarity of a human birth involves three steps: recognizing the leisures and endowments, realizing the difficulty of obtaining them, and considering their deep significance. When we have studied how karma operates, we realize how difficult it is to guarantee a human birth. This fleeting opportunity is the only one that allows us to fulfill the heart's deepest desire and realize the supreme possibility of full awakening.

"Although we have obtained this unique opportunity for spiritual growth, we squander our human birth. Continually disturbed by the meaningless actions of this life, we lose the immense benefit of realizing liberation, which is carried off by laziness: We return empty-handed from a land of jewels." (LGB)

Impermanence and Death

Because we are unable to truly believe that our lives will end, we must deliberately turn to meditation on impermanence. Terdag Lingpa advises us to look at three points: that death is certain, that the time of death is uncertain, and that only the Dharma is useful to us at the time of death.

Although we all acknowledge that death will come, rarely do we allow this knowledge to permeate our being. Withholding this knowledge from ourselves confines us to superficial aspects of existence. "With the passing of each day, we move closer and closer to death, yet as each day elapses, our mind-stream only grows rougher." (LGB)

Death is inescapable, the one certain fact of existence. And yet we are unable to predict when this might occur. What will come first, tomorrow or our death? With awareness of this unpredictability, we would live differently, finding each moment a precious opportunity to deepen understanding and appreciation.

At the time of death, our wealth, our friends and family can afford us no protection. We depart alone, accompanied by the force of our own actions and whatever wisdom we may have gained from studying and practicing the Dharma.

Defects of Samsara

Terdag Lingpa points out three themes for contemplating the defects of samsara: the suffering of the lower realms, the suffering of the higher realms, and suffering in general. Following the law of cause and effect, we will reap what we have sown and in the end, the result is always sufffering of one kind or another. Nowhere in the three realms can we find lasting happiness.

"A human being, true to his real nature,
having seen this disgusting state of affairs,
should banish all thoughts
that delight in samsara
in order to realize deliverance." (KB I:III)

Cause and Effect

To develop contemplation on the law of cause and effect, Terdag Lingpa advises study of three more points: the general understanding of karma, the specific understanding of which actions lead to which results, and serious consideration of the four noble truths.

"Having thoroughly given up cause and effect
with all their sidelines that initiate samsara,
apply yourself earnestly to the cause and effect
that ensures deliverance,
and you will quickly realize the highest positive good. . . .

"Deliverance depends on ourselves
and so does the means to it.
There is no chance that others will deliver us

incidentally, just as nobody can stop
the dream of a person asleep.
If this were possible,
samsara would already have been emptied
by the rays of compassion radiating
from the Buddha and his sons.

"Therefore, you yourself must put on the armor of effort.
The time to exert yourself
and to set out on the road to deliverance has come." (KB I:III)

Further Readings

Cūḷakammavibhaṅga Sutta, Majjhima Nikāya CXXXV. On analyzing karma.

Suhṛllekha, by Nāgārjuna. *Golden Zephyr.*

Śikṣasamuccaya, by Śāntideva. Chapter I, pp. 32–36. Prayers used by the Bodhisattva to dedicate merit to others.

"The Four Demons," by Ma-gcig Lab-sgron-ma. In *Footsteps on the Diamond Path* (Crystal Mirror I–III), pp. 119–125.

Ngal-gso-skor-gsum, by Klong-chen-pa. *Kindly Bent to Ease Us,* volume I, chapter III; volume II, chapter II. On becoming concerned with liberation.

Dam-chos-yid-bzhin-nor-bu-thar-pa-rin-po-che'i-rgyan, by sGam-po-pa. *The Jewel Ornament of Liberation,* chapters IV–VI. On impermanence, suffering, and karma.

Rin-chen-them-skas, by gTer-bdag-gling-pa. *Jewel Ladder.* On turning the mind toward the Dharma.

Kun-bzang-bla-ma'i-zhal-lung. *Kun-zang La-may Zhal-lung,* 2 volumes, chapters I, II, III, and IV. Detailed discussions of human birth, impermanence, samsara, and karma.

Nges-don-sgron-me, by Kong-sprul-blo-gros-mtha'-yas. *The Torch of Certainty,* chapter I. On turning the mind toward the Dharma.

SECTION SIXTEEN

Reality of Freedom

CHAPTER THIRTY-SIX

Victory of Freedom

The truth of cessation proclaims that victory over the delusion and confusion of samsara can be achieved. Others have gone before us: the Lord Buddha, who is known as the Jina (the Conqueror), the Bodhisattvas, and the Arhats. They are masters of the mind, expressing truth through their teachings and embodying truth in their lives.

Studying the Third Noble Truth

Studying the lives of the masters who have reached extraordinary stages of freedom from emotionality, we hear the truth of cessation. From a perspective enmeshed in the realms of suffering, descriptions of freedom and knowledge realized by the Enlightened Ones may seem impossible until we have also studied the path that leads to cessation. Understanding that these accomplishments result from a precise and proven process of transformation, we can let the beauty of greater freedom and knowledge touch our hearts and inspire our own efforts. In the midst of our difficulties and discouragement, images and events from the life stories of great masters return to memory, reminding us of higher possibilities for human beings.

Śrāvaka Path of No More Learning

At the stage of the Śrāvaka path called no more learning, the Arhats know that they have removed the residues of the kleśas and are free of karma that would propel them into another rebirth in samsara. The cause of suffering has been totally eliminated, and there is cessation, the end of suffering. This is complete peace and certain knowledge that the emotions will no longer stir, for the flame of desire has been extinguished.

Released from the realm of desire, the realm of form, and the realm of formlessness, the Arhat has completely renounced the world: He is beyond the world and removed from the world. The training of the Śrākava path is complete.

Sixteen Arhats

At the time of the parinirvāṇa, sixteen Arhats, all close disciples of the Buddha, vowed to remain in the world to uphold the teachings of Śākyamuni Buddha until such time as his teachings would disappear. Appearing to devoted students of the Dharma over the centuries, the sixteen Arhats continue to extend countless blessings. Their presence in the world has supported the Sangha and enabled the Dharma to survive many difficulties. Their images give special blessings in troubled times; thus representations of the sixteen Arhats have been greatly revered, particularly in China and Tibet. The meditation practices and prayers for invoking their blessings have been handed down in an unbroken lineage to the present day.

The Excellence of the Arhat

While aiming at nirvana that pacifies the sufferings of samsara, the path of the Śrāvaka results in excellence. The Abhidharmakoṣabhāṣya explains excellence as absence of all pain, as absolutely good, and as the highest. (AKB VII:13a)

"The Arhat's wandering is at an end: He is free from sorrow, completely free. Sorrow no longer exists for the one who has cut all bonds.

"The Arhat does not need possessions: He gives everything away. His sphere of action is wide open and unmarked, completely free. Like the path of a bird across the sky, his way is hard to trace.

"The Arhat is as firm as the earth's foundation; firm in his spiritual practice, he is like a blade of tempered steel. Clear and undisturbed as a deep pond, such a being is not bound to the world.

"The Arhat is without ambition: He knows the uncreated. He has severed the links of embodiment and is free from longing, free from place or position. This is the best of men." (DP VII:1,3,6,8)

Nirvana

Nirvana is known as cessation based on comprehension, the extinction of the afflictions, the cessation brought about by prajñā. (AKB I:6a,II:55c–d) The Milindapañha offers these similes to describe nirvana: Nirvana shares one quality with the lotus, two with water, three with medicine, ten with space, three with the wish-fulfilling gem, and five with the mountain.

Just as the lotus is unstained by water, so nirvana is unstained by the emotional afflictions. Just as cool water allays fever, the coolness of nirvana allays the fever of the passions. Just as water removes the thirst of humans and animals who are exhausted, thirsty, and overwhelmed with heat, so nirvana removes the craving for sense pleasures, for further becoming, and for the cessation of becoming. Just as medicine cures the ills of poison, so nirvana protects against the poison of the emotional afflictions. Just as medicine puts an end to sickness, nirvana puts an end to all sufferings. Just as medicine gives security from suffering, so too does nirvana.

Like space, nirvana is neither born, nor decays, dies, passes away nor is renewed. Both are unconquerable, and neither can be stolen. Both are unsupported; both are ways to journey on; both are unobstructed and infinite. Just as a wish-fulfilling gem grants all desires, nirvana brings joy and light. Just as a mountain is lofty and exalted, so is nirvana. Just as a mountain peak is inaccessible, so nirvana cannot be touched by the emotional afflictions. Just as no seeds can grow on the mountain peak, so no afflictions can grow in nirvana. Just as a mountain is utterly unshakable, so nirvana is complete equanimity, free from all desire to please or displease. (MP XV)

Powers and Knowledge of the Arhat

With awakening (bodhi) there arises the knowledge of the destruction of all the emotional afflictions and the knowledge of the nonarising of the emotional afflictions in the future. By these two knowledges, one abandons ignorance and knows there is nothing more to be accomplished. At this moment, one steps on to the path of no more learning as an Arhat. (AKB VI:67a–b, 76d)

Ten Dharmas and Five Pure Skandhas

There are ten special dharmas that belong to One with No More to Learn: the eight members of the eightfold path together with genuinely pure liberation and knowledge of genuinely pure liberation. (AKB VI:75–76, AS II)

"One with No More to Learn is completely liberated from all bonds . . . Thus, it is only the One with No More to Learn who can be said to possess genuinely pure liberation and knowledge of genuinely pure liberation." (AKB VI:75c–d)

The five pure skandhas of the Arhat are: the skandha of moral discipline, the skandha of samādhi, the skandha of prajñā, the skandha of liberation, and the skandha of the knowledge of liberation. These five pure skandhas include the ten dharmas of One with No More to Learn. (AKB I:27,VI:75b,76c–d, AS II, DN XXXIV)

With and Without Ornament

An Arhat who has conquered all the emotional afflictions by means of prajñā is called an Arhat without ornament. If he has conquered the afflictions by also mastering the stages of dhyāna (see chapter 42), he is called an Arhat who is liberated from two sides, "free in both ways." This Arhat is ornamented with the

TEN DHARMAS AND FIVE PURE SKANDHAS

Skandha of moral discipline
1. genuinely pure speech
2. genuinely pure conduct
3. genuinely pure livelihood

Skandha of samādhi
4. genuinely pure effort
5. genuinely pure mindfulness
6. genuinely pure samādhi

Skandha of prajñā
7. genuinely pure view
8. genuinely pure thought

9. *Skandha of liberation*

10. *Skandha of the knowledge of liberation*
knowledge of destruction of afflictions
knowledge of nonarising of afflictions

three wisdoms and the six superknowledges, through the practices associated with the eight deliverances, the eight dominant āyatanas, and the ten all-encompassing āyatanas. (AS II, KJ 58b.2)

The Mahānidāna Suttanta explains: "Now when once a brother, Ānanda, has mastered these eight deliverances in order and has also mastered them in reverse order, and again in both orders consecutively, so that he is able to lose himself in and emerge from any one of them whenever he chooses, wherever he chooses, and for as long as he chooses—when too by rooting out the kleśas, he enters into and abides in that emancipation of heart, that emancipation of mind which he by himself here in this present world has come to know and realize—then such a brother, Ānanda, is called free in both ways (ubhatobhāgavimutto)." (DN XV)

Six Superknowledges Superknowledges include five that arise both in advanced practitioners and Arhats: divine hearing, divine sight that knows the death and rebirth of all beings, memory of past existences, knowledge of the mind of others, and supernatural abilities. The sixth superknowledge, the knowledge of the destruction of the afflictions, belongs only to the Arhat.

Three Wisdoms Three of the superknowledges are called the three wisdoms of the One with No More to Learn. They bring about the end of unknowing with regard to the three times: knowledge of past lives (the past), knowledge of the birth and death of all beings (the future), and knowledge of deliverance, the destruction of the afflictions (the present). (AKB VII:45c–d, KJ 59a.1)

Eight Deliverances The first two deliverances oppose attachment to visible things in the realm of desire and in the first dhyāna. The third deliverance is cultivated in the fourth dhyāna. In the formless absorptions, there are three more deliverances. The eighth deliverance is the cessation of feeling and perception which turns one away from all conditioned things. The eight deliverances remove afflictions and bring mastery of the absorptions (AKB VIII:32a–c,34a–b, AS IV).

Eight Dominant Āyatanas The eight dominant āyatanas are associated with the eight deliverances. By means of the deliverance, there is the release from all attachment to objects of emotionality. Attaining the dominant āyatana, the Arhat gains complete domination so that emotions no longer arise in the presence of the object. (AKB VIII:35, AS IV)

Ten All-Encompassing Āyatanas The Arhat also possesses ten all-encompassing āyatanas. These ten refer to the kasinas of earth, water, fire, wind, blue, yellow, red, white, space, and consciousness. It is by means of concentrations based on these kasinas that one obtains the deliverances. (AKB VIII:36)

There are numerous other knowledges and qualities that develop as one reaches liberation: freedom from emotionality, ten special knowledges, knowledge resulting from resolve, four exact knowledges, three samādhis, and mastery of nine stages of absorption. (AKB VII:35c, KJ 59a.2–3)

With and Without Remainder

Though all the afflictions are eliminated, an Arhat retains the physical and mental supports for living: This is called nirvana with a remainder. When this individual's life comes to an end, he abandons his physical form and enters nirvana without any remainder. (AKB II:4, VI:37a–c)

Bodhisattva Path of No More Learning

The aim of the Bodhisattva path is neither to dwell in the cessation and peace of nirvana nor to dwell in the turmoil and confusion of samsara. Practicing the Mahāyāna teachings, the Bodhisattva attains the perfect enlightenment of the Buddha that transcends both nirvana and samsara.

The Mahāyāna recognizes certain outstanding Arhats, however, as Bodhisattvas who have deliberately manifested in the manner of the Śrāvaka (sprul-pa'i-nyan-thos). Śāriputra, Maudgalyāyana, the seven patriarchs, and the sixteen Arhats, for example, were Śrāvakas in form but Bodhisattvas in realization.

The Bodhisattva on the path of no more learning has attained Buddhahood. Having attained the samādhi that resembles a diamond, having cut through the roots of everything that must be transformed with the great transformation that arises from the three realizations, he removes the two kinds of obscuration and manifests the truth that has reached the end of the path: The Bodhisattva obtains the bodies of the Buddha, the five families, the five Buddha wisdoms, the five pure skandhas, and the ten no more learning dharmas, and innumerable qualities, forms of knowledge, and accomplishments.

Further Readings

Abhidharmakoṣabhāṣya, by Vasubandhu. Chapters VII, VIII. On knowledges and absorptions in the advanced stages of the path.

Abhidharmasamuccaya, by Asaṅga. Chapter II. On the noble truth of cessation.

Dhammapada. Chapter VII. On the Arhat.

The Three Jewels and History of Dharma Transmission (Crystal Mirror VI), pp. 218–247. On the sixteen Arhats.

SECTION SEVENTEEN

Path of Liberation

CHAPTER THIRTY-SEVEN

The Truth of the Path

After considering the basic operation of samsara, and after recognizing that an alternative is possible (the first, second, and third noble truths), we can develop an understanding of the path of liberation from samsara set forth in the fourth noble truth.

Studying the Fourth Noble Truth

When we see the complete map of the path and understand the fundamental approach articulated in the Abhidharma, the instructions and guidelines on what to study or how to practice are easier to apply. We need to know what is involved at each level: the purposes, the practices, and the results. We also need to understand how various types of practices and teachings available in the West fit into the larger perspective of the Buddhist path to enlightenment. The tree of knowledge that grows from such a foundation will have solid roots; study and practice will be effective; and the fruit of our efforts will contribute to the transmission of the Dharma.

THE FIVE PATHS

Path of preparation

Path of linking

Path of seeing

Path of meditation

Path of no more learning

The Five Paths

The path of transformation set forth by the Buddha includes five stages. The first is preparation; this is followed by a stage that links preparation with directly seeing the truth. Seeing is followed by a stage of meditating upon what has been seen; this gives rise to a path where there is no more to learn, for the training is complete.

Traversing the five paths, the individual relies on the thirty-seven wings of enlightenment, special practices based on the three trainings. The Buddha often summarized the path to enlightenment by reminding his disciples of these thirty-seven practices.

"O Monks . . . those things which I have discovered and proclaimed should be thoroughly learned by you, practiced, developed, and cultivated so that this holy life may endure for a long time, that it may be for the benefit and happiness of the world, out of compassion for the world, for the well being of gods and human beings. And what are those things?" (DN XVI)

The thirty-seven wings are the four foundations of mindfulness, the four genuine restraints, the four bases of supernatural powers, the five spiritual faculties, the five spiritual powers, the seven branches of enlightenment, and the eightfold path.

Both the Śrāvaka and the Bodhisattva follow the five paths, but there are differences in practice and understanding that Mahāyāna schools discuss in various ways. Lama Mipham summarizes how the Bodhisattva sets forth, completely certain that he must find an alternative to samsaric existence and knowing that he must perfect extraordinary practices:

"By completely understanding the two kinds of selflessness in great depth, and by practicing the stages of the path, the perfections, and the inexhaustible Mahāyāna practices in all their vastness, he takes the path to heart. Having accomplished the unity of the depth of wisdom and the vastness of skillful means, having achieved the understanding of sameness that does not conceptualize in the manner of samsara and nirvana or faults and virtues, he attains the fruit of nonlocalizable nirvana—this is why he leaves home. This is what entering the excellent path of the Mahāyāna is like." (KJ 77b.4)

Although from the Mahāyāna perspective, the Śrāvaka perspective is limited, the achievements of those following the way of the Śrāvaka are extraordinary; some sources say the accomplished Arhat has completed eight of the ten stages of the Bodhisattva path. Moreover, the teachings of the Śravakayāna form the basic foundation for all forms of Buddhist study and practice.

Lama Mipham explains that it is essential to refute the philosophical system that is based on a smaller vision and an orientation toward self-benefit, and so takes a partial ground, path, and goal to be the whole truth. But since the Śrāvaka path of practice and the liberations are genuine, these teachings are not to be discarded by the Bodhisattvayāna, but are commonly accepted as necessary for completing the higher stages. (GTD 11b.3)

CHAPTER THIRTY-EIGHT

Path of Preparation

The path is entered by beginning the three trainings. The way of the Śrāvaka commences with taking formal vows. Disillusioned with the immensity of the sufferings of samsara, the Śrāvaka accepts the discipline of a monk or nun and begins training in morality. Declaring one's intention to renounce the causes of suffering, one takes the medicine of the path, which is the antidote for the disease of suffering.

Twelve Practices

The Śrāvaka way of life is characterized by careful observance of the Vinaya rules and by twelve ways of acting that are excellent examples of renunciation. The Visuddhimagga devotes an entire chapter to these ascetic practices which perfect the special quality of being content with few material goods. (VM II)

The twelve ways of acting are: wearing clothes that have been discarded by others, owning only three robes, wearing felt or wool, begging for food, eating only once a day, eating moderately, remaining isolated, dwelling at the foot of trees, staying in exposed places, staying in cemeteries, sleeping sitting up, and staying wherever one happens to be.

Subjects of Contemplation

Training in meditative concentration begins with practices that calm and focus body and mind. Then gross attachments are removed by contemplating ugliness and by mindfulness of breathing. The Visuddhimagga gives forty different subjects of contemplation: ten kasinas, ten kinds of foulness, ten recollections, four immeasurables, four formless absorptions, one perception, and one defining.

The ten kasinas are objects constructed to represent the four elements—earth, water, fire, wind; the four colors—blue, yellow, red, white; and light and space.

The ten kinds of foulness are various stages of decay of the human body, such as disintegrating corpse and skeleton. Concentration on these especially develops the ability to curb desire.

The ten recollections are of the Buddha, Dharma, Sangha, the recollection of virtue, generosity, deities, mindfulness of death, mindfulness of the body, mindfulness of breathing, and recollection of peace. Meditation on these develops not only concentration but wisdom.

The four immeasurables are loving kindness, compassion, sympathetic joy, and equanimity. Meditation on these develops many qualities and special powers as well as concentration.

The four formless absorptions are the last four levels of meditation known as boundless space, boundless consciousness, nothingness, and neither perception nor nonperception.

One perception is the perception of the repulsiveness of food and nourishment. This type of meditation breaks the fascination with sense desires.

One defining means defining the four elements. This type of practice sees all the substances of the body as a collection of the elements.

To train properly in concentration one must work with a suitable subject. Not all of the forty are effective for everyone. The Visuddhimagga gives six types of temperaments: greedy, hateful, deluded, faithful, intelligent, and speculative, and explains in detail how to recognize each type and which subjects are best for each type of individual. (VM III:74ff)

For a person of greedy temperament, contemplation on the ten kinds of foulness and recollection of the body are eleven appropriate subjects. For one of hateful temperament, contemplation of the four immeasurables and four colored kasinas are eight appropriate subjects. For one of deluded temperament and for one of speculative temperament, mindfulness of breathing is the most suitable subject. The first six recollections are suitable for one of faithful temperament. One with intelligent temperament should use the mindfulness of death, recollection of peace, the one defining, and the one perception. The remaining kasinas and the formless absorptions are suitable for individuals of any temperament. (VM III:121)

Four Foundations for Mindfulness

Having developed concentration through the subjects of contemplation, the Śrāvaka begins training in wisdom by focusing on the four foundations of mindfulness: body, feeling, mind, and dharmas. The four mindfulnesses are taught to oppose the four errors: belief that our ordinary experience is pure, that it brings happiness, that it is permanent, and that it is associated with a self. The four mindfulnesses are the first set of practices among the wings of enlightenment.

The Arthaviniścaya Sūtra explains that one contemplates the body, feelings, mind, and dharmas internally, externally, and both internally and externally. The practice is undertaken with a mind that is clearly conscious, ardent, mindful, and free of both covetousness and dejection. (AVS XIII)

The Mahāsatipaṭṭhāna Sutta explains that the mindfulness of dharmas includes the five hindrances that obstruct the three trainings, the five skandhas, the six organ āyatanas, the seven branches of enlightenment, and the four noble truths. (DN XXII)

The four mindfulnesses are based on prajñā, the discernment of dharmas. This discernment develops in the fourth mindfulness into recognizing that all things are impermanent, suffering, empty, and not-self, and this understanding leads directly to the analysis of the four truths on the path of linking. (AKB VI:15–16)

Bodhisattva Path of Preparation

Lama Mipham explains how the Bodhisattva enters the path of preparation: "Arising from the power of the inner Buddha nature and from an ocean of faith, comes the heartfelt decision to set out towards the complete and perfect enlightenment of the Buddha for the sake of benefiting all sentient beings. Like entering the ocean, he plunges in, wishing to purify, ripen, and bring to completion the potential for enlightenment in himself and all others over countless periods of time." (KJ 77b.3)

To purify the emotions, the Bodhisattva practices antidotes to attachment, aversion, confusion, pride, and conceptualizing. If attachment is strong, the focus is the thirty-six impure things, the nine unpleasant things, and special meditations on the skeleton. If aversion is strong, the focus is on loving kindness; if confusion is strong, the focus is on the meaning of interdependent co-operation; if pride is strong, the focus is on the divisions of the various realms and understanding one's place within the many worlds of existence; if conceptualizing is strong, the focus is on following the breath.

With instruction from a Mahāyāna master, one can learn how to work skillfully with emotional energy without repressing it. The Mahāyāna possesses innumerable ways of working with emotionality, using, for example, counteragents such as the four immeasurables, penetrating the delusive aspects of emotion, and refining the emotional energies. (KJ 62a.5, KB I:VII)

The Mahāyāna practice of the mindfulnesses has a different focus than the Śrāvakayāna practice. While the Śrāvakas focus mainly on their own bodies, the Bodhisattvas focus on their own and other's bodies. In mindfulness of the body, Śrāvakas focus on the truth of suffering, while the followers of the Bodhisattva path focus on how conventionally the body is like an illusion and how ultimately it is free from all extremes: permanent/impermanent, suffering/not suffering, self/no-self, empty/not-empty. Lama Mipham explains how this practice culminates: "The mindfulness practice of the Bodhisattva settles into the realm of reality through nonconceptual primordial wisdom." (KJ 87a.4)

Mahāyāna texts abound in examples of Bodhisattva preparatory practices such as developing the roots of virtue, stimulating courage, practicing refined forms of restraint, and zealous study of the Mahāyāna teachings. (MSG III:1–6)

CHAPTER THIRTY-NINE

Path of Linking

From the knowledge that develops from the practice of the four mindfulnesses on the path of preparation there arise four further levels of understanding called the path of linking. These four levels of understanding connect the preparation stage with the path of seeing. (AKB VI:16–19c)

The fourth of the four mindfulnesses, mindfulness of dharmas, leads directly to a focus on the four truths. Each of the four truths has four distinctive aspects, making sixteen aspects in all. These sixteen aspects are the major focus of all four levels of the path of linking.

The four levels of the path of linking are: heat, summit, patience, and supreme worldly dharmas. In proceeding from level to level, knowledge develops, then begins to "burn" brightly, spreading like a fire that consumes ignorance.

The level of heat develops through weak, medium, and strong stages up to the point where the summit arises. After the summit there arises the third level, patience, in which the practitioner opens to knowledge. Patience is called an acquiescence, agreement, or receptivity. A fourth level, supreme worldly dharmas, connects directly to the path of seeing. These four levels are also known as the levels that bring certainty (nirvedhabhāgīya), where doubts are abandoned and certainty is gained. The Abhidharmakoṣabhāṣya explains: "Nirvedha signifies definitively known, the noble path. Through it, the truths are distinguished, and doubts are abandoned." These four levels arise not from the wisdom based on hearing and reflecting, but from wisdom arising out of meditative practice. (AKB VI:20a–b)

Sixteen Aspects of the Truths

The sixteen aspects are described as follows: Suffering, impermanence, emptiness, and selflessness are the four aspects of the truth of suffering. One Vaibhāṣika tradition of commentary explains that focusing on suffering means to note the painful nature of experience. Focusing on impermanence means seeing how things arise in dependence on causes. Focusing on emptiness means to see that experience actually opposes the belief of anything belonging to a self. Focusing on selflessness is to see how experience opposes a belief in a self.

A commentary by Saṁghabhadra explains that meditation on the four aspects of suffering, impermanence, emptiness, and selflessness cures individuals who hold to the four errors: that within experience can be found bliss, permanence, something belonging to a self, and the existence of a self.

Cause, arising, appearance, and condition are the four aspects of the truth of origination. Focusing on the cause is to understand the cause as a seed that will grow. Focusing on arising is to see what immediately arises from the seed. Focusing on appearance is to see the series of seed, shoot, and stalk. Focusing on condition is to understand the surrounding conditions just as the surrounding conditions for the creation of a jug include clay, sticks, potter's wheel, twine, water, etc.

Saṁghabhadra explains that meditation on the aspects of cause and arising counters the view that there is only one cause; cause is a complex of causes and conditions. The aspect of appearance counters the view that there is evolution of something existent or that something existent transforms itself. The aspect of condition counters the view that the world is created by a creator.

Cessation, quiescence, excellence, and renunciation of samsara are the four aspects of the truth of cessation. Focusing on cessation is to understand the destruction of impurity. Focusing on quiescence is to see the destruction of the three fires of craving, anger, and delusion. Focusing on excellence is to realize the absence of all pain. Focusing on renunciation is to understand that all the causes of pain are disconnected.

Saṁghabhadra explains that the aspect of cessation counters the view that deliverance is not really possible. The aspect of quiescence counters the view that deliverance would still include some type of suffering. The aspect of excellence counters the view that happiness obtained in the worldly practices of meditation is the ultimate bliss. The aspect of renunciation counters the view that deliverance is subject to disappearing.

Path, method, attainment, and liberation are the four aspects of the truth of the path. Focusing on the path means to understand that there is traversing toward something (nirvana). Focusing on the method is to know there are resources and means. Focusing on the attainment is to realize that there is accurate and correct achievement. Focusing on liberation is to understand passing beyond in a definitive way.

Saṁghabhadra explains that the aspect of path opposes the view that there is no path to follow. The aspect of method opposes the view that a false path is the right path. The aspect of attainment opposes the view that there is some other path that will bring true liberation. The aspect of liberation opposes the view that the path is subject to disappearance. (AKB VII:13)

The Śrāvaka Path of Linking and the Thirty-Seven Wings

The wings of enlightenment that come into play during the path of linking are the four genuine restraints, the four bases for supernatural powers, the five spiritual faculties, and the five spiritual powers. (AKB VI:67b–70)

On the first level of the path of linking (the heat), there is an increase of energy due to the practice of the four genuine restraints. The principle of progress is that one's resources are now devoted toward the positive and are no longer wasted in the negative. The four genuine restraints offer a clear methodical approach in four steps: not to allow nonvirtue that has not yet arisen to arise; to abandon nonvirtuous acts and qualities that have already arisen; to develop virtuous acts and qualities that have not yet arisen; and to maintain, stabilize, and expand virtue that has already arisen.

On the second level of the path of linking (the summit), the supernatural powers are developed through the practice of samādhi, and these become the support for success along the path. The four bases for these supernatural powers are samādhis developed by cultivating willingness, effort, intention, and analysis. Due to the operation of these supernatural powers, the roots of good that one obtains cannot be lost. (AKB VI:70,VII:42a–d)

In the third level of the path of linking (patience), the five spiritual faculties predominate: faith, effort, mindfulness, samādhi, and prajñā. One who has reached this level can no longer fall into lower realms of rebirth, for the nonvirtuous actions and emotional afflictions that lead to those realms have been abandoned. (AKB VI:23b)

At the fourth level of the path of linking (the supreme worldly dharmas), these same faculties have become powers that overcome all obstacles that prevent linking to the path of seeing.

Bodhisattva Path of Linking

The Mahāyāna considers these stages differently, putting the four mindfulnesses, the four genuine restraints, and the four bases for supernatural powers on the path of preparation as lower, middle, and high levels (KJ 59b.1) The path of linking relies especially upon the five spiritual faculties and the five spiritual powers.

The Bodhisattva practice of the four genuine restraints differs from the Śrāvaka practice. The Bodhisattva transforms especially his attitude and orientation so that it does not become limited and small-minded; he transforms confusion and hesitation so that his faith grows boundlessly; he transforms any holding on to beliefs in "me and mine;" and he transforms the patterns of discrimination so that he does not foster dualistic conceptions. (MSG III:6)

Mahāyāna texts describe the path of linking in terms of the development of samādhi and prajñā that completely penetrate the illusion of self-nature for any element of reality. The Abhidharmasamuccaya and the Mahāyānasaṁgraha explain that on each of these four levels of the path of linking the Bodhisattva is practicing distinctive samādhis of light and brilliance (AS II, MSG III:13). Within these samādhis, the Bodhisattva's wisdom shines brightly and grows until it penetrates the fog of illusion.

On the path of linking, the Bodhisattva's commitment to reaching the full enlightenment of a Buddha is like a blazing fire. Intent on developing immaculate wisdom and unimaginable powers derived from samādhi, the Bodhisattva works energetically and tirelessly to be able to be of benefit to all beings. (PP II)

CHAPTER FORTY

Path of Seeing

One who enters the path of seeing leaves behind the quality of being an ordinary person and becomes a noble person. Some schools say this occurs just before the path of seeing is entered, while others say the decisive point is just after entering the path of seeing.

Moments of the Path

The actual insight into the four truths is direct perception. This insight takes place in sixteen successive moments. These sixteen moments of the path of seeing are the first completely pure moments of the path; all the moments of insight belonging to the previous levels are impure.

From out of the practice of the supreme worldly dharmas there arises a patience that is no longer impure but pure. This patience is an opening to the reality of suffering where the resistance to the truth is dropped (moment one). Immediately thereafter arises the actual Dharma knowledge of suffering in the realm of desire (moment two).

This Dharma knowledge is followed by another, consecutive moment of patience (moment three), which is directed toward the reality of suffering in the form and formless realms; immediately thereafter arises the Dharma knowledge of suffering in those realms. This is the first pure Dharma knowledge (moment four).

These four moments take place in regard to each of the four truths, making sixteen in all. The patience in regard to knowledge of the origin of suffering in the desire realm (moment five) is followed by Dharma knowledge of the origin of suffering in the desire realm (moment six). A consecutive patience in regard to knowledge of the origin of suffering in the two higher realms (moment seven) is followed by Dharma knowledge of the origin of suffering in the two higher realms (moment eight).

The patience in regard to knowledge of the extinction of suffering in the desire realm (moment nine) is followed by the Dharma knowledge of the extinction of suffering in that realm (moment ten). A consecutive patience in regard to the knowledge of the extinction of suffering in the two higher realms (moment eleven) is followed by Dharma knowledge of the extinction of suffering in the two higher realms (moment twelve).

The patience in regard to knowledge of the path which opposes suffering in the desire realm (moment thirteen) is followed by the Dharma knowledge of that path (moment fourteen). A consecutive patience in regard to knowledge of the path in the two higher realms (moment fifteen) is followed by the Dharma knowledge of the path bearing on those two realms (moment sixteen).

Sixteenth Moment

There are numerous views among the early Abhidharma masters about the exact dynamics of the path of seeing and the path of meditation. One view is that the first fifteen moments belong to the path of seeing, while the sixteenth moment is the path of meditation. (AKB VI:28c–d) The first pure knowledge of the truths is realized in the fifteen moments, and the power of truth actively cuts off emotional afflictions that can be removed by seeing. The sixteenth moment is meditation on the truths that have now all been seen; this leads into the path of meditation. The path of meditation counters each of the remaining afflictions that can only be removed by meditation.

As the true nature of reality becomes clear on the path of seeing, the seven branches of enlightenment come into play. These seven branches or aspects are mindfulness, investigation, effort, joy, alert ease, samādhi, and equanimity. Although these aspects have existed before, now they operate in a pure fashion for the first time. (AKB VI:71a–b)

Bodhisattva Path of Seeing

The Bodhisattva entering the path of seeing steps onto the first stage of the Bodhisattva path. The first two of the five paths, the path of preparation and the path of linking, are preliminary to entering the Bodhisattva path proper. While the first stage of the Bodhisattva path begins on the path of seeing, the second stage through the tenth stage of the Bodhisattva path belong to the path of meditation. The path of no more learning is the Buddha stage.

The Mahāyānasūtrālaṁkāra says of the entrance to the path of seeing: "The Bodhisattva obtains then a consciousness which is free from the grip of duality, transworldly, unsurpassable, without differentiation, and spotless." (MSA XIV:28)

Like the Śrāvaka, the Bodhisattva practices the seven branches of enlightenment at this stage. The Mahāyānasūtrālaṁkāra explains: "Like a Cakravartin king surrounded by the seven jewels, the Bodhisattva with his virtuous qualities is always surrounded by the seven branches of enlightenment." (MSA XVIII:62)

Lama Mipham describes the Bodhisattva's understanding of the four noble truths on the path of seeing: The Bodhisattva sees the emptiness of all dharmas, completely free from all conceptual elaboration, with spotless wisdom and patience purified of all passion. He has the eye of the Dharma. From this knowledge arise faith, discipline, and all the virtuous qualities of the Noble Ones. (AS II, KJ 60b.2)

The Mahāyānasūtrālaṁkāra describes one way of understanding the transformation that takes place as the Bodhisattva enters the path of seeing. When the Bodhisattva sees the selflessness of all dharmas on the path of seeing, he sees the sameness of all dharmas, and thus he regards all beings as the same as himself. Free of the limited view of self that has no meaning, he instead comes to a great view of self that has great meaning: that self and others are the same. (MSA XIV:31–41)

CHAPTER FORTY-ONE

Worldly Path of Meditation

The path of meditation is the fourth of the five paths, comprising numerous stages of meditative concentration. This path has two aspects: the worldly path, which includes various non-Buddhist approaches to liberation from suffering, and the transworldly path, which is the path of the Buddha.

Worldly paths teach one to enter the various levels of meditation but do not join this meditation to the knowledge of the four truths. Thus, the worldly approach does not lead to complete liberation from suffering, though it can produce some degree of freedom from emotionality and supernatural powers.

The worldly path of meditation can be regarded as a gradual and temporary release from each of the three realms. One who learns how to enter the first dhyāna can temporarily abandon the desire realm. Likewise, one who learns how to enter the first formless absorption can temporarily escape the form realm. But after progressing through the four formless absorptions, the practitioner reaches the limit of the three realms. Breaking through this limit requires insight into the four truths. (AKB V:6a–d,68a–c)

Numerous yogic techniques were practiced extensively in ancient India at the time of the Buddha. The Buddha examined each of the systems that used these techniques, following their instructions and perfecting the practices. Passing through all the stages of the form realm and entering into the four absorptions of the formless realm, the Buddha experienced wonders and marvels, hundreds of samādhis, and the supernatural powers that arise from the practice of deep samādhi.

In the Lalitavistara the Buddha explains that these practices do not lead to distaste for the world, the absence of desire, or the cessation of rebirth; they do not lead to superior knowledge, nirvana, or perfect enlightenment. (LAL XVII)

Though the various stages of samādhi are not sufficient in themselves, they are important aids to liberation when linked to knowledge of the four truths. In the Lalitavistara the Buddha explains that calming desire is essential before the highest wisdom can manifest. One tormented by desire who pursues the highest truth is like a man trying to make a fire with green wood. For one who has calmed desire, wisdom emerges just as flames burst forth easily from dry wood. The union of samādhi and prajñā is like a spreading fire that consumes all ignorance. (LAL XVII)

The development of prajñā, through hearing, reflecting, and meditation, is supported by the ability to remain focused and concentrate deeply. At deeper stages of samādhi, the mind begins to function differently, allowing a different quality of knowledge to emerge. The Abhidharmakoṣabhāṣya explains: "Dhyāna is the application of a pure mind to a single object . . . The nature of meditative concentration (dhyāna) is concentration (samādhi)." And further: "By reason of dhyāna the ascetic is concentrated and capable of upanidhyāna, truly knowing. As it is said in the Sūtra, 'He who is concentrated knows truly.'" (AKB VIII:1d–e)

All minds possess concentration, which is a mental event among the ten omnipresent, but weak samādhi is not fully one-pointed. The preparation for the first stage of dhyāna is a gradual stabilizing of the mind through distinct levels of concentration until it becomes totally focused on its object in a one-pointed manner. This completely concentrated attention is the threshold of the first stage of dhyāna.

Stages of Dhyāna

On the worldly path of meditation, one enters into the first stage of dhyāna by noting the defects of the existing state of mind and contemplating the peacefulness of the first stage of dhyāna. One moves through each stage of dhyāna, abandoning the lower sphere by recognizing it as coarser and the higher state as more refined. This process develops not from a focus on the four truths but from a focus on the coarser-finer spectrum of experience.

Each of the four stages of meditative concentration in the dhyānas has a different character. All stages are characterized by concentration (samādhi). In addition, the first stage of meditative concentration is characterized by four factors: investigation, analysis, mental happiness, and bliss. The second stage possesses only mental happiness and bliss; the third stage possesses only bliss, which is abandoned on the fourth stage.

The Abhidharmakoṣabhāṣya explains how investigation (and analysis), mental happiness, and bliss are gradually eliminated: "The second, third, and fourth dhyānas are characterized by the successive abandoning of each of these three parts." (AKB VIII:2b)

If the four stages of dhyāna are not impure, they contain in addition several other important factors. The second stage contains the internal purity of faith. Internal purity of faith arises when the movement and agitation connected with investigation and analysis come to an end. In moving out of the first stage into the second stage, the practitioner has seen that the lower levels can be abandoned and that the higher levels are more worthy. This is called faith.

The third stage contains equanimity, a joy that is free from movement toward any object; mindfulness that protects this equanimity; and awareness that is associated with this mindfulness. The fourth stage contains pure mindfulness, pure equanimity, and the feeling of neither suffering nor happiness.

The four stages of meditative concentration have eight faults which disturb them. In the beginning investigation and analysis produce agitation; when investigation and analysis are set aside, there remain the disturbances of mental unhappiness and physical discomfort and the disturbances of breathing in and breathing out. In the third stage, mental happiness actually becomes a disturbance. When mental happiness is set aside, one enters the fourth stage, which contains no faults. Like a lamp in a protected place, concentration is unwavering. (AKB VIII:2,7,8,9)

Stages of Absorption

Like the four meditative concentrations, the four formless meditations or absorptions are stages of a progressive concentration that proceeds to abandon each lower sphere and move toward the higher. The sphere of boundless space is entered by letting go of the fourth stage of meditative concentration. This is abandoned for the sphere of boundless consciousness, which in turn is abandoned for the sphere of nothingness, and then the sphere of neither perception nor nonperception. The first three are named for the objects one considers in the first three abodes. In the fourth abode, there is scarcely any conceptuality remaining, and thus it is named the sphere of neither perception nor nonperception. The formless meditations do not contain the various shifting factors of the four dhyānas. By practicing the dhyānas and absorptions, and developing various strengths (small, medium, great), one can gain rebirth in the form and formless realms. (AKB VIII:2c–e, AS II, KJ 63a.2)

Nine Levels

The nine levels are the desire realm, the four stages of dhyāna, and the four formless absorptions. Together these constitute all of samsaric existence. These are the realms where beings can take birth and so are called levels of existence (upapatti); they are also realms of meditation, and so are called levels of absorption (samāpatti). (AKB VI:48a–b, VIII:1a)

Two Absorptions

Two special absorptions are the absorption of extinction, which is a cessation of feeling and perception, and the absorption of nonperception. These are both states where the mind's functioning is arrested. Followers of the Buddha do not cultivate the absorption of nonperception, which is regarded by some traditions of yoga as deliverance. This state is considered an abode within the fourth stage of meditation where meditators can stay for a long time without making real progress toward liberation.

The Abhidharmakoṣabhāṣya says: "The Noble Ones consider this absorption a precipice, a calamity, and do not value entering it. On the contrary, ordinary people identify nonperception with true deliverance; they have no idea of 'going out' from it. Hence they cultivate the absorption that leads to it." (AKB II:42)

The Śrāvakas consider the absorption of extinction a temporary tranquility similar to nirvana. It is found at the highest level of the formless realm, at the peak of the sphere of neither perception nor nonperception. The one who has practiced this absorption can obtain nirvana in his current existence. The Abhidharmakoṣabhāṣya explains: "It is produced only by the Noble Ones, not by ordinary people. These latter cannot produce it because they fear annihilation and because this absorption can only be produced through the power of the path; in fact it is the ascetic who has seen nirvana who is determined to obtain it." (AKB II:43, VI:43c–d)

Four Immeasurables

Qualities that can be developed by dwelling in these stages of meditation and absorption include the four immeasurables: loving kindness, compassion, sympathetic joy, and equanimity. They are called immeasurable because they apply to an immeasurable number of beings, create immeasurable merit, and produce immeasurably positive results. (AKB VIII:29a–31d)

There is a preparatory stage of the four immeasurables that can be practiced by beginners, but these are said only to "resemble" the real immeasurables; the real immeasurables are practiced in various stages of dhyāna. The immeasurables disrupt but do not remove conflicting emotions. The Śrāvaka practices these four after the emotional afflictions of the desire realm have been abandoned.

Loving kindness and compassion are defined as the absence of hatred. Sympathetic joy is intense satisfaction, and equanimity is basically the absence of desire. The objects of these meditations are the happiness, unhappiness, and joy of all beings. Thinking that beings are happy, the practitioner enters into loving kindness; thinking that they are suffering, he enters into compassion; thinking that they are joyful, he enters into joyfulness; thinking that beings are equally worthy, he enters the meditation of equanimity.

Five Superknowledges

From the practice of meditation, there develop five superknowledges: divine hearing or clairaudience that hears sounds both near and far, clairvoyance or divine sight that knows the death and rebirth of all beings, memory of past existences, knowledge of the mind of others, and supernatural abilities such as flying through space or becoming invisible. A sixth superknowledge belongs to the Arhat.

The Abhidharmakoṣabhāṣya discusses at length the types of meditations and absorptions and how the practitioner moves between the stages, gaining mastery. It explains which meditations are undefiled and transworldly, which are pure, which are associated with emotional afflictions, and which counter emotional afflictions. (AKB VIII)

Easy Route

The stages of meditative concentration may be cultivated at the early stages of the five paths. This approach is called the "easy route" because it joins and balances calm and insight and allows the whole path to be traversed in a smooth fashion. In contrast, the path of preparation and the path of linking can be practiced without complete training in meditative stabilization and absorptions. Progress is then more difficult and the practitioner will have to work harder and longer on the path of meditation. (AKB VI:66a–d)

CHAPTER FORTY-TWO

Transworldly Path of Meditation

The transworldly path begins with the path of seeing and the direct personal insight into the four truths. The transworldly path is called "uncorrupt" for it alone does not lead to emotional instability. All things connected with the worldly path remain corrupt, even positive mental events and virtuous actions and practices. Until the four truths are seen, even virtue tends toward a kind of instability.

The Abhidharmakoṣabhāṣya says: "The defilements are removed through seeing the four truths and through meditation." (AKB VI:1a–b)

After progressing through the path of seeing, the Śrāvaka enters the transworldly path of meditation, using the stages of meditation to focus again and again on the four truths. In this way the Śrāvaka removes the afflictions that can be abandoned by meditation. (AKB VI:28c–31b,47c–49c) As emotional afflictions drop away, the eightfold path can be purely practiced for the first time. (AKB VI:71a–b)

Removing Afflictions by Meditation

The afflictions that can be removed by meditation are classified into categories of weak, medium, and strong: weak-weak, weak-medium, weak-strong; medium-weak, medium-medium, medium-strong; strong-weak, strong-medium, and strong-strong. Afflictions in these nine categories exist in relation to the desire realm, to the four levels of the form realm, and to the four levels of the formless realm. This gives nine levels where the mind might be abiding, with nine strengths in each, or eighty-one tendencies all together. The most gross and obvious are easier to remove; the weakest, most subtle defilements are the most difficult to remove and are abandoned last.

Thus the path of meditation is made up of three paths. The weak path is powerful enough to remove the strong and obvious afflictions. The strong path is what is required for removing the most subtle, weakest afflictions. The middling path is for removing the afflictions of medium strength. (AKB VI:33b–d)

The Abhidharmakoṣabhāṣya explains that when one washes a piece of cloth, the darker stains are washed out first, while the most subtle stains persist the longest. In the same way, a great darkness is dramatically illuminated with a small glimmer of light; to dispel the small darkness of a shadow requires a very bright light.

Four Courses

There are four courses outlined in the texts: one that is difficult for those of slow intelligence; one that is difficult for those of swift intelligence; one that is easy for those of slow intelligence; and one that is easy for those of swift intelligence. (AKB VI:66a–d, AVS XI, AS II)

For one with weak higher faculties (the five spiritual faculties of faith, effort, mindfulness, concentration, and wisdom) and intense emotionality, every moment is filled with suffering. Such a one reaches the destruction of emotional afflictions very slowly. One with sharp spiritual faculties who is intensely emotional can destroy the emotional afflictions quite quickly, but the course is difficult and painful. One almost free of emotional affliction but with sluggish spiritual faculties destroys the emotional afflictions slowly, but in a state of ease without great suffering. The one who is largely free from emotionality and also possesses sharp spiritual faculties will progress swiftly and easily toward the destruction of afflictions with little suffering.

Entering the Stream

If a Śrāvaka has experienced the fifteen moments of the path of seeing, but not yet removed the afflictions that can be removed by meditation, he is a candidate for the state known as Stream Enterer; in the sixteenth moment of the path of seeing, he becomes a Stream Enterer. An individual reaching this stage will be reborn no more than seven times.

If through the practice of the worldly path, the Śrāvaka who is experiencing the path of seeing has already removed certain afflictions and mastered certain stages of meditation, he is a candidate for the state of Once Returner, which he achieves upon the sixteenth moment. If even additional categories of afflictions are removed beforehand, the Śrāvaka is a candidate for the state of Nonreturner which he reaches in the sixteenth moment.

The Once Returner returns only one more time to samsara. The Nonreturner may obtain nirvana in the following ways: in the interval between this life and the next; at the point of rebirth because the path has become spontaneous and powerful; or taking rebirth, he makes strong efforts; or taking rebirth, he only needs to make a small effort; or taking rebirth in the form or formless realms, he obtains nirvana from there. (AKB VI:29–39)

Diamond Concentration

The ninth category of afflictions, the final bond to samsara, is finally broken by a meditative absorption called Vajropamasamādhi, the highest absorption, which is like a diamond. This state can be produced from within any one of nine stages of meditation. At the moment that the Noble One has destroyed the ninth category, there arises the knowledge of destruction (kṣayajñāna). Now the individual is an Arhat, one who has no more to learn: He does not need to attain another state or to continue to apply the three trainings. (AKB VI:44d)

Eight Noble Ones

The Stream Enterer, the Once Returner, the Nonreturner, and the Arhat, together with the candidates for each of these four, are known as the eight Noble Ones. Only the eighth, the Arhat, has achieved the final path of no more learning.

After the knowledge of destruction has arisen, and the individual has become an Arhat, there may also arise the knowledge of the future nonarising of the defilements. This only occurs if the Arhat is "immovable," and can no longer regress from the state of Arhat. (AKB VI:44d,56a) The knowledge of destruction and the knowledge of nonarising are called bodhi, awakening. By the first knowledge, one knows that the work has been done; by the second knowledge one knows that there is nothing more to be accomplished. By these two knowledges, one abandons ignorance. (AKB VI:67a–b).

The thirty-seven wings that assist and support bodhi, as mentioned above, are the four mindfulnesses, the four genuine restraints, the four bases for supernatural power, the five spiritual faculties, the five spiritual powers, the seven branches of enlightenment, and the eightfold noble path. (AKB VI:67b–70)

Bodhisattva Path of Meditation

The path of meditation begins with the second stage of the Bodhisattva Path, the Immaculate, and includes the remaining stages up through the tenth stage. After progressing through the path of seeing, the Bodhisattva soars on the two wings of the Mahāyāna, wisdom and compassion. Uniting penetrating knowledge of the emptiness of all dharmas with the practices of profound samādhi, the Bodhisattva enters innumerable beautiful samādhis described in many Mahāyāna Sūtras. (AS II, KJ 63b.3) The Bodhisattva often utilizes the fourth dhyāna, for the superknowledges are active there. The fourth dhyāna is deeply calm and also clear and penetrating. The higher formless absorptions become ever more calm but are not as clear as the fourth dhyāna.

ŚRĀVAKA PATH

Path of Preparation
Four Foundations of Mindfulness

Path of Linking
Heat: Four Genuine Restraints
Summit: Four Bases of Supernatural Powers
Patience: Five Spiritual Faculties
Supreme Worldly Dharmas: Five Spiritual Powers

Path of Seeing
Seven Branches of Enlightenment

Path of Meditation
Eightfold Path

Path of No More Learning

BODHISATTVA PATH

Path of Preparation
Four Foundations of Mindfulness
Four Genuine Restraints
Four Bases of Supernatural Powers

Path of Linking
Five Spiritual Faculties
Five Spiritual Powers

Path of Seeing
Seven Branches of Enlightenment

Path of Meditation
Eightfold Path

Path of No More Learning

The Mahāyānasaṁgraha explains: "How does the Bodhisattva practice the path of meditation? In the ten Bodhisattva stages that conform with the descriptions in the texts and which are the summation of all the Sūtras, the Bodhisattva practices for thousands of kalpas by means of calm and transworldly insight. This knowledge bears upon the characteristics of all dharmas without conceptualizing, while there also arises a posterior (conceptualized) knowledge. Through this practice his body and mind are transformed, and then he makes efforts to obtain the three bodies of a Buddha." (MSG III:14)

The follower of the Mahāyāna eventually reaches the path of no more learning, which is the perfect enlightenment of a Buddha. Longchenpa explains:"When you have come to the end of the cultivation of these four stages of learning comprising the thirty-seven wings that lead to awakening, you pass into nirvana that is not localized anywhere, the path of no more learning. There has never been anyone who has become a Buddha without having traveled these paths and traversed these stages." (KB I:XI)

Further Readings

Mahāsatipaṭṭhāna Sutta, Digha Nikāya XXII. On the foundations of mindfulness.

Sāmaññaphala Sutta, Digha Nikāya II. Poetic descriptions of the stages of meditation.

Phyag-chen-zla-ba'i-'od-zer, by Dwags-po bKra-shis-rnam-rgyal. *Mahāmudrā,* book I, chapters I–IV. On calm and insight.

Dam-chos-yid-bzhin-nor-bu-thar-pa-rin-po-che'i-rgyan, by sGam-po-pa. *The Jewel Ornament of Liberation,* chapter XVIII. Overview of the five paths.

Footsteps on the Diamond Path (Crystal Mirror I–III), pp. 126–141. Lama Mipham's various meditation instructions.

SECTION EIGHTEEN

Diamond Light

CHAPTER FORTY-THREE

Expressions and Preconceptions

After the enlightenment, the Lord Buddha, the Fully Awakened One, dwelled in complete silence for seven weeks. At last, considering whether to attempt expressing the inexpressible, he declared:

"My profound path goes against the current;
it is difficult to see.
Those blind with passion will not see it;
even hearing it they would gain no benefit."

But the king of the gods approached the Buddha and beseeched him in the name of all beings to teach:

"O Muni, you must open wide the door to immortality,
for they are ready to listen
to the immaculate Buddhadharma." (LAL XV)

The Enlightened One consented and began to teach, first at Deer Park in Sārnāth and then throughout India. Those who listened each heard the teachings according to his or her own inner understanding. Able to free themselves from the limitations of the ordinary discriminating mind, the Bodhisattvas alone were capable of perceiving the full implications of śūnyatā, knowledge of complete reality.

"Free from all spoken language, inexpressible, immeasurable, incomparable, incommensurable; it is like space. Not nihilistic, not eternalistic . . ." (LAL XV)

Finding the Right Words

The more subtle the knowledge, the more difficult it is to express in language. The successful transmission of the wisdom of the Buddha from one culture to another depends both on inner understanding and on the careful use of suitable words that lead the practitioner to understand what is "inexpressible."

When Buddhism was transmitted to Tibet, master translators who were also realized practitioners developed Tibetan terminology capable of expressing the full meaning of the original texts. They used terms with great precision, relying on their inner understanding, as well as on the commentaries passed down through the centuries. Knowing the different meanings possible at different stages of the path, they established a vocabulary capable of embracing the entire range of Buddhist thought.

The Western world has not yet developed the vocabulary to express many of the insights of Buddhism. Even our most suitable English words do not yet have the depth of associations needed to convey the full meaning of the traditional terms. Some English words that are now in use reverberate strongly with meanings derived from science, Christianity, or other dominant Western influences. Without experience in meditative practice or study of the canonical texts and commentaries, we hear only the common meaning of the word and make only the familiar associations.

Śūnyatā, for example, is often translated into English as "emptiness." Commonly accepted meanings for "empty" include containing nothing, not occupied or inhabited, unfrequented; null, lacking reality, substance, or value; hollow, devoid of sense, destitute of effect, idle, having no purpose or result. Synonyms for empty are vacant, vacuum, blank, and void. But none of these meanings tells us much about śūnyatā; in fact, they encourage preconceptions that can be deeply misleading. Like a sculptor refining a form by chipping away the stone, we must remove one preconception after another in order to glimpse the true meaning of śūnyatā. Preconceptions seem to reside at the basis of ordinary thinking as preestablished patterns upon which we unthinkingly rely. One such pattern, for example, involves notions of oneness, beginnings and endings, and cause and effect.

The One and the Many

For centuries the traditional Western way of understanding existence has been in terms of God as creator, the prime mover, and first cause. The existence of this creator explains existence or guarantees its reality.

Buddhism explains "existence" in terms of a multiplicity of causes. It can be argued that what is singular cannot be a cause. What is unitary is without relation, without distinctions, without causes, without other. How or why would one act?

Nāgārjuna explains in the Bodhicittavivaraṇa: "Why would an efficacious creator be dependent on something other than himself? He would of course produce things all at once. A creator who depends on something other than himself is neither eternal nor efficacious." (BCV 8)

Once the one acts, he is no longer one, for there is now, in addition to the one, the intention of the one, the mode of action of the one, and the result of this action. Other logical and existential difficulties quickly follow from this line of thought: Is the creation the same or different from the creator? How can the unchanging one be associated with the changing many? Is the creator perfect and the creation imperfect? We are now deeply in the midst of dualism and all its attendant difficulties.

No Beginning No Ending

The beginning of the beginning would be the first cause. If there is no singularity at the beginning of everything, then there is no beginning. If there is no beginning, there cannot be an end. Experience would have limits and rhythms, but these rhythms would have no source and no end-point.

According to Nāgārjuna: "The Great Ascetic said: The extreme limit of the past cannot be discerned. Samsara is without bounds; indeed there is no beginning and no ending of that. How could there be a middle to what has no before or after? It follows that past, future, and present do not obtain." (MMK XI:1–2)

Cause and Effect

If something has come about by itself, it would already exist and not need to "come about." If it came about through something completely other than itself, then anything could come from anything: A sprout could arise from a stone as well as from a seed.

If something comes about from both itself and from something other, there is contradiction: If it is produced from itself, it already exists; if it is produced from something else, it must be nonexistent at the time of its cause. Finally, something that is produced neither from itself nor from something else would be uncaused. If things were produced without causes, then they would randomly arise and experience would be chaos.

Nāgārjuna explains: "That which has been born cannot be born. Nor can that which is unborn be born. What is being born now, being partly born partly unborn, cannot be born either." (SST 5)

Not-Seeing

These brief observations suggest how it can be demonstrated logically that what we call "experience" cannot come about. It has never arisen; it has never ceased; it cannot be caused; it cannot begin or end. Still, we hold a view of existent things; more than that, we actually experience the world of things. What could the basis for this experience be? Do we simply invent it? Is experience self-validating, needing no basis?

Logic can show that experience cannot take place in the way that we believe it does. But we are not convinced. This not-seeing, this not-being-convinced is the guarantee of the reality of experiencing.

The Buddha taught that experience is like a dream. During a dream, experience appears to be taking place; stories are developing with beginnings and endings. If we awaken, the dream is not there. It is not even accurate to say it is nonexistent, as though it had once existed and now had ceased. From the perspective of waking knowledge, the dream is completely unborn.

Nor is it accurate to say we make up experience, as though mind or self were the cause. Mind, self, and subject are just stories within the dream.

Again, Nāgārjuna explains: "Just as a teacher by his magical powers formed a magical form, and this magical form formed again another magical form—just so the "one who forms" is himself formed magically." (MMK XVII:31)

No Basis

Our daily life brings us experiences characterized by differing degrees of confusion and delusion. For example, intense suffering creates a world of its own that dramatically shifts when suffering lightens. We step out of that dark heavy world into a very different world where our thoughts and feelings and even our senses operate in different patterns. Buddhist texts describe the experience of beings in the six different destinies as utterly different; what appears to a human as a glass of water is ambrosia to the gods, and filth to the hungry ghosts.

The variation in consciousness in relation to different types of meditative practice also demonstrates that what we call reality changes. The "reality" of the Buddha is not the same as the experience of the ordinary person. The reality of the Śrāvaka is different from the reality of the Bodhisattva. Passing through ten stages of the path, the Bodhisattva experiences distinct realities, each with different characteristics.

The question then arises: Which experience is the real one? We imagine that there must be a fundamental reality that somehow is differently perceived by different beings, perhaps due to different sense organs or different conditioning. But we want to find an ultimate basis, a firm foundation upholding the process of interpretation.

The Abhidharma tells us that the world of experience arises from karma and kleśa, but what is the ultimate source of these two? Nāgārjuna says: "Karma and kleśa arise from thought (kalpana, rnam-rtog); thought arises from conceptual elaboration (prapañca, spros-pa); conceptual elaboration comes to an end in śūnyatā." (MMK XVIII:5)

Discrimination and Interpretation

How does the mind make discriminations? Every language has different names for "blue." The word "blue" is just a pointer, but what is it pointing at? Where does "blue" come from? Labels are based on distinctions that separate out one "thing" from another "thing." We distinguish "blue" from all other colors: not-red, not-black, not-white, not-yellow. What remains is "blue." But where does the red of not-red come from? Red is also distinguished in the same way so that red is: not-blue, not-black, not-white, not-yellow.

The essence of distinguishing is negation. One must be able to say "is-not" in order to assert "is." Exist depends on not-exist. Is-not is the means to establish is. Each of these existents, however, depends on the negation of all those other than itself. Simple opposites are obviously interdependent: light and dark, high and low. High is not-low and low is not-high. But all distinctions are similarly created.

If we focus on distinguishing blue, we find blue. It seems to exist. As long as we temporarily ignore that the red of not-red is also created by making distinctions that refer back to blue, it appears that not-red is a solid witness for blue. But the discovery of blue is based on the discovery of red, which is based on the discovery of black, and so forth. There is no independent verification in the process of discrimination.

In the world of appearance things take turns verifying one another, and we do not notice the trick. There is no independent basis, and yet appearance has not disappeared. These distinctions appear to establish something but in truth, establish nothing. Interdependent co-operation is appearance and emptiness.

CHAPTER FORTY-FOUR

Light of Understanding

For ordinary perception grounded in duality, existence and nonexistence are mutually exclusive and contradictory. When the Heart Sūtra says "Form is emptiness," we imagine emptiness is accepted while form is rejected. Removing one term and pinning down the other term, we avoid contradiction, which is how we reach an understanding. Since ordinary perception does not experience emptiness in form, we may imagine that emptiness is other than form, somewhere else, perhaps beyond form. But the Sūtra says there is not something other than form that is empty. Emptiness is nowhere else than in the form. The two are inseparable, but not in the way that two horns are together on the head of an ox; and not in the way that two strands of rope are intertwined; and not even as two sides of a single coin, for there are no sides in complete reality. The relationship of form and emptiness is even closer than that.

Nāgārjuna points out: "As sweetness is the very nature of sugar and hotness that of fire, we maintain that the nature of things is śūnyatā." (BCV 57)

Nothing and Something

How can the nature of something be nothing? This seems to be saying white is black; and moreover, the very essence of white is black. Our ordinary way of understanding "nothing" is as the opposite of "something," as the absence of something: There used to be something present, but it is no longer there. Something and nothing define each other by mutual exclusion. Śūnyatā does have meaning, but it does not mean nothing, for the distinction-making that establishes something and nothing belongs to the realm of convention and imagination.

Samsaric System

Based on this interdependent verification, a vocabulary develops together with a logic and a narrative. All these discriminations exist within the samsaric system.

Nāgārjuna explains: "Just as pleasure and pain depending on an object in a dream do not have a real object, so neither that which arises in interdependent co-operation nor that upon which it arises in dependence exists." (SST 14)

Projections project each other, thoughts confirm one another, constituting a patterning that includes the operation of the senses, feelings, memories, and logic.

Within this closed samsaric system, the self seems established as the central controller governing the circuits of the system. This illusion is sustained by the completeness with which the patterns of projection occupy the mind. The patterns instantly proliferate to fill the space of the mind. We cannot even imagine being unoccupied with the projections, and this unimaginability guarantees that we will not awaken.

Totally involved in self, we misunderstand śūnyatā. We concretize it, explain it, try to single it out. Śūnyatā is experiential realization, nondual, beyond the two extremes, and not communicable in language. For beings completely immersed in discriminations and language, the Dharma must tell a story about śūnyatā to point to it at all. This pointing is done through negation. Śūnyatā is: no-thing, nonreal, nonself, nonsubstantial, not-originated, not-produced, neither-real-nor-nonreal. But the dualistic mind easily misunderstands this approach.

Candrakīrti explains: ". . . the purpose of śūnyatā is to quiet conceptual elaborations. You, however, speculate that the meaning of śūnya is nonexistence, and this only reinforces the network of conceptual elaboration. You do not understand the purpose of śūnyatā . . . How caṇ śūnyatā, whose very nature is the undoing of conceptual elaborations, actually exist as 'nonexistence'?" (PRA XXIV)

Awakening from Interpretation

Śūnyatā cannot be captured in concepts or perception, for the labeling process joins one thing with another thing in a subtle interpretation that limits rather than opens experience. These mind processes do not have access to śūnyatā, but prajñā and samādhi can open the door. One can gradually examine and analyze the five skandhas, exploring the architecture of the mind, taking apart the structure brick by brick until the entire construction of self is penetrated. Moreover, one can directly and one-pointedly contemplate the meaning of existence and the nature of interpretation.

Once we awaken to śūnyatā, we recognize that identity is illusion. The five skandhas are transitory and insubstantial, and the story of the self is invention. Likewise, the projections with which the self is involved are fictions, overestimations and underestimations, dramatizations based on limited perspectives.

Upon awakening, there seems to be "absence of self" or "self as not existing," but a closer look clearly shows no loss has been incurred. If experience has no real history, then no one is gaining or losing anything. There is no property to be stolen, no self to be lost or found. With this way of understanding, there is a break in the clouds of confusion and the light of śūnyatā shines through.

In this light, the clouds of emotionality can be penetrated; the realm of illusion can be transformed through the power of enlightening experience. Now it becomes truly relevant to say that not-knowing is the cause of suffering. Now the expression "emptiness" becomes more than a philosophical term.

Turning to the light again and again, one begins to inhabit the realm of wisdom. Desire, attachment, discrimination, identity of self and other all become profoundly questionable. In the Vimalakīrtinirdeśa Sūtra, the Bodhisattva of wisdom and the layman Vimalakīrti engage these questions:

"Mañjuśrī: What is the root of desire and attachment?

Vimalakīrti: Unreal construction is the root of desire.

Mañjuśrī: What is the root of unreal construction?

Vimalakīrti: False concepts are the root.

Mañjuśrī: What is the root of false concept?

Vimalakīrti: Baselessness.

Mañjuśrī: What is the root of baselessness?

Vimalakīrti: Mañjuśrī, when something is baseless, how can it have any root? Therefore, all things stand on the root which is baseless." (VK VII)

Inviting Light into Life

Inviting this new light into life cuts the roots of samsaric illusion and transforms "personality." Out of the understanding of emptiness arises compassion for those still deluded by the nightmare. Protected by the realization of śūnyatā, the Bodhisattva participates in the world of illusion, continuing on and on until all sentient beings reach complete liberation.

This is the way of the Mahāyāna path of transcendent wisdom. From the realization of śūnyatā arises the practice of the perfections, which accumulates virtue and wisdom. Traversing the five paths and the ten stages, one eventually realizes the complete awakening of the Buddha and the three bodies of the Enlightened Onc.

Completely indestructible and uninterrupted, the diamond light of śūnyatā is the most potent antidote to samsara. While illusion may continue for a long time within the confines of the story, illusion is temporary: It is śūnyatā that "continues." As powerful as the delusion of samsara is, śūnyatā is yet more powerful, for it cuts through delusion but itself is not cut.

Personified as the goddess Prajñāpāramitā in the Mahāyāna Sūtras, sūnyatā is known as the Mother of the Buddhas and Bodhisattvas. Source of light, she leads all beings away from darkness. Protectress, she cannot be defeated. Antidote to birth and death, she sets in motion the wheel of the Dharma. Perfect refuge, she makes us seek the safety of the wings of enlightenment.

"Like drops of dew touched by the rays of the sun,
all our theorizing vanishes once we meet you." (PPS)

Further Readings

Ratnaguṇasaṁcayagāthā. Verse summary of the 8,000 Line Prajñāpāramitā.

Heart Sūtra. Fundamental Prajñāpāramitā teachings.

Diamond Sūtra. Fundamental Prajñāpāramitā teachings.

Yuktiṣaṣitikā, by Nāgārjuna.

Śūnyatāsaptati, by Nāgārjuna.

Reference Materials

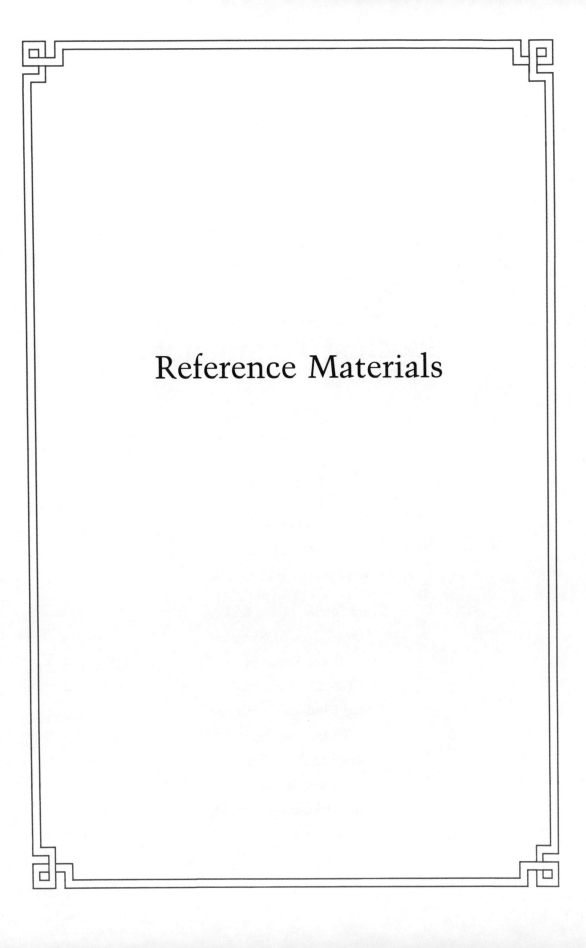

Buddhist Terminology

Three Bodies of the Buddha
sku-gsum
trikāya

dharmakāya	chos-sku	dharmakāya
sambhogakāya	longs-spyod-rdzogs-pa'i-sku	sambhogakāya
nirmāṇakāya	sprul-pa'i-sku	nirmāṇakāya

MVP 115, GL 211–240

Ten Stages of the Bodhisattva Path
byang-chub-sems-dpa'i-rnams-kyi-sa-bcu
daśabhūmi

the joyous	rab-tu-dga'-ba	pramuditā
the immaculate	dri-ma-med-pa	vimalā
the illuminating	'od-byed-pa	prabhākarī
the radiant	'od-'phro-ba-can	arciṣmatī
the hard to conquer	shin-tu-sbyang-dka'	sudurjayā
the manifest	mngon-du-gyur-pa	abhimukhī
the far-reaching	ring-du-song-ba	duraṁgamā
the immovable	mi-g.yo-ba	acalā
the excellent intelligence	legs-pa'i-blo-gros	sādhumatī
the cloud of dharma	chos-kyi-sprin	dharmameghā

MVP 885, DBS, ASL II

Stages of the Śrāvaka
nyan-thos-kyi-gang-zag-gi-rim-pa
śrāvaka-pudgala-kramā

stream enterer	rgyun-du-zhugs-pa	śrotāpanna

once returner	lan-cig-phir-'ong-ba	sakṛdāgāmin
non-returner	phir-mi-'ong-ba	anāgāmin
arhat	dgra-bcom-pa	arhat

MVP 1008, AKB VI:29–53,45b

Qualities of the Arhat
dgra-bcom-pa'i-yon-tan

three wisdoms	rig-pa-gsum	trividyā
six superknowledges	mngon-shes-drug	ṣaḍabhijñā
eight deliverances	rnam-par-thar-pa-brgyad	aṣṭa-vimokṣa
ten dharmas of one with no more to learn	mi-slob-pa'i-chos-bcu	daśa-aśaikṣa-dharma
eight dominant āyatanas	zil-gyis-gnon-pa'i-skye-mched-brgyad	aṣṭa-abhibhvāyatana
ten all-encompassing āyatanas	zad-par-gyi-skye-mched-bcu	daśa-kṛtsnāyatana
free of emotion	nyon-mongs-med-pa	araṇa
knowledge from resolve	smon-nas-shes-pa	praṇidhi-jñāna
four exact knowledges	yang-dag-par-rig-pa-bzhi	catvāri-pratisamvid
nine successive absorptions	mthar-gyis-gnas-pa'i-snyoms-'jug-dgu	navānupūrva-vihāra-samāpatti

AKB VII:35a–56d,35c, AS II,IV, VM XIV, KJ 59a.1, WE 36

Six Superknowledges
mngon-shes-drug
ṣaḍ-abhijñā

clairvoyance	lha'i-mig-gi-mngon-shes	divyacakṣur-abhijñā
clairaudience	lha'i-rna-ba'i-mngon-shes	divyaśrota-abhijñā

knowledge of the minds of others	pha-rol-gyi-sems-shes-pa'i-mngon-shes	paracitta-abhijñā
supernatural abilities	rdzu-'phrul-gyi-bya-ba-shes-pa'i-mngon-shes	ṛddhi-abhijñā
knowledge of past lives	sngon-gyi-gnas-rjes-su-dran-pa'i-mngon-shes	pūrvanivāsānu-smṛti-abhijñā
knowledge of the cessation of corruption	zag-pa-zad-pa'i-mngon-shes	āsravakṣa-abhijñā

AKB VII:42a–d, MVP 201, WE 41

Five Incomparable Skandhas
mi-mnyam-pa-dang-mnyam-pa'i-phung-po-lnga
asama-sama-pañca-skandha

skandha of morality	tshul-khrims-kyi-phung-po	śīla-skandha
skandha of contemplation	ting-'dzin-gyi-phung-po	samādhi-skandha
skandha of wisdom	shes-rab-kyi-phung-po	prajñā-skandha
skandha of liberation	rnam-par-grol-ba'i-phung-po	vimukti-skandha
skandha of knowledge of liberation	rnam-par-grol-ba'i-ye-shes-mthong-ba'i-phung-po	vimukti-jñāna-darśana-skandha

DN XXXIV, AKB I:20a–22b, VI:75b,76c–d, AS II, MVP 103, WE 36

Three Types of Nirvana
mya-ngang-las-'das-kyi-rnam-grangs
nirvāṇa-trāya-paryāyā

nirvana with remainder	phung-po-lhag-ma-dang-bcas-pa'i-mya-ngan-las-'das-pa	sopadhi-śeṣa-nirvāṇa
nirvana without remainder	phung-po-lhag-ma-med-pa'i-mya-ngan-las-'das-pa	nirupadhi-śeṣa-nirvāṇa

nonlocalized nirvana	mi-gnas-pa'i-mya-ngan-las-'das-pa	apratiṣṭhita-nirvāṇa

MVP 1724, AKB VI:37a–c, AS II, KJ 58a.6, WE 36

Two Types of Arhat
dgra-bcom-pa
arhat

unornamented	dgra-bcom-rgyan-med	niralaṁkāra
ornamented	dgra-bcom-rgyan-bcas	sālaṁkāra

AKB VI:64a–b, AS II,IV, KJ 58b.2, WE 36

Three Vehicles
theg-pa-gsum
triyāna

vehicle of Śrāvakas	nyan-thos-kyi-theg-pa	śrāvakayāna
vehicle of Pratyekabuddhas	rang-sangs-rgyas-kyi-theg-pa	pratyeka-buddhayāna
vehicle of Bodhisattvas	byang-chub-sems-dpa'i-theg-pa	bodhisattvayāna

AS IV, MSA I, GL 19, LKV XX, MVP 1249, WE 13–14

Twofold Holy Dharma
dam-pa'i-chos
saddharma

explanations	lung	āgama
realization	rtogs	adhigama

AKB VIII 39a–b, WE 3

Three Collections
sde-snod-gsum
tripiṭaka

vinaya	'dul-ba'i-sde-snod	vinaya-piṭaka
sūtra	mdo'i-sde-snod	sūtra-piṭaka
abhidharma	chos-mngon-pa'i-sde-snod	abhidharma-piṭaka

AS II, BU I:34–38, WE 4,12

Twelve Branches of Scripture
gsung-rab-yan-lag-bcu-gnyis
dvādaśāṅgapravacana

Single topic discourses	mdo'i-sde	sūtra
discourses in verse	dbyangs-kyis-bsnyad-pa'i-sde	geya
prophecies	lung-du-bstan-pa'i-sde	vyākaraṇa
verse summaries	tshigs-su-bcad-pa'i-sde	gāthā
spoken to maintain the Dharma	ched-du-brjod-pa'i-sde	udāna
guidelines following a specific incident	gleng-gzhi'i-sde	nidāna
life stories	rtogs-pa-brjod-pa'i-sde	avadāna
historical accounts	de-lta-bu-byung-ba'i-sde	itivṛttaka
previous lives of the Buddha	skyes-pa'i-rabs-kyi-sde	jātaka
long complex sūtras	shin-tu-rgyas-pa'i-sde	vaipulya
wondrous acts	rmad-du-byung-ba'i-chos-kyi-sde	adbhutadharma
topics of specific knowledge	gtan-la-phab-par-bstan-pa'i-sde	upadeśa

AS II, MVP 1266, BU I:33, DR 76, WE 3

Three Kinds of Teachings
bka'-gsum

spoken by the Buddha	gsungs-pa	vāc
spoken with the blessing of the Buddha	byin-gyis-brlabs-pa	adhiṣṭhāna
spoken with the mandate of the Buddha	rjes-su-gnang-ba	anujñāta

BU I:40, DR 74, WE 4

Three Trainings
bslab-pa-gsum
triśikṣā

moral discipline	tshul-khrims	śīla
meditative concentration	ting-nge-'dzin	samādhi
wisdom	shes-rab	prajñā

VM I,III,XIV, AKB VI:43c–d, MSG:VI,VII,VIII, AS III, DR 70–73, WE 11,12

Three Kinds of Prajñā
shes-rab-gsum
trividhāḥ prajñā

prajñā arising from hearing	thos-pa-las-byung-ba'i-shes-rab	śrutamayī-prajñā
prajñā arising from reflecting	bsam-pa-las-byung-ba'i-shes-rab	cintāmayī-prajñā
prajñā arising from meditating	bsgom-pa-las-byung-ba'i-shes-rab	bhāvanāmayī-prajñā

AKB VI:5a–d, AS III, VM XIV:14, MVP 1550, WE 11

Three Marks
mtshan-nyid-gsum
trilakṣaṇa

selfless	bdag-med-pa	anātman
impermanent	mi-rtag-pa	anitya
suffering	sdug-bsngal	duḥkha

AN III, DP XX:5–7, AKB VI:16, AS II, WE 10

Four Truths
bden-pa-rnam-bzhi
catuḥsatya

truth of suffering	sdug-bsngal-gyi-bden-pa	duḥkha-satya
truth of the origin of suffering	kun-'byung-gi-bden-pa	samudaya-satya
truth of cessation of suffering	'gog-pa'i-bden-pa	nirodha-satya
truth of the path	lam-gyi-bden-pa	mārga-satya

AS II, KJ 34a.5–65b, WE 9

Four Laws of the Dharma
chos-kyi-sdom-bzhi
catur-dharmoddāna

everything compounded is impermanent	'du-byed-thams-cad-mi-rtag-pa	sarvasaṁskṛta-anitya
everything corrupt is suffering	'du-byed-zag-bcas-thams-cad-sdug-bsngal-ba	sarvāsrava-duḥkha
all things are empty and without self	chos-thams-cad-stong-zhing-bdag-med-pa	sadharma-śūnyamanātmaka

nirvana is peace	mya-ngan-las-'das-pa-zhi-ba	nirvāṇa-śāntaka

MSA XVIII, KJ 92a.3, WE 10

Ten Topics of Expert Knowledge
mkhas-par-bya-ba'i-gnas-bcu

skandhas	phung-po	skandha
dhātus	khams	dhātu
āyatanas	skye-mched	āyatana
interdependent co-operation	rten-cing-'brel-bar-'byung-ba	pratītya-samutpāda
possible and impossible	gnas-dang gnas-ma-yin-pa	sthānāsthāna
indriyas	dbang-po	indriya
temporality	dus	adhvan
truth	bden-pa	satya
ways to enlightenment	theg-pa	yāna
conditioned and nonconditioned	'dus-byas-dang-'dus-ma-byas	saṁskṛta-asaṁskṛta

MAV III:17a–22b, KJ 2a.1, KJD, WE 10

Five Paths
lam-lnga
pañca-mārga

path of preparation	tshogs-lam	sambhāra-mārga
path of linking	sbyor-lam	prayoga-mārga
path of seeing	mthong-lam	darśana-mārga
path of meditation	bsgom-lam	bhāvanā-mārga
path of no more learning	mi-slob-pa'i-lam	aśaikṣa-mārga

AKB VI:65b–d, AS II, KJ:59a.4, WE 37

Thirty-seven Wings of Enlightenment
byang-chub-kyi-chos-sum-cu-rtsa-bdun
saptatriṁśa-bodhipakṣa-dharma

four foundations of mindfulnesses	dran-pa-nye-bar-bzhag-pa-bzhi	catuḥ-smṛtyupasthāna
four genuine restraints	yang-dag-par-spong-ba-bzhi	catuḥ-samyak-prahāṇa
four bases for supernatural power	rdzu-'phrul-gyi-rkang-pa-bzhi	catvāra-ṛddhipāda
five spiritual faculties	dbang-po-lnga	pañcendriya
five spiritual powers	stobs-lnga	pañca-bala
seven branches of enlightenment	byang-chub-kyi-yan-lag-bdun	sapta-bodhyaṅga
eightfold noble path	'phags-pa'i-lam-yan-lag-brgyad	aṣṭā ga-mārga

AKB VI:66c–d, AS II, WE 37

Four Foundations of Mindfulness
dran-pa-nye-bar-bzhag-pa-bzhi
catuḥ-smṛtyupasthāna

mindfulness of body	lus-dran-pa-nye-bar-bzhag-pa	kāya-smṛtyupasthāna
mindfulness of feelings	tshor-ba-dran-pa-nye-bar-bzhag-pa	vedanā-smṛtyupasthāna
mindfulness of mind	sems-dran-pa-nye-bar-bzhag-pa	citta-smṛtyupasthāna
mindfulness of dharmas	chos-dran-pa-nye-bar-bzhag-pa	dharma-smṛtyupasthāna

AKB VI:14a–d, AS II, MVP 952, KJ 84a.1, WE 38

Four Genuine Restraints
yang-dag-par-spong-ba-bzhi
catuḥ-samyak-prahāṇa

not to initiate non-virtuous actions not yet generated	mi-dge-ba'i-chos-ma-skyes-pa-mi-bskyed-pa
give up nonvirtuous actions not yet generated	mi-dge-ba'i-chos-skyes-pa-spang-bar-byed-pa
bring about virtuous actions not yet generated	dge-ba'i-chos-ma-skyes-pa-bskyed-pa
not to allow virtuous actions already arisen to degenerate	dge-ba'i-chos-skyes-pa-mi-nyam-par-byed-pa

AKB VI:68d–70, AS II, MVP 957, KJ:84b.2, WE 39

Four Bases for Supernatural Power
rdzu-'phrul-gyi-rkang-pa-bzhi
catvāra-ṛddhipāda

samādhi based on willingness	'dun-pa'i-ting-nge-'dzin	chanda-samādhi
samādhi based on mind	sems-kyi-ting-nge-'dzin	citta-samādhi
samādhi based on effort	brtson-'grus-kyi-ting-nge-'dzin	vīrya-samādhi
samādhi based on analysis	dpyod-pa'i-ting-nge-'dzin	mīmāṁsā-samādhi

AKB VI:68d–70, AS II, MVP 966, VM III:24, KJ 84b.4, WE 39

Five Spiritual Faculties
dbang-po-lnga
pañcendriya

spiritual faculty of faith	dad-pa'i-dbang-po	śraddhendriya
spiritual faculty of effort	brtson-'grus-kyi-dbang-po	vīryendriya
spiritual faculty of mindfulness	dran-pa'i-dbang-po	smṛtīndriya
spiritual faculty of meditative concentration	ting-nge-'dzin-gyi-dbang-po	samādhīndriya
spiritual faculty of wisdom	shes-rab-kyi-dbang-po	prajñendriya

AKB VI:68d–70, AS II, KJ 85a.4, WE 39

Five Spiritual Powers
stobs-lnga
pañcabala

spiritual power of faith	dad-pa'i-stobs	śraddhā-bala
spiritual power of effort	brtson-'grus-kyi-stobs	vīrya-bala
spiritual power of mindfulness	dran-pa'i-stobs	smṛti-bala
spiritual power of meditative concentration	ting-nge-'dzin-gyi-stobs	samādhi-bala
spiritual power of wisdom	shes-rab-kyi-stobs	prajñā-bala

AKB VI:68b–70, AS II, MVP 982, KJ 85a.6, WE 39

Seven Branches of Enlightenment
byang-chub-kyi-yan-lag-bdun
saptabodhyaṅga

branch of enlightened mindfulness	dran-pa-yang-dag-byang-chub-kyi-yan-lag	smṛti-saṁbodhyaṅga
branch of enlightened investigation	chos-rab-tu-rnam-par-'byed-pa-yang-dag-byang-chub-kyi-yan-lag	dharma-pravicaya-saṁbodhyaṅga
branch of enlightened effort	brtson-'grus-yang-dag-byang-chub-kyi-yan-lag	vīrya-saṁbodhyaṅga
branch of enlightened joy	dga'-ba-yang-dag-byang-chub-kyi-yan-lag	prīti-saṁbodhyaṅga
branch of enlightened alert ease	shin-tu-sbyangs-pa-yang-dag-byang-chub-kyi-yan-lag	praśrabdhi-saṁgbodhyaṅga
branch of enlightened contemplation	ting-nge-'dzin-yang-dag-byang-chub-kyi-yan-lag	samādhi-saṁbodhyaṅga
branch of enlightened equanimity	btang-snyoms-yang-dag-byang-chub-kyi-yan-lag	upekṣā-saṁbodhyaṅga

AKB VI:68b–70, MVP 988, KJ 85b.1, WE 40

Eightfold Noble Path
'phags-pa'i-lam-yan-lag-brgyad
aṣṭāṅgamārga

genuinely pure view	yang-dag-pa'i-lta-ba	samyag-dṛṣṭi
genuinely pure thought	yang-dag-pa'i-rtog-pa	samyak-saṁkalpa
genuinely pure speech	yang-dag-pa'i-ngag	samyag-vāk
genuinely pure conduct	yang-dag-pa'i-las-kyi-mtha'	samyak-karmānta
genuinely pure livelihood	yang-dag-pa'i-'tsho-ba	samyag-ājīva

genuinely pure effort	yang-dag-pa'i-rtsol-ba	samyag-vyāyāma
genuinely pure mindfulness	yang-dag-pa'i-dran-pa	samyak-smṛti
genuinely pure meditative concentration	yang-dag-pa'i-ting-nge-'dzin	samyak-samādhi

AKB VI:70, AS II, MVP 996, KJ 86b.1, WE 9

Four Levels That Bring About Certainty
nges-par-'byed-pa'i-cha-dang-mthun-pa-bzhi
catur-nirvedha-bhāga-krama

heat	drod-ba	uṣmagata
summit	rtse-mo	mūrdhān
patience	bzod-pa	kṣānti
supreme worldly dharmas	'jig-rten-pa'i-chos-kyi-mchog	laukikāgriya-dharma

AKB VI:17-20, AS II, MVP 1210, KJ 59b.2, WE 39

Sixteen Aspects of the Four Noble Truths
'phags-pa'i-bden-pa-bzhi-rnam-pa-bcu-drug-tu-phye-ba
ṣoḍaśabhurākārāirvisāritānicatvāry-ārya-satya

suffering	sdug-bsngal	duḥkha
impermanence	mi-rtag-pa	anitya
emptiness	stong-pa	śūnyatā
selflessness	bdag-med-pa	anātmaka
cause	rgyu	hetu
arising	kun-'byung-ba	samudaya
appearance	rab-tu-skye-ba	prabhava
condition	rkyen	pratyaya
cessation	'gog-pa	nirodha
quiescence	zhi-ba	śānta
excellence	gya-nom-pa	praṇīta

renunciation	nges-par-'byung-ba	niḥsaraṇa
path	lam	mārga
method	rigs-pa	nyāya
attainment	sgrub-pa	pratipatti
liberation	nges-par-'byin-pa	nairyāṇika

MVP 1189–1204, cf.AKB VII:13a, KJD 7a.5, WE 39

Sixteen Moments of Knowledge
ye-shes-skad-cig-ma-bcu-drug
ṣoḍḍaśa-citta-kṣaṇa

patience in regard to dharma knowledge of suffering	sdug-bsngal-la-chos-shes-pa'i-bzod-pa	duḥkhadharma-jñāna-kṣānti
dharma knowledge of suffering	sdug-bsngal-la-chos-shes-pa	duḥkhadharma-jñāna
patience in regard to consecutive knowledge of suffering	sdug-bsngal-la-rjes-su-shes-pa'i-bzod-pa	duḥkhānvaya-jñāna-kṣānti
consecutive knowledge of suffering	sdug-bsngal-la-rjes-su-shes-pa	duḥkhānvaya-jñāna
patience in regard to dharma knowledge of origin	kun-'byung-la-chos-shes-pa'i-bzod-pa	samudaya-dharma-jñāna-kṣānti
dharma knowledge of origin	kun-'byung-la-chos-shes-pa	samudaya-dharma-jñāna
patience in regard to the consecutive knowledge of origin	kun-'byung-la-rjes-su-shes-pa'i-bzod-pa	samudayānvaya-jñāna-kṣānti
consecutive knowledge of origin	kun-'byung-la-rjes-su-shes-pa	samudayānvaya-jñāna
patience in regard to dharma knowledge of cessation	'gog-pa-la-chos-shes-pa'i-bzod-pa	nirodha-dharma-jñāna-kṣānti
dharma knowledge of cessation	'gog-pa-la-chos-shes-pa	nirodha-dharma-jñāna

patience in regard to consecutive knowledge of cessation	'gog-pa-la-rjes-su-shes-pa'i-bzod-pa	nirodhānvaya-jñāna-kṣānti
consecutive knowledge of cessation	'gog-pa-la-rjes-su-shes-pa	nirodhānvaya-jñāna
patience in regard to dharma knowledge of the path	lam-la-chos-shes-pa'i-bzod-pa	mārga-dharma-jñāna-kṣānti
dharma knowledge of the path	lam-la-chos-shes-pa	mārga-dharma-jñāna
patience in regard to consecutive knowledge of the path	lam-la-rjes-su-shes-pa'i-bzod-pa	nirodhānvaya-jñāna-kṣānti
consecutive knowledge of the path	lam-la-rjes-su-shes-pa	mārgānvaya-jñāna

AKB VI:25c-28d, AS II, MVP 1216, KJ 60a.1, WE 40

Two Paths

worldly path	'jig-rten-pa'i-lam	laukika-mārga
transworldly path	'jig-rten-las-'das-pa'i-lam	lokottaramārga

AKB VI:1, AS II, KJ 61a.2, 63b.5, WE 41,42

Three Nonconditioned
'dus-ma-byas-gsum
trividham-asaṁskṛtam

cessation based on comprehension	so-sor-brtags-'gog	pratisaṁkhyā-nirodha
cessation not based on comprehension	so-sor-brtags min-'gog-pa	apratisaṁkhyā-nirodha
space	nam-mkha'	ākāśa

AKB I:6a–d, AS I, MVP 2185, 2186, KJ 12a.3, WE 23

Five Factors of Meditative Concentration
[bsam-gtan-gyi-yan-lag-lnga]
[catvāri-dhyāna]

investigation	rtog-pa	vitarka
analysis	dpyod-pa	vicāra
mental happiness	dga'-ba	prīti
bliss	bde-ba	sukha
one-pointedness	sems-rtse-gcig-pa-nyid	cittaikāgratā

AKB VIII:2a–b, 7–9, AS II, MVP 1477, KJ 61b.6, WE 11,41

Four Formless Absorptions
gzugs-med-pa'i-snyoms-par-'jug-pa-bzhi
[catur-arūpya-samāpatti]

sphere of boundless space	nam-mkha'-mtha'-yas-skye-mched	ākāśānantya-āyatana
sphere of boundless consciousness	rnam-shes-mtha'-yas-skye-mched	vijñānānantya-āyatana
sphere of nothingness	ci-yang-med-pa'i-skye-mched	ākiṁcanya-āyatana
sphere of neither perception nor non-perception	'du-shes-med-'du-shes-med-min-skye-mched	naivasaṁjñā-na-asaṁjñā-āyatana

AKB VIII:2c–4d, AS II, MVP 1491, KJ 62b.5, WE 41

Two Absorptions
snyoms-par-'jug-pa-gnyis
samāpatti-dvaya

absorption of nonperception	'du-shes-med-pa'i-snyoms-'jug	asaṁjñā-samāpatti

absorption of the cessation of feeling and perception	'du-shes-dang-tshor-ba-'gog-pa'i-snyoms-'jug	saṁjñā-vedita-nirodha-samāpatti

AKB II:42a–43g, AS I, MVP 1502,1500, KJ 12a.6, WE 41

Four Immeasurables
tshad-med-bzhi
catur-apramāṇa

loving kindness	byams-pa	maitrī
compassion	snying-rje	karuṇā
sympathetic joy	dga'-ba	muditā
equanimity	btang-snyoms	upekṣā

AKB VIII:29a–31e, AS IV, MVP 1503, KJ 81b.3, WE 41

Eight Types of Prātimokṣa Vows
so-thar-rigs-brgyad
aṣṭaprātimokṣasaṁvara

ordained monk	dge-slong	bhikṣu
ordained nun	dge-slong-ma	bhikṣūṇī
male novice	dge-tshul	śrāmaṇera
female novice	dge-tshul-ma	śrāmaṇerikā
beginners not of age	dge-slob-ma	śikṣāmāna
layman	dge-bsnyen	upāsaka
laywoman	dge-bsnyen-ma	upāsikā
layman and laywomen temporary vows	bsnyen-gnas	upavāsa, upavāsī

AKB IV:15, AS II, KJ 41a.4, WE 5

Three Realms
khams-gsum
tridhātu

desire realm	'dod-pa'i-khams	kāmadhātu
form realm	gzugs-kyi-khams	rūpadhātu
formless realm	gzugs-med-pa'i-khams	arūpadhātu

AKB III:1a-d, AS II, MVP 3071, WE 29

Six Destinies
'gro-ba-rigs-drug
ṣaḍgati

hell	dmyal-ba	naraka
hungry ghosts	yi-dwags	pretā
animals	dud-'gro	tiryak
humans	mi	manuṣya
demigods	lha-ma-yin	asura
gods	lha	deva

AKB III:1a–c, 4a–b, 58, 65–71, AS II, KZLZ I:III, WE 29

Five Degenerations of the Kāliyuga
rtsod-dus-kyi-snyigs-ma-lnga
pañca-kaṣāya

degenerating lifespan	tshe'i-snyigs-ma	āyuḥ-kaṣāya
degenerating views	lta-ba'i-snyigs-ma	dṛṣṭī-kaṣāya
degenerating emotionality	nyon-mongs-pa'i-snyigs-ma	kleśa-kaṣāya
degenerating basis of being	sems-can-gyi-snyigs-ma	sattva-kaṣāya

degenerating time	dus-kyi-snyigs-ma	kalpa-kaṣāya

AKB III:94a-b, MVP 2335, KJ 39a.4, WE 30

Twelve Links of Interdependent Co-operation
rten-cing-'brel-bar-'byung-ba'i-yan-lag-bcu-gnyis
dvādaśāṅga-pratītyasamutpāda

ignorance	ma-rig-pa	avidyā
karmic propensities	'du-byed	saṁskāra
consciousness	rnam-par-shes-pa	vijñāna
name and form	ming-dang-gzugs	nāma-rūpa
six organ āyatanas	skye-mched-drug	ṣaḍāyatana
contact	reg-pa	sparśa
feeling	tshor-ba	vedanā
craving	sred-pa	tṛṣṇā
grasping	len-pa	upādāna
existence	srid-pa	bhava
birth	skye-ba	jāti
old age and death	rga-shi	jarā-maraṇa

AKB III:20a–37b, VM XVII:105,310–313, LAL XXVI, AS I, AVS V, MVP 2241, KJ 18a.6, WE 25-26

Five Categories of the Knowable
[shes-bya-lnga]
[pañca-jñeyadharma]

form	gzugs	rūpa
mind	sems	citta
mental events	sems-byung	caitta
nonassociated forces	ldan-min-'du-byed	viprayukta-saṁskāra
nonconditioned	'dus-ma-byas	asaṁskṛta

AKB II:34a–36d, AS I, GTD 14b.3, WE 17,21

Five Skandhas
phung-po-lnga
pañca-skandha

skandha of form	gzugs-kyi-phung-po	rūpa-skandha
skandha of feeling	tshor-ba'i-phung-po	vedanā-skandha
skandha of perception	'du-shes-kyi-phung-po	saṁjñā-skandha
skandha of motivational factors	'du-byed-kyi-phung-po	saṁskāra-skandha
skandha of consciousness	rnam-par-shes-pa'i-phung-po	vijñāna-skandha

AKB I:7–15, AS I, PSP, MVP 1831, KJ 2a.3, WE 18–22

Four Great Elements
'byung-ba-chen-po-bzhi
catvāri-mahābhūta

earth	sa	pṛthivī
water	chu	ab
fire	me	tejas
air	rlung	vāyu

AKB I:12–13, AS I, MVP 1837, KJ 2b.2, WE 18

Eleven Resultant Forms
'bras-gzugs bcu-gcig

five sense organs	dbang-po-lnga	pañcendriya
five sense objects	don-lnga	pañca-viṣaya
one nonmanifesting	rnam-par-rig-byed-min-pa'i-gzugs	avijñapti

AKB I:35a–b, AS I, PSP, KJ 2b.3, WE 18

Five Sense Organs
dbang-po-lnga
pañcendriya

eye	mig-gi-dbang-po	cakṣur-indriya
ear	rna-ba'i-dbang-po	śrotrendriya
nose	sna'i-dbang-po	ghrāṇendriya
tongue	lce'i-dbang-po	jihvendriya
body	lus-kyi-dbang-po	kāyendriya

AKB I:14a–b,18d, AS I, PSP, KJ 2b.5, WE 18

Five Sense Objects
don-lnga
pañca-viṣaya

visible form	gzugs	rūpa
sound	sgra	śabda
smell	dri	gandha
taste	ro	rasa
tangibles	reg-bya	spraṣṭa

AKB I14a–b,18d, AS I, PSP, KJ 3a.1, WE 18

Five Objects of Mind That are Form
chos-kyi-skye-mched-pa'i-gzugs-lnga
[pañcarūpa-dharmāyatana]

imaginary form	kun-btags-pa'i-gzugs	parikalpita
form arising from power of meditation	dbang-'byor-ba'i-gzugs	vaibhūtvika
form arising from aggregation (atoms)	bsdus-pa-las-gyur-pa	abhisaṁkṣepika

space-form appearance of clear space	mngon-par-skabs-yod-pa'am-gsal-ba	abhyavakāśika
form arising from a vow	yang-dag-par-blangs-pa-las-byung-ba	sāmādānika

AS I, PSP, KJ 3b.5, WE 18

Three Types of Feelings

pleasant	bde-ba	sukha
unpleasant	sdug-bsngal	duḥkha
neutral	btang-snyoms	aduḥkha-sukha

AKB I:14c, AS I, PSP, KJ 5a.2, MBP 20–21, WE 19

Five Types of Feelings

physical pleasure	bde-ba	sukha
mental pleasure	yid-bde	saumanasya
physical pain	sdug-bsngal	duḥkha
mental pain	yid-mi-bde	daurmanasya
indifference	btang-snyoms	upekṣā

AS I, KJ 5a.2, MBP 20–21, WE 19

Six Types of Perception

perception with characteristics	mtshan-ma-dang-bcas-pa'i-'du-shes	sanimitta-saṁjñā
perception without characteristics	mtshan-ma-med-pa'i-'du-shes	animitta-saṁjñā
lesser perception	chung-ngu'i-'du-shes	parītta-saṁjñā
vast perception	rgya-chen-po'i-'du-shes	mahadgatā-saṁjñā

immeasurable perception	tshad-med-pa'i-'du-shes	apramāṇa-saṁjñā
perception of nothingness	ci-yang-med-pa'i-'du-shes	ākiṁcit-saṁjñā

AS I, KJ 5b.1, MBP 24–25, WE 20

Three Poisons
dug-gsum
triviṣa

confusion	gti-mug	moha
attachment	'dod-chags	rāga
aversion	zhe-sdang	dveṣa

Five Types of Motivational Forces Associated with Mind
sems-dang-mtshungs-ldan-gyi-'du-byed
pañca-citta-samprayukta-saṁskāra

omnipresent events	sa-chen-po-pa	mahābhūmika
virtuous events	dge-ba'i-sa-mang	kuśala-mahābhūmika
nonvirtuous events	mi-dge-ba'i-sa-pa	akuśala-mahābhūmika
emotionally afflicted events	nyon-mongs-chen-po'i-sa-pa	kleśa-mahābhūmika
lesser emotions	nyon-mongs-chung-ngu'i-sa-pa-rnams	parītta-kleśa-bhūmika

AKB II:23c–31c, cf.KJ 5b.4, WE 21

Ten Omnipresent Events
sa-chen-po-pa
daśa-mahābhūmika

feeling	tshor-ba	vedanā

intention	sems	cetanā
perception	'du-shes	saṁjñā
interest	'dun-pa	chanda
contact	reg-pa	sparśa
discernment	shes-rab	prajñā
mindfulness	dran-pa	smṛti
attention	yid-la-byed-pa	manaskāra
determination	mos-pa	adhimokṣa
concentration	ting-nge-'dzin	samādhi

AKB II:24, cf.AS I, cf.PSP, cf.MBP 19–38, WE 21

Ten Virtuous Events
dge-ba'i-sa-mang
daśa-kuśala-mahābhūmika

faith	dad-pa	śraddhā
conscientiousness	bag-yod-pa	apramāda
alert ease	shin-tu-sbyangs-pa	praśrabdhi
equanimity	btang-snyoms	upekṣā
self-respect	ngo-tsha-shes-pa	hrī
propriety	khrel-yod-pa	apatrāpya
non-attachment	ma-chags-pa	alobha
non-hatred	zhe-sdang-med-pa	adveṣa
non-violence	rnam-par-mi-'tshe-ba	avihiṁsā
effort	brtson-'grus	vīrya

AKB II:25, cf.AS I, cf.PSP, cf.MBP 38–64, WE 21

Two Nonvirtuous Events
mi-dge-ba'i-sa-pa
akuśala-mahābhūmika

lack of respect	ngo-tsha-med-pa	āhrīkya

impropriety	khrel-med-pa	anapatrāpya

AKB II:26c-d, cf.AS I, cf.PSP, cf.MBP 82, WE 21

Six Emotionally Afflicted Events
nyon-mongs-chen-po'i-sa-pa
ṣaṭ-kleśa-mahābhūmika

confusion	gti-mug	moha
nonconscientiousness	bag-med-pa	pramāda
laziness	le-lo	kausīdya
faithlessness	ma-dad-pa	aśraddhā
torpor	rmugs-pa	styāna
restlessness	rgod-pa	auddhatya

AKB II:26a–c, cf.AS I, cf.PSP, cf.MBP 64–81, WE 21

Ten Lesser Emotions
nyon-mongs-chung-ngu'i-sa-pa
daśa-parītta-kleśa-bhūmika

vindictiveness	khro-ba	krodha
resentment	khon-du-'dzin-pa	upanāha
spite	'tshig-pa	pradāśa
malice	rnam-par-'tshe-ba	vihaṁsā
jealousy	phrag-dog	īrṣyā
dishonesty	g.yo	śāṭhya
deceit	sgyu	māyā
hypocrisy	'chab-pa	mrakṣa
avarice	ser-sna	mātsarya
haughtiness	rgyags-pa	mada

AKB II:27, cf.AS I, cf.PSP, cf.MBP 82–99, WE 21

Eight Variables
gzhan-'gyur
aniyata

worry	'gyod	kaukṛtya
sleepiness	gnyid	middha
investigation	rtog-pa	vitarka
analysis	dpyod-pa	vicāra
desire	'dod-chags	rāga
anger	khong-khro	pratigha
pride	nga-rgyal	māna
doubt	the-tshom	vicikitsā

AKB II:27, cf.AS I, cf.PSP, cf.MBP 99–107, WE 21

Fourteen Nonassociated Motivational Forces
ldan-min-'du-byed
viprayukta-saṁskāra

acquisition	thob-pa	prāpti
nonacquisition	ma-thob-pa	aprāpti
similarity of state	skal-mnyam	sabhāgatā
absorption of nonperception	'du-shes-med-pa'i-snyoms-'jug	asaṁjña-samāpatti
nonperception	'du-shes-med-pa	asaṁjñā
absorption of cessation	'gog-pa'i-snyoms-'jug	nirodha-samāpatti
the life force	srog-gi-dbang-po	jīvitendriya
birth	skye-ba	jāti
duration	gnas-pa	sthiti
aging	rga-ba	jarā
impermanence	mi-rtag-pa	anityatā

names of things	ming-gi-tshogs	nāmakāya
phrases	tshig-gi-tshogs	padakāya
letters	yi-ge-tshogs	vyañjanakāya

AKB II:35–48d, AS I, PSP, KJ 9b.2, WE 21

Additional Nonassociated Motivational Forces

ordinary being	so-so'i-skye-bo	pṛthagjana
continuity	'jug-pa	pravṛtti
diversity	so-sor-nges-pa	pratiniyama
relatedness	'byor-'brel-ba	yoga
rapidity	mgyogs-pa	jāva
order	go-rim	anukrama
temporality	dus	kāla
spatiality	yul	deśa
countabiity	grangs	saṁkhyā
collection	tshogs-pa	sāmagrī

AS I, KJ 10b.2, WE 21

Six Consciousnesses
rnam-shes-tshogs-drug
ṣaḍ-vijñāna

eye-consciousness	mig-gi-rnam-par-shes-pa	cakṣur-vijñāna
ear-consciousness	rna-ba'i-rnam-par-shes-pa	śrotra-vijñāna
nose-consciousness	sna'i-rnam-par-shes-pa	ghrāṇa-vijñāna
tongue-consciousness	lce'i-rnam-par-shes-pa	jihva-vijñāna
body-consciousness	lus-kyi-rnam-par-shes-pa	kāya-vijñāna
mind-consciousness	yid-kyi-rnam-par-shes-pa	mano-vijñāna

AKB I:16a–d, AS I, PSP, MVP 2016, KJ 10b.6, WE 22

Eighteen Dhātus
khams-bco-brgyad
aṣṭadaśa-dhātu

eye dhātu	mig-gi-khams	cakṣur-dhātu
form dhātu	gzugs-kyi-khams	rūpa-dhātu
eye-consciousness dhātu	mig-gi-rnam-par-shes-pa'i-khams	cakṣur-vijñāna-dhātu
ear dhātu	rna-ba'i-khams	śrotra-dhātu
sound dhātu	sgra'i-khams	śabda-dhātu
ear-consciousness dhātu	rna-ba'i-rnam-par-shes-pa'i-khams	śrotra-vijñāna-dhātu
nose dhātu	sna'i-khams	ghrāṇa-dhātu
smell dhātu	dri'i-khams	gandha-dhātu
nose-consciousness dhātu	sna'i-rnam-par-shes-pa'i-khams	ghrāṇa-vijñāna-dhātu
tongue dhātu	lce'i-khams	jihva-dhātu
taste dhātu	ro'i-khams	rasa-dhātu
tongue-consciousness dhātu	lce'i-rnam-par-shes-pa'i-khams	jihvā-vijñāna-dhātu
body dhātu	lus-kyi-khams	kāya-dhātu
tangibles dhātu	reg-bya'i-khams	spraṣṭavya-dhātu
body-consciousness dhātu	lus-kyi-rnam-par-shes-pa'i-khams	kāya-vijñāna-dhātu
mind dhātu	yid-kyi-khams	mano-dhātu
dhātu of dharmas	chos-kyi-khams	dharma-dhātu
mind-consciousness dhātu	yid-kyi-rnam-par-shes-pa'i-khams	mano-vijñāna-dhātu

AKB I:17c–d, AS I, PSP, MVP 2040, KJ 12b.4, WE 23

Twelve Āyatanas
skye-mched-bcu-gnyis
dvādaśa-āyatana

āyatana of the eye	mig-gi-skye-mched	cakṣur-āyatana
āyatana of form	gzugs-kyi-skye-mched	rūpa-āyatana
āyatana of the ear	rna-ba'i-skye-mched	śrotra-āyatana
āyatana of sound	sgra'i-skye-mched	śabda-āyatana
āyatana of the nose	sna'i-skye-mched	ghrāṇa-āyatana
āyatana of smell	dri'i-skye-mched	gandha-āyatana
āyatana of the tongue	lce'i-skye-mched	jihva-āyatana
āyatana of taste	ro'i-skye-mched	rasa-āyatana
āyatana of the body	lus-kyi-skye-mched	kāya-āyatana
āyatana of tangibles	reg-bya'i-skye-mched	spraṣṭavya-āyatana
āyatana of mind	yid-kyi-skye-mched	mano-āyatana
āyatana of mental objects	chos-kyi-skye-mched	dharma-āyatana

AKB I:24, AS I, PSP, MVP 2027, KJ 14a.6, WE 24

Twenty-two Indriyas
dbang-po-nyi-shu-rtsa-gnyis
dvāviṁśatīndriya

indriya of the eye	mig-gi-dbang-po	cakṣur-indriya
indriya of the ear	rna-ba'i-dbang-po	śrotrendriya
indriya of the nose	sna'i-dbang-po	ghrāṇendriya
indriya of the tongue	lce'i-dbang-po	jihvendriya
indriya of the body	lus-kyi-dbang-po	kāyendriya
indriya of mind	yid-kyi-dbang-po	mano'ndriya
indriya of life	srog-gi-dbang-po	jīvitendriya

indriya of male	pho'i-dbang-po	puruṣendriya
indriya of female	mo'i-dbang-po	strī-indriya
indriya of pain	sdug-bsngal-gyi-dbang-po	duḥkhendriya
indriya of pleasure	bde-ba'i-dbang-po	sukhendriya
indriya of mental happiness	yid-bde-ba'i-dbang-po	saumanasyendriya
indriya of mental unhappiness	yid-mi-bde-ba'i-dbang-po	daurmanasyendriya
indriya of equanimity	btang-snyoms-kyi-dbang-po	upekṣendriya
indriya of faith	dad-pa'i-dbang-po	śraddhendriya
indriya of effort	brtson-'grus-kyi-dbang-po	vīryendriya
indriya of mindfulness	dran-pa'i-dbang-po	smṛtī-indriya
indriya of meditative concentration	ting-nge-'dzin-gyi-dbang-po	samādhī-indriya
indriya of wisdom	shes-rab-kyi-dbang-po	prajñendriya
indriya that brings about knowing the unknown	mi-shes-pa-kun-shes-par-byed-pa'i-dbang-po	anājñātam ājñāsyāmī-indriya
indriya of what is unknown	mi-shes-pa'i-dbang-po	ājñendriya
indriya of possessing all-knowingness	kun-shes-pa-dang-ldan-pa'i-dbang-po	ājñātāvi-īndriya

AKB II:1–6, AS I, MVP 2059, KJ 27b.4, WE 27

Five Classifications of Action

corrupt, uncorrupt	zag-bcas-zag-med	sāsrava, anāsrava
pleasant, unpleasant, indifferent	bde-sdug-btang-snyoms	sukhavedanīya, duḥkhavedanīya, aduḥkhavedanīya
virtuous, nonvirtuous, indeterminate	dge-ba-mi-dge-ba-lung-ma-bstan	kuśala, akuśala, avyākṛta

meritorious, demeritorious, nonagitated	bsod-nams-yin-min-mi-g.yo-ba	puṇya, apuṇya, āniñya
manifest and nonmanifest	rnam-par-rig-byed-yin-min	vijñapti, avijñapti

AKB IV: 2a,8b–c,45a–d,57a–d,59c–d, AS II, MVP 2188–89,1913,1887, KJ 40b.1–43b.2, WE 32

Ten Nonvirtuous Actions
mi-dge-ba-bcu
akusala

three of mind: covetousness, ill-will, wrong views	brnab-sems-gnod-sems-log-lta	abhidhyā, vyāpāda, mithyādṛṣṭi
three of speech: harsh words, slander, idle talk, lying	tshig-rtsub-phra-ma-ngag-bkyal-rdzun	pārusya, paiśunya, abaddha-pralāpa, mṛṣā-vāda
three of body: killing, stealing, sexual misconduct	srog-gcod-ma-byin-len-log-g.yem	prāṇātighāta, adattādāna, kāmamithyācārya

AKB IV:65a–71d, AS II, KZLZ I:IV, cf.MVP 1685, KJ 46a.2, WE 32

Five Mortal Transgressions
mtshams-med-pa-lnga
pañcānantarya

patricide	pha-gsod-pa	pitṛghāta
matricide	ma-gsod-pa	mātṛghāta
killing an arhat	dgra-bcom-pa-gsod-pa	arhadghāta
causing division in the sangha	dge-'dun-gyi-dbyen-byas-pa	saṅghabheda

maliciously causing Tathāgata to bleed	de-bzhin-gshegs-pa'i-sku-la-ngan-sems-kyis-khrag-'byin-pa	tathāgatasyātike duṣṭacittarudhir-otpādanam

AKB IV:96, MVP 2323, KJ 47b.6. KZLZ I:IV, WE 32

Five False Views
lta-ba-nyon-mongs-can
dṛṣṭi-saṁkleśa

belief in an I and a mine within the transitory skandhas	'jig-tshogs-la-lta-ba	satkāya-dṛṣṭi
view holding to an extreme	mthar-'dzin-pa'i-lta-ba	antagrāha-dṛṣṭi
perverted view	log-par-lta-ba	mithyā-dṛṣṭi
holding a limited view in esteem	lta-ba-mchog-'dzin	dṛṣṭi-parāmarśa
holding ascetic practices and discipline to be paramount	tshul-khrims-dang-brtul-zhugs-mchog-'dzin	śīlavrata-parāmarśa

AKB V:7–9d, AS I, MVP 1954–1959, KJ 7a.2, WE 33

Six Root Afflictions
rtsa-ba'i-nyon-mongs-drug

desire	'dod-chags	rāga
anger	khong-khro	pratigha
ignorance	ma-rig-pa	avidyā
pride	nga-rgyal	māna
false views	lta-ba-nyon-mongs-can	dṛṣṭi-saṁkleśa
doubt	the-tshom	vicikitsā

AKB V:1a–2a, AS II, MVP 1944, 1945, 1946, 1953, 1954, 1960, KJ 49a.3, WE 33

Three Kinds of Suffering
sdug-bsngal-gsum
traya-duḥkhatā

suffering of suffering	sdug-bsngal-gyi-sdug-bsngal	duḥkha-duḥkhatā
suffering of the conditioned	'du-byed-kyi-sdug-bsngal	saṁskāra-duḥkhatā
suffering of change	'gyur-ba'i-sdug-bsngal	vipariṇāma-duḥkhatā

AK:VI:3, MVP:2228, KZLZ:III, WE 9

Eight Worldly Dharmas
'jig-rten-chos-brgyad
aṣṭa-loka-dharma

gain	rnyed-pa	lābha
loss	ma-rnyed-pa	alābha
fame	snyan-pa	yaśa
disgrace	mi-snyan-pa	ayaśa
praise	bstod-pa	praśaṁsā
blame	smad-pa	nindā
pleasure	bde-ba	sukha
pain	sdug-bsngal	duḥkha

MVP 2341, KJ 39a.3, WE 33

Tibetan-Sanskrit-English Word List

kun-nas-dkris-ba, paryavasthāna, wrappings
kun-sbyor, saṁyojana, fetters
skye-mched, āyatana, āyatana
skyes-bu, pṛthagjana, ordinary person
khams, dhātu, dhātu
khams-gsum, tridhātu, three realms
'gro-ba-rigs-drug, ṣaḍgati, six destinies
rgyu-gzugs, causal forms
mngon-shes, abhijñā, superknowledge
chu-bo, ogha, floods
chos-kyi-sdom-bzhi, catur-dharmoddāna, four laws of the Dharma
chos-'khor-gsum, dharmacakrapravartana, three turnings
'ching-ba, bandhana, bonds
'jig-rten-gyi-khams, lokadhātu, world-systems
nyan-thos-kyi-theg-pa, Śrāvakayāna, Śrāvaka vehicle
nyon-mongs, kleśa, afflictions, emotional afflictions

snyoms-'jug, samāpatti, absorption
ting-nge-'dzin, samādhi, meditative concentration
gti-mug, moha, confusion
rtog-pa, vitarka, investigation
rtogs, adhigama, realization
rten-cing-'brel-bar-'byung-ba, pratītyasamutpāda, interdependent co-operation
lta-ba-nyon-mongs-can, dṛṣṭi-saṁkleśa, false views
stong-pa-nyid, śūnyatā, emptiness
thabs, upāya, skill in means
dad-pa, śraddhā, faith
'dul-ba, vinaya
dus, kāla, adhvan, time
dran-pa, smṛti, mindfulness
bde-ba, sukha, pleasure
bdag-med-pa, anātman, selflessness
bden-pa, satya, truth
'dod-chags, rāga, desire, attachment
'dod-pa'i-khams, kāmadhātu, desire realm
'du-byed, saṁskāra, karmic propensities
'du-shes, saṁjñā, perception
'du-shes-med-pa, asaṁjñā, nonperception
'dun-pa, chanda, interest
'dus-byas-dang-'dus-ma-byas, saṁskṛta-asaṁskṛta, conditioned and nonconditioned
ldan-min-'du-byed, citta-viprayukta-saṁskāra, nonassociated motivational forces
sdug-bsngal, duḥkha, pain, suffering
sde-snod-gsum, tripiṭaka, three collections
nam-mkha', ākāśa, space
rnam-par-thar-pa, vimokṣa, deliverances
rnam-par-rig-byed-yin-min, vijñapti, avijñapti, manifest and nonmanifest
rnam-par-shes-pa, vijñāna, consciousness
snod-dang-bcud, bhājana-loka-sattva-loka, world and beings
dpyod-pa, vicāra, analysis

phung-po, skandha

bag-nyal, anuśayas, latent emotions

byang-chub-sems-dpa'i-theg-pa, Bodhisattvayāna, Bodhisattva vehicle

byang-phyogs-so-bdun, saptatriṁśa-bodhipakṣa, thirty-seven wings of enlightenment

dbang-po, indriya, organ or indriya

'bras-gzugs, resultant form

'byung-ba-chen-po, mahābhūta, great element

ma-rig-pa, avidyā, ignorance

mi-dge-ba, akuśala, nonvirtuous

smon-lam, praṇidhāna, aspiration

tshad-med-bzhi, catur-apramāṇa, four immeasurables

tshul-khrims, śīla, moral discipline

tshor-ba, vedanā, feeling

zag-bcas-zag-med, sāsrava,anāsrava, corrupt and uncorrupt

gzugs-kyi-khams, rūpadhātu, form realm

gzugs-med-pa'i-khams, arūpyadhātu, formless realm

bzod-pa, kṣanti, patience

yang-dag-par-rig-pa, pratisamvid, exact knowledge

yid-la-byed-pa, manaskāra, attention

ye-shes, jñāna, knowledge

las, karma, karma

lung, āgama, explanations

len-pa, upādāna, grasping

shes-rab, prajñā, wisdom, discernment

sems, cetanā, intention

sems, citta, mind,

sems-dang-mtshungs-ldan-gyi-'du-byed, citta-samprayukta-saṁskāra, motivational forces associated with mind

srid-pa, bhava, existence

bsam-gtan, dhyāna, meditation

bsod-nams, puṇya, merit

English-Tibetan-Sanskrit Word List

āyatana, skye-mched, āyatana
absorption, snyoms-'jug, samāpatti
afflictions, emotional afflictions, nyon-mongs, kleśa
analysis, dpyod-pa, vicāra
aspiration, smon-lam, praṇidhāna
attention, yid-la-byed-pa, manaskāra
bonds, 'ching-ba, bandhana
causal forms, rgyu-gzugs
world-systems, 'jig-rten-gyi-khams, lokadhātu
collections, three, sde-snod-gsum, tripiṭaka
concentration, meditative, ting-nge-'dzin, samādhi
conditioned and nonconditioned, 'dus-byas-dang-'dus-ma-byas, saṁskṛta-asaṁskṛta
confusion, gti-mug, moha.
consciousness, rnam-par-shes-pa, vijñāna
corrupt and uncorrupt, zag-bcas-zag-med, sāsrava, anāsrava

deliverance, rnam-par-thar-pa, vimokṣa
desire, 'dod-chags, rāga
desire realm, 'dod-pa'i-khams, kāmadhātu
destinies, six, 'gro-ba-rigs-drug, ṣaḍgati
dhātu, khams, dhātu
discernment, shes-rab, prajñā
elements, four great, 'byung-ba-chen-po-bzhi, catvāri mahābhūta
emptiness, stong-pa-nyid, śūnyatā
existence, srid-pa, bhava
explanations, lung, āgama
faith, dad-pa, śraddhā
false views, lta-ba-nyon-mongs-can, dṛṣṭi-saṁkleśa
feeling, tshor-ba, vedanā
fetters, kun-sbyor, saṁyojana
floods, chu-bo, ogha
form realm, gzugs-kyi-khams, rūpadhātu
formless realm, gzugs-med-pa'i-khams, arūpyadhātu
grasping, len-pa, upādāna
ignorance, ma-rig-pa, avidyā
immeasurables, four, tshad-med-bzhi, catur-apramāṇa
indriya, dbang-po, indriya
intention, sems, cetanā
interdependent co-operation, rten-cing-'brel-bar-'byung-ba, pratītyasamutpāda
interest, 'dun-pa, chanda
investigation, rtog-pa, vitarka
karma, las, karma
karmic propensities, 'du-byed, saṁskāra
knowledges, super, mngon-shes, abhijñā
knowledges, exact, yang-dag-par-rig-pa, pratisamvid
knowledge, ye-shes, jñāna
latent emotions, bag-nyal, anuśaya
laws of the Dharma, four, chos-kyi-sdom-bzhi, catur-dharmoddāna
manifest and nonmanifest, rnam-par-rig-byed-yin-min, vijñapti, avijñapti
meditation, bsam-gtan, dhyāna

meditative concentration, ting-nge-'dzin, samādhi

merit, bsod-nams, puṇya

mind, sems, citta

mindfulness, dran-pa, smṛti

moral discipline, tshul-khrims, śīla

motivational forces associated with mind, sems-dang-mtshungs-ldan-gyi-'du-byed, citta-samprayukta-saṁskāra

nonassociated motivational forces, ldan-min-'du-byed, citta-viprayukta-saṁskāra

nonmanifesting form, rnam-par-rig-byed-min-pa'i-gzugs, avijñaptirūpa

nonperception, 'du-shes-med-pa, asaṁjñā

nonvirtuous actions, ten, mi-dge-ba-ni-bcu-yin

ordinary person, skyes-bu, pṛthagjana.

organ, dbang-po, indriya

perception, 'du-shes, saṁjñā

patience, bzod-pa, kṣanti

pleasure, bde-ba, sukha

realization, rtogs, adhigama

realms, three, khams-gsum, tridhātu

resultant form, 'bras-gzugs

selflessness, bdag-med-pa, anātman

skandha, phung-po, skandha

skill in means, thabs, upāya

space, nam-mkha', ākāśa

suffering, sdug-bsngal, duḥkha

time, dus, kāla, adhvan

truth, bden-pa, satya

turnings, three, chos 'khor-gsum, dharmacakrapravartana

vehicle of Bodhisattvas, byang-chub sems-dpa'i-theg-pa, Bodhisattvayāna

vehicle of Listeners, nyan-thos-kyi-theg-pa, Śrāvakayāna

wings of enlightenment, thirty-seven, byang-phyogs-so-bdun, saptatriṁśad-bodhipakṣa

wisdom, discernment, shes-rab, prajñā

vinaya, 'dul-ba, vinaya
world and beings, snod-dang-bcud, bhājana-loka-sattva-loka
wrappings, kun-nas-dkris-ba, paryavasthāna

Bibliography and Abbreviations

Canonical Texts and Commentaries

AN Anguttara Nikāya. *The Book of Gradual Sayings,* translated by F. L. Woodward and E. M. Hare. 5 volumes. Reprint ed. London: Pali Text Society, 1972–1982.

ASL Abhisamayālaṁkāra, by Maitreyanātha (NE 3786). *Abhisamayālaṁkāra,* translated by Edward Conze. Rome: IsMEO, 1954. (Serie Orientale Roma 6).

AVS Arthaviniścaya Sūtra (NE 317). Berkeley: Dharma Publishing, forthcoming.

AKB Abhidharmakoṣabhāṣya, by Vasubandhu (NE 4089–4090). *Abhidharmakośabhāsyām,* translated from the French translation of Louis de la Vallé Poussin by Leo M. Pruden. 4 volumes. Berkeley: Asian Humanities Press, 1988–1990.

AS Abhidharmasamuccaya, by Asaṅga (NE 4049). *Le Compendium de la super-doctrine (Philosophie),* (Abhidharmasamuccaya) d'Asaṅga, translated by Walpola Rahula. Paris: Ecole Française d'Éxtreme-Orient, 1971. Reprinted 1980.

BCA Bodhisattvacaryāvatāra (NE 3871), by Śāntideva. *Entering the Path of Enlightenment,* translated by Marion L. Matics. New York: Macmillan, 1970. See also: *A Guide to the Bodhisattva's Way of Life,* translated by Stephen Batchelor and Sherpa Tulku. Dharamsala: Library of Tibetan Works and Archives, 1979.

BCV Bodhicittavivaraṇa, by Nāgārjuna (NE 1800). "Bodhicittavivaraṇa," in *Master of Wisdom, Writings of the Buddhist Master Nāgārjuna,* translations and studies by Chr. Lindtner. Berkeley: Dharma Publishing, 1986.

DN Digha Nikāya. *Dialogues of the Buddha,* translated by T. W. and C. A. F. Rhys-Davids. 3 volumes. Reprint ed. London: Pali Text Society, 1977. See also: *Thus Have I Heard, The Long Discourses of the Buddha,* translated by Maurice Walshe. London: Wisdom, 1987.

DP Dhammapada. *Dhammapada, Translation of Dharma Verses with the Tibetan Text.* Berkeley: Dharma Publishing, 1985.

DS Vajracchedikā Sūtra (NE 16). "Diamond Sūtra," in *Buddhist Wisdom Books,* translated by Edward Conze. London: Allen and Unwin, 1975.

DSB Daśabhūmika Sūtra. Traditionally included in the Avataṁsaka Sūtra (NE 44). *The Flower Ornament Scripture,* translated by Thomas Cleary. 3 volumes. Boston: Shambhala, 1985–1990.

GL rGyud-bla-ma (Mahāyānottara Tantraśāstra NE 4024). "The Sublime Science of the Great Vehicle to Salvation, being a Manual of Buddhist Monism: The Work of Ārya Maitreya with a Commentary by Āryāsaṅga," translated by E. Obermiller. *Acta Orientalia* 9 (1930):81–306. Reprinted, Shanghai: 1940.

GZ Suhṛllekha, by Nāgārjuna and bShes-spring-gi-mchan-'grel-padma-dkar-po'i-phreng-ba, by Lama Mi-pham. *Golden Zephyr* ("A Letter to a Friend" and "Garland of White Lotus Flowers"), translated by Leslie Kawamura. Berkeley: Dharma Publishing, 1975.

HS Prajñāpāramitāhṛdaya (NE 21), "Heart Sutra," in *Buddhist Wisdom Books,* translated by Edward Conze. London: Allen and Unwin, 1975.

JAT Jātakamāla, by Āryaśūra (NE 4150). *The Marvelous Companion: Life Stories of the Buddha, by Āryaśūra.* Berkeley: Dharma Publishing, 1983.

LAL Lalitavistara Sūtra (NE 95). *The Voice of the Buddha: The Beauty of Compassion,* translated by Gwendolyn Bays. Berkeley: Dharma Publishing, 1983.

LGB Bla-ma-rgyang-'bod, by Kong-sprul Blo-gros-mtha'-yas. Manuscript copy.

LKV Laṅkāvatāra Sūtra (NE 107). *The Laṅkāvatāra Sūtra: A Mahāyāna Text,* translated from the Sanskrit by D.T. Suzuki. Boulder: Prajñā Press, 1978.

MAV Madhyāntavibhaṅga Kārikā and Ṭīkā (NE 4021, 4027), by Maitreyanātha and by Vasubandhu. "Commentary on the Separation of the Middle from Extremes," translated by Stefan Anacker, in *Seven Works of Vasubandhu, the Buddhist Psychological Doctor.* Delhi: Motilal Banarsidass, 1984. (Religions of Asia Series, No. 4.)

MN Majjhima Nikāya. *The Middle Length Sayings,* translated by I.B. Horner. Reprint ed. London: Pali Text Society, 1975–1982.

MMK Mūlamadhyamakakārikā, by Nāgārjuna (NE 3824). In *Emptiness: A Study in Religious Meaning,* by Frederick Streng. New York: Abingdon Press, 1967.

MP Milindapañha, *Milinda's Questions,* translated by I. B. Horner. 2 volumes. London: Pali Text Society, 1969. See also *The Debate of King Milinda, An Abridgement of the Milinda Pañha,* by Bhikkhu Pesala. Delhi: Motilal Banarsidass, 1991.

MSA Mahāyānasūtrālaṁkāra, by Maitreya (NE 4020). *Mahāyānasūtrālaṁkāra: Exposé de la doctrine du grand vehicule selon le systeme Yogācāra,* volume II, translated by Sylvain Levi. Paris: Champion, 1911.

MSG Mahāyānasaṁgraha, by Asaṅga (NE 4048). *Le Somme du grand vehicule,* translated by Etienne Lamotte. 2 volumes. Louvain: Université de Louvain, 1973.

MVS Mahāvaṁsa. *The Great Chronicle of Ceylon,* translated by Wilhelm Geiger. First published 1912; reprinted Colombo: Ceylon Government Information Department, 1950; New Delhi: Asian Educational Services, 1986.

MVP Mahāvyutpatti (NE 4346). *Mahāvyutpatti,* prepared by R. Sakaki. 2 volumes. Tokyo: Suzuki Research Foundation, 1916.

PP Prajñāpāramita Sūtras (NE 8, 9,10). *The Large Sūtra on Perfect Wisdom, with the Divisions of the Abhisamayālaṁkāra,* translated by Edward Conze. Reprint edition. Berkeley: University of California, 1975. Abridged translation of the Pañcaviṁśatisāhasrikā.

PRA Prasannapadā, by Candrakīrti (NE 3860). *Lucid Exposition of the Middle Way,* translation of 16 chapters by Mervyn Sprung. Boulder: Prajñā Press, 1979.

PPS Prajñāpāramitāstotra, by Nāgārjuna (NE 1127). In *Buddhist Texts Through the Ages,* edited by Edward Conze. New York: Harper and Row, 1964.

PSP Pañcaskandhaka Prakaraṇa, by Vasubandhu (NE 4059). "A Discussion of the Five Aggregates," translated by Stefan Anacker, in *Seven Works of Vasubandhu, the Buddhist Psychological Doctor.* Religions of Asia Series, No. 4. Delhi: Motilal Banarsidass, 1984.

RGS Prajñāpāramitā Ratnaguṇasaṁcayagāthā (NE 13). In *The Perfection of Wisdom in Eight Thousand Lines and its Verse Summary,* translated by Edward Conze. Bolinas: Four Seasons Foundation, 1973.

SL Suhṛllekha, by Nāgārjuna (NE 4182). In *Golden Zephyr.* See GZ.

SS Śīkṣāsamuccaya, by Śāntideva (NE 3940). *Siksha-Samuccaya, A Compendium of Buddhist Doctrine,* translated by Cecil Bendall and W. H. D. Rouse. Delhi: Motilal Banarsidass, 1971.

SST Śūnyatāsaptati, by Nāgārjuna (NE 3827). "Śūnyatāsaptati," in *Master of Wisdom, Writings of the Buddhist Master Nāgārjuna,* translations and studies by Chr. Lindtner. Berkeley: Dharma Publishing, 1986.

TSK Triṁśikākārikā, by Vasubandhu (NE 4055). "The Thirty Verses," translated by Stefan Anacker, in *Seven Works of Vasubandhu, the Buddhist Psychological Doctor.* Religions of Asia Series, No. 4. Delhi: Motilal Banarsidass, 1984.

VK Vimalakīrtinirdeśa Sūtra (NE 176). *The Holy Teaching of Vimalakīrti, A Mahāyāna Scripture,* translated by Robert A. F. Thurman. University Park and London: Pennsylvania State University Press, 1986.

VY Vyākhyāyukti, by Vasubandhu (NE 4061).

YS Yuktiṣaṣṭikā, by Nāgārjuna (NE 3825). "Yuktiṣaṣṭikā," in *Master of Wisdom, Writings of the Buddhist Master Nāgārjuna,* translations and studies by Chr. Lindtner. Berkeley: Dharma Publishing, 1986.

VM Visuddhimagga, by Buddhaghosa. *The Path of Purification,* translated by Bhikkhu Ñāṇamoli. Second Edition. Colombo: A. Semage, 1964.

Works by Tibetan Masters

CC Sems-kyi-dpyod-pa-rnam-par-sbyong-ba-so-sor-brtag-pa'i-dpyad-sgom-'khor-lo-ma and dBu-ma'i-lta-khrid-zab-mo, by Mi-pham 'Jam-dbyangs-rnam-rgyal-rgya-mtsho. *Calm and Clear* ("The Wheel of Analytic Meditation" and "Instructions on Vision in the Middle Way"), translated by Tarthang Tulku. Berkeley: Dharma Publishing, 1973.

DR bsTan-pa'i-rnam-gzhag and Chos-'byung, (gSang-sngags-snga-'gyur-rnying-ma'i-bstan-pa'i-rnam-gzhag-mdo-tsam-brjod-pa legs-bshad-snang-ba'i-dga'-ston and Gangs-ljongs rgyal-bstan yongs-rdzogs-kyi phyi-mo-snga-'gyur rdo-rje-theg-pa'i bstan-pa rin-po-che ji-ltar-byung-ba'i-tshul-dag-cing gsal-bar-brjod-pa lha-dbang-g.yul-las-rgyal-ba'i rnga-bo-che'i-sgra-dbyangs.) by bDud-'joms 'Jigs-bral-ye-shes-rdo-rje (Dudjom Rinpoche edition, Kalimpong, 1978). *The Nyingma School of Tibetan Buddhism: Its Fundamentals and History,* translated by Gyurme Dorje and Matthew Kapstein. 2 volumes. Boston: Wisdom Publications, 1991.

DT Jo-mo-la-gdams-pa'i-chos-skor. *Dakini Teachings, Padmasambhava's Oral Instructions to Lady Tsogyal,* recorded and concealed by Yeshe Tsogyal, and revealed by Nyang Ral Nyima Odzer and Sangye Lingpa. Translated by Erik Pema Kunsang. Boston and Shaftesbury: Shambhala, 1990.

GTD Yid-bzhin-mdzod-kyi-grub-mtha'-bsdus-pa, by Mi-pham 'Jam-dbyangs-rnam-rgyal-rgya-mtsho (gSung-'bum published by rDzong-gsar mKhyen-brtse). Partial translation in *Buddhist Philosophy in Theory and Practice,* by Herbert V. Guenther. Boulder: Shambhala, 1976.

KB Ngal-gso-skor-gsum, by Klong-chen-pa (Dodrupchen edition). *Kindly Bent to Ease Us,* translated by Herbert Guenther, 3 volumes. Berkeley: Dharma Publishing, 1975.

KJ mKhas-pa'i-tshul-la-'jug-pa'i-sgo-zhes-bya-ba'i-bstan-bcos, by Mi-pham 'Jam-dbyangs-rnam-rgyal-rgya-mtsho (gSung-'bum published by rDzong-gsar mKhyen-brtse).

KJD mKhas-'jug-gi-sdom-byang, by Mi-pham 'Jam-dbyangs-rnam-rgyal-rgya-mtsho (gSung-'bum published by rDzong-gsar mKhyen-brtse).

KZLZ Kun-bzang-bla-ma'i-zhal-lung, by dPal-sprul O-rgyan 'Jigs-med-chos-kyi-dbang-po (gSung-'bum from Dudjom Rinpoche's library). *Kunzang La-may Zhal-lung,* translated by Sonam T. Kazi. 2 volumes. Upper Montclair: Diamond-Lotus Publishing, 1989, 1993.

JL Rin-chen-them-skas, by sMin-gling gTer-chen 'Gyur-med-rdo-rje (gTer-bdag-gling-pa). *The Jewel Ladder,* translated by Tsepak Rigzin. Dharamsala: Library of Tibetan Works and Archives, 1990.

JO Dam-chos-yid-bzhin-gyi-nor-bu-thar-pa-rin-po-che'i-rgyan, by sGam-po-pa. *The Jewel Ornament of Liberation,* translated by Herbert V. Guenther. Berkeley: Shambhala, 1971.

MBP Sems-dang-sems-byung-gi-tshul-gsal-par-ston-pa-blo-gsal-mgul-rgyan, by Ye-shes-rgyal-mtshan. *Mind in Buddhist Psychology,* translated by Herbert V. Guenther and Leslie S. Kawamura. Berkeley: Dharma Publishing, 1975.

MM Nges-don-phyag-chen-po-sgom-rim-legs-bshad-zla-ba'i-'od-zer, by Dwags-po bKra-shis-rnam-rgyal. *Mahāmudrā,* translated by Lobsang P. Lhalungpa. London and Boston: Shambhala, 1986.

OD "The Opening of the Dharma," by 'Jam-dbyangs mKhyen-brtse Chos-kyi-blo-gros. In *Four Essential Buddhist Texts,* translated by Geshe Ngawang Dhargye, et. al. Dharamsala: Library of Tibetan Works and Archives, 1982.

STG Grub-brgyud-shing-rta-chen-po-brgyad-kyi-smin-grol-snying-po-phyogs-gcig-bsdus-pa-gdams-ngag rin-po-che'i-mdzod-kyi-dkar-chag-bkra-shis-grags-pa'i-rgya-mtsho, by Kong-sprul Blo-gros-mtha'-yas (dPal-spungs edition).

TC Nges-don-sgron-me, by Kong-sprul Blo-gros-mtha'-yas. *Torch of Certainty,* translated by Judith Hanson. Boulder and London: Shambhala, 1977.

Biographical and Historical Works

BA Deb-ther-sngon-po, by 'Gos Lo-tsā-ba (Lokesh Chandra edition, 1974). *The Blue Annals,* translated by George N. Roerich. Second edition. Delhi: Motilal Banarsidass, 1976.

BU Chos-'byung, by Bu-ston Rin-po-che. *History of Buddhism,* translated by E. Obermiller. Heidelberg: Institut für Buddhismuskunde, 1931. (Materialien zur Kunde des Buddhismus, 18)

HT *Buddhist Records of the Western World,* by Hsüan-tsang. Translated from the Chinese by Samuel Beal. Delhi: Motilal Banarsidass, 1981. First published 1884.

IT *A Record of the Buddhist Religion as Practiced in India and the Malay Archipelago (A.D. 671–695),* by I-tsing. Translated by J. Takakusu. Delhi: M. Manoharlal, 1966. First published Oxford, 1896.

SDS Saddhamma Saṁgaha. *A Manual of Buddhist Historical Traditions,* translated by Bimala Churn Law. Delhi: Bharatiya Publishing House, 1980.

TAR rGya-gar-chos-'byung, by Tāranātha. *History of Buddhism in India,* translated by Lama Chimpa and Alaka Chattopadyaya. Simla: Indian Institute of Advanced Study, 1970.

Western Works on Biography, History, and Buddhist Literature

Ancient Tibet, Research Materials from the Yeshe De Project. Berkeley: Dharma Publishing, 1986.

Buddha, Dharma, Sangha in Historical Perspective. Berkeley: Dharma Publishing, 1984. (Crystal Mirror VII)

Buddhism in China: A Historical Survey, by Kenneth Ch'en. New York: Princeton University Press, 1964. Reprinted 1972, 1973.

The Buddhist Conquest of China: The Spread and Adaptation of Buddhism in Early Medieval China, by E. Zurcher, 2 volumes. Leiden: E. J. Brill, 1972. Originally published 1959.

The Eternal Legacy: An Introduction to the Canonical Literature of Buddhism, by Sangharakshita. London: Tharpa Publications, 1985.

Footsteps on the Diamond Path. Berkeley: Dharma Publishing, 1992. (Crystal Mirror I–III, revised and expanded edition)

The Foundation of Japanese Buddhism, by Daigan and Alicia Matsunaga. 2 volumes. Los Angeles: Buddhist Books International, 1974, 1976.

The Indianized States of Southeast Asia, by G. Coedès, translated by Susan Brown Cowing. Honolulu: University Press of Hawaii, 1968.

Holy Places of the Buddha. Berkeley: Dharma Publishing, forthcoming. (Crystal Mirror IX)

The Life of the Buddha and the Early History of His Order, derived from Tibetan works in the bKah-hgyur and bsTan-hgyur, by W. Woodville Rockhill. London: Kegan Paul, Trench, Trübner and Co., 1884.

The Life of the Buddha as it Appears in the Pāli Canon, by Bhikkhu Ñāṇamoli. Kandy: Buddhist Publications Society, 1972.

Light of Liberation, A History of Buddhism in India. Berkeley: Dharma Publishing, 1992. (Crystal Mirror VIII)

Lineage of Diamond Light. Berkeley: Dharma Publishing, 1977. (Crystal Mirror V, revised edition, 1991)

Lives of Eminent Korean Monks, translated by Peter H. Lee. Cambridge: Harvard University Press, 1969.

The Three Jewels and History of Dharma Transmission. Berkeley: Dharma Publishing, 1984. (Crystal Mirror VI)

Tibet in Pictures, by Li Gotami Govinda. 2 volumes. Berkeley: Dharma Publishing, 1979.

Tibetan Civilization, by R. A. Stein. Stanford: University Press, 1972.

Zen and Japanese Culture, by D.T. Suzuki. Princeton: University Press, 1973.

Note

NE: *The Nyingma Edition of the Tibetan Canon,* a 1981 reprint of the sDe-dge edition, with supplementary texts. *See* p. 57, *supra.*

WE *Ways of Enlightenment.* The list of Buddhist Terminology contained in the Reference Materials gives citations to chapters of this volume.

Canonical texts, commentaries, and works by Tibetan authors are cited by divisions in roman or arabic numerals. KJ, KJD, and GTD are cited to the folio and line of the Tibetan editions. Citations to BU, DR, HT, and MBP are to page numbers in the English translation; citations to MVP are to entry numbers in the translation.

Index

Nyingma Institute
1815 Highland Place, Berkeley, CA 94709
(510) 843–6812

The Nyingma Institute was founded in 1972 by Tarthang Tulku, an accomplished lama who was the first to carry the lineage of the Nyingma school to America. For over twenty years Nyingma Institute has sought to make available the wisdom and compassion of this enlightened lineage. The educational programs at Nyingma Institute reflect the vision of its founder:

"The Tibetan Buddhist tradition has always held that intellectual effort, in whatever form, is valuable only insofar as it aids growth and realization as a human being. These objectives can only be accomplished through a thorough understanding of the nature and functioning of the human mind and by the exposure of self-imposed limitations that prevent openness, balance, and compassion. The study of Tibetan Buddhism is far more than the undertaking of an academic discipline in the Western sense. It is a comprehensive learning process that relates to every possible situation and to every moment in our lives."

Following this tradition, education at Nyingma Institute places equal emphasis on study, meditation, and work. Classes, workshops, and residential retreats offer a unique blend of opportunities to integrate awareness into everyday life. Enriched by the beauty and blessings of the meditation garden, prayer wheels, and stupa, Nyingma Institute, located in the Berkeley hills overlooking the San Francisco Bay, is a place of refuge and tranquility.